THE HIGH MEDIEVAL
DREAM VISION

THE HIGH MEDIEVAL DREAM VISION

Poetry, Philosophy, and Literary Form

Kathryn L. Lynch

STANFORD UNIVERSITY PRESS
Stanford, California   1988

Stanford University Press
Stanford, California

© 1988 by the Board of Trustees of the
Leland Stanford Junior University

Printed in the United States of America

CIP data appear at the end of the book

Published with
the assistance of Wellesley College

For my father, Frank W. Lynch

PREFACE

In this book, I develop a model for reading the high medieval dream vision that addresses its broad discursive function within its age. I argue that an analysis of medieval vision poetry must begin with a study of the contemporary philosophy and poetic theory that informed it; accordingly, my introduction and first two chapters provide the background and terms that I have found necessary to my understanding of the complex relationship between these two fields of discourse and individual poems. Although this synthetic approach means that I must limit myself to treating in detail only the most central of these poems and only those that embody a certain high medieval viewpoint, the model for reading outlined here has a wider application than I have had the space or time to give it. My hope is that others will also find this model useful for reading, thinking about, and writing on additional texts within the genre I have described and in related genres—texts by Godfrey of Saint Victor, Jean de Hanville, Brunetto Latini, Petrarch, Chaucer, Langland, Christine of Pizan, James I of Scotland, and so on. I hope that my discussion of how the paradigmatic structure of the literary vision echoed central epistemological structures in scholastic philosophy can help open a new discussion of the role that the dream vision played within the larger hierarchy of medieval genres.

Happily, such a discussion of genre seems already to have begun. Until quite recently, little attention had been devoted to exploring the influence that literary visions exerted upon one another, beginning with the genre's prototype, Boethius's *De consolatione philosophiae*. However, a very recent study, Michael D. Cherniss's *Boethian Apocalypse: Studies in Middle English Poetry*, also speaks to this gap in scholarship. Cherniss's fine book unfortunately did not appear until mine was in the final stages of editing and so could not be incorporated into my discussion. Nevertheless, his work is related to mine in such interesting ways that I cannot resist commenting briefly on it here. Cherniss concentrates on the formal rather than historical features of the genre, thus providing a description of the literary vision's formal possibilities that reaches into the fifteenth century. At times my more historical and functional interests, such as my concern with medieval epistemology and theories of the imagination, lead me to praise the very features in a text with which he finds fault; yet I trust our two studies will be seen, in the largest sense, to complement each other. Any disagreement should be potentially fruitful as a stimulus to further discussion.

Discussion of this kind has been extremely useful to me in the past, for this book, originally my doctoral thesis, has been during the past eight years part of a dialogue with several readers—some of them known and some anonymous. I feel privileged to acknowledge their help here. As my dissertation directors at the University of Virginia, V. A. Kolve and Hoyt N. Duggan gave me both the intellectual support and the freedom necessary to pursue the large topic of the dream vision while providing the direction I needed to narrow and focus my ideas. The advice of A. C. Spearing, a visiting professor during the early stages of my thinking about dream visions, also helped to keep me on track. I was fortunate, too, for the arrival of Barbara Nolan during the middle of the dissertation project and for her encouragement and suggestions as a third member of my committee. Winthrop Wetherbee, of Cornell University, read parts of the manuscript at that time and again later, liberally and tactfully sharing his learning with me.

I owe much as well to three anonymous readers for Stanford University Press, whose scrupulous comments on my manuscript helped to clarify and elaborate my argument, and to my colleague William E. Cain at Wellesley College, for his help with the introductory theoretical chapter. Also at Wellesley, Rachel Jacoff read the Dante chapter and offered many useful suggestions; Katharine Park generously shared her writing and expertise on medieval and Renaissance faculty psychology; and Mark Petrini assisted in checking over some of the Latin translations. My students—especially those in a seminar on medieval vision literature in the fall of 1985—have been a constant source of energy and ideas. Corinna Nichols and Tanya Durilin, who served as my research assistants during one particularly hectic phase of revision, deserve special recognition for their skill and stamina. I am grateful for a grant from the Dana Foundation that helped compensate Tanya for her assistance, and similarly for a grant from Wellesley College that supported my work in the summer of 1984 and defrayed a portion of the production costs of this book. Without the library staff at Wellesley—Joan Stockard, Sally Linden, Claire Loranz, and Nancy Strong—my research would have been much more difficult. And finally, my writing has benefited from the competence and patience of my editors, Helen Tartar and Karen Brown Davison, and other members of the editorial staff at Stanford University Press.

Over the past few years, I have also been fortunate to have close friends whose emotional support has sustained me and given me the confidence to complete this work: James M. Kee at the College of the Holy Cross, Louise Fradenburg at Dartmouth College, Sandy Feinstein at Southwestern College, Jessica Feldman and Charlene Sedgwick at the University of Virginia, and Marilyn Sides at Wellesley College. Jim Kee and Sandy Feinstein have also read and commented on large sections of this book, a task that goes beyond friendship. Above all, though, I am grateful to my family: to my parents Frank and Marilyn Lynch, who have done whatever they could to lighten the burden of work and parenthood; to my children Michael and Madeline, who have cheerfully shared me with my work and who seem to be turning out pretty well in spite of it; and to my husband Robert McDonnell, whose love and unflagging belief in me keeps me going when all else fails.

K.L.L.

CONTENTS

A Note on Texts and Translations   xiii

Introduction: The Medieval Vision and Modern Scholarship   1

1
The Marriage of Matter and Form in High Medieval Philosophy and Poetics   21

2
A Grammar of Dream and Vision for Medieval Poetry   46

3
Myth and Vision in the *De planctu naturae*   77

4
Mirror or Mirage? Jean de Meun and the Satire of Visionary Failure   113

5
The *Purgatorio*: Dante's Book of Dreams   146

6
John Gower's Fourteenth-Century Philosophical Vision   163

Notes   201
Works Cited   237
Index   253

A NOTE ON TEXTS AND TRANSLATIONS

Translations are my own unless otherwise attributed. When a foreign language text forms the main subject of discussion in a chapter, I have provided quotations in both the original language and the English translation in the body of my text. For other foreign language texts, I have generally given only the English translation, except for words or phrases whose translation would be awkward or would detract from a point about verbal nuance. Even here, however, the originals or appropriate references can normally be found in my notes. As for the texts themselves, I have tried to choose editions that are both reliable and easily available, frequently preferring editions in the Loeb Classical Library series for works that are not under close scrutiny here. For works that form the focus of my discussion, however—for instance, Boethius's *De consolatione philosophiae*—I have sacrificed availability for the goal of scholarly accuracy.

Quotations from the five main texts discussed in this book are from the following sources:

Confessio Amantis
John Gower, *The Complete Works of John Gower*, ed. G. C. Macaulay, 4 vols. (Oxford, 1899–1902)

De consolatione philosophiae
Boethius, *Philosophiae consolatio*, ed. Ludwig Biehler, *Corpus Christianorum*, 94 (Turnholt, 1957)
Boethius, *The Consolation of Philosophy*, trans. Richard Green (Indianapolis, 1962)

De planctu naturae
  Alain de Lille, *De planctu naturae*, ed. Nikolaus M. Häring, *Studi Medievali*, series 3, 19 (1978): 797–879
Commedia
  Dante Alighieri, *The Divine Comedy*, ed. and trans. Charles S. Singleton, 3 vols., 6 parts (Princeton, 1970–75)
Le Roman de la rose
  Guillaume de Lorris and Jean de Meun, *Le Roman de la rose*, ed. Félix Lecoy, 3 vols. (Paris, 1965–70)
  Guillaume de Lorris and Jean de Meun, *The Romance of the Rose*, trans. Charles Dahlberg (Princeton, 1971)

THE HIGH MEDIEVAL
DREAM VISION

INTRODUCTION

The Medieval Vision and Modern Scholarship

Like the novel for the modern era, the vision narrative for the Middle Ages was an enormously popular and enduring literary form. Along with romance, it was perhaps the genre of the age; or, one might equally say, the period from the twelfth century through the fourteenth was the Age of the Dream Vision. During this time, a great many authors, both English and continental, tried their hand at vision poems; the genre includes such influential works as the *Roman de la rose*, most of Chaucer's early poetry, the major works of Guillaume de Machaut, the Middle English *Pearl*, *Piers Plowman*, and, as I will argue, even Dante's *Commedia*. Though the greatness of these poems is irrefutable, the reasons for that greatness remain somewhat puzzling, hinting at some specialized intent these poets shared that we no longer quite grasp. In response, this book will isolate that intent and account in part for the appeal of one group of these poems.

Why should so many poets—and so many great ones—have chosen to work in the vision form? This question, one on which I will focus, does not allow an immediate or straightforward answer. According to a recent conservative count, over 225 visions were written from the sixth century through the fifteenth, if one does not distinguish between literary and nonliterary visions. The concentration is even higher for the years after 1100, when about 70 percent of all visions and 90 percent of the literary ones were probably composed.[1]

Introduction

It hardly needs to be said that so great a number of texts produced over so many hundreds of years must be characterized by a staggering diversity, presenting a serious problem to scholars attempting a unified survey or description of the genre. This diversity does indeed seem to have been a stumbling block to students of the field. First of all, the form has not attracted nearly the attention that its quality and volume demand. There are a mere half-dozen full-length scholarly studies that treat the vision exclusively,[2] a telling figure when set alongside the plentiful modern studies of medieval drama, romance, lyric, and even the didactic forms of sermon and exempla. Second, those studies that have taken the medieval vision as their main subject have generally had to sacrifice depth to achieve some measure of comprehensiveness.

One positive result of this trade-off is that the immense task of identifying, cataloguing, classifying, and describing members of the genre has largely been done, and done admirably. In *The Vision of Hell*, for example, D. D. R. Owen provides an excellent survey of medieval infernal journeys in French and Anglo-Norman literature throughout the medieval period, whereas A. C. Spearing in *Medieval Dream-Poetry* concentrates on fourteenth- and fifteenth-century English and Scots dream visions. Fine treatments even more comprehensive in scope are supplied by Peter Dinzelbacher in his magisterial *Vision und Visionsliteratur im Mittelalter* and by Francis X. Newman in a regrettably unpublished dissertation, "*Somnium*: Medieval Theories of Dreaming and the Form of Vision Poetry." I do not mean to imply that these writers have not been alert to interpretation or generic function as well—A. C. Spearing, for example, stresses the genre's propensity for artistic self-consciousness. Their main goal, however, has not been to define the genre but to make the vision available against the background of a larger tradition, and this goal they have largely achieved. Unfortunately, the method employed by these scholars suggests that ultimately the boundaries of the tradition are so hazily defined and its membership so highly differentiated that no overriding principle of generic unity can emerge.

To be sure, prudence requires some agreement with Spearing when he acknowledges that "the dream-framework may be used for a number of different purposes, and in some cases, no doubt, it is no more than a literary convention, taken over through sheer inertia on the poet's part."[3] But even an uninspired or exhausted poet does not operate so mechanically; a poet makes choices among conventions for specific reasons, though they may not always be the best ones and though he may not be fully conscious of them. Spearing's concession indicates not chaos in the tradition but a need to narrow the field of works treated, to uncover not just the diversity of conventions represented in vision literature but the principles that underlie their creation and reception. Recognition of this need seems to lie behind Constance Hieatt's *The Realism of Dream Visions* and Paul Piehler's *The Visionary Landscape*, two slightly earlier studies that provide a more detailed analysis of fewer works in an attempt to explain the economy of medieval visions by reference to a myth criticism and psychological theory that universalizes the impulses behind artistic creation. But, though it yields results on its own terms, this procedure is at base ahistorical, in Piehler's formulation, "ultra-historic,"[4] and so tends to trivialize the confrontation between a modern sensibility and a medieval one. For example, the first of nine propositions put forth by Piehler in his introduction is that "medieval visionary allegory offers its readers participation in a process of psychic redemption closely resembling, though wider in scope than, modern psychotherapy."[5] Or as Hieatt argues, "It is possible to find a medieval precedent for almost all the various facets of our [modern] dream theory."[6] In this unfortunate reduction medieval writers tend to become mere forerunners of Freud and Jung, and differences such as those between the "supernatural" in a medieval world view and the "unconscious" in a modern one become simply differences of "terminology."[7]

Only one study—Barbara Nolan's *The Gothic Visionary Perspective*—identifies a limited tradition and locates it in a well-defined historical period. She notes in late medieval spiritual quests, stretching across both the visual and verbal arts, a similar tendency to chart the "actual historical movement of all mankind toward universal joy in the heavenly city,"[8] and she limits her discussion of literary works primarily to three, the *Vita nuova*, *Pearl*, and *Piers Plowman*. Her treatment comes, I think, closest to my own. By attending to historical change and by tracing significant intersections among the arts, she demonstrates the historical cohesiveness of the spiritual quest. This historicity, however, not her specific analyses, constitutes the main virtue of her approach, for readers are finally not shown the limits of the theory's application, nor are they given a precise definition of the literary or generic norms against which to gauge change or innovation. Thus, a wide range of works in different media at times seem more or less indistinguishable from one another. A fuller and more differentiated understanding of the visionary perspective can come from a closer focus on issues of the vision's form or genre, on the conventions that offered a range of possibilities for the poet who set out to write a "dream vision."

My method, therefore, will be to limit myself to a manageable subgenre (a term I will explain shortly) of visionary literature by focusing here primarily on five writers—Boethius, Alain de Lille, Jean de Meun, Dante, and John Gower—with occasional references to other poets who, by drawing on this core set of writers, formed part of a self-conscious tradition. These are poets, as Piehler says, who "regard themselves as part of a cumulative tradition, in which each allegorist recapitulates, refines and develops the thought and imagery of his predecessors."⁹ This is not, then, a book about Pauline visions of Hell or about the French love vision in the thirteenth and fourteenth centuries, though I am not attempting to deny that philosophical elements enter into these traditions. Like most literary genres, the philosophical—one might alternatively call it Boethian—vision mingled in many poems with other subgenres of the larger vision genre, creating admixtures and ultimately generating new forms of expression. Nor is this a book about Chaucer and Langland, who are later than the "high medieval" visionaries studied here, at least in spirit even when they intersect in time. More thoroughly and in radically new ways, these later poets stretch the form and turn it in on itself to express a view of the world and art significantly different from that of their predecessors. These later medieval vision poets, who I believe work in a self-reflexive or "tertiary" form of the philosophical vision, I wish to examine in a future study. Here I will be concerned chiefly with those poems in which the generic norms of the *high* medieval philosophical vision dominate; by this method, I intend to identify precisely the character and function of those norms.

A Definition of Genre

The first instrument required is a notion of genre defined rigorously enough to allow identification of significant normative functions and comparisons among works. Benedetto Croce and other skeptics aside, genre criticism is an indispensable scholarly tool, when one means by genres simply the types that make communication possible, the sets of expectations, the systems of conventions or shared properties, against which a reader judges and evaluates an author's performance.[10] As E. D. Hirsch observes, "Only such a bridge can unite the particularity of meaning with the sociality of interpretation."[11] Just as no linguistic utterance is possible without the rules of language that govern it—as, roughly speaking, *parole* is required to produce *langue*—so also no literary work can exist detached from the kind or type that sets the rules of its game. If we are to understand the game a poet plays, then first we must describe its rules.

This recourse to the language of "rules," however, should not suggest that genres themselves are prescriptive or immutable classes. Though no work can be isolated from its kind—i.e., no work exists sui generis—neither are there available timeless, a priori classes or categories capable of describing the generic possibilities available to writers through all time. Though humans no doubt share habits of mind, psychic structures, needs, and impulses throughout the ages, no theory—from Northrop Frye's to Paul Hernadi's—has succeeded in uncovering these common factors systematically enough to reveal the "order of verbal art" that lies beneath centuries of diverse works.[12] Even if such an order could be uncovered, its historical value would be dubious, for it would still be subject to the same criticisms I have already leveled against the ahistorical and universalizing psychological and myth criticism of Piehler and Hieatt.

A genre, rather, seems to be made up of a repertoire of features that evolve slowly over time. Drawing upon this repertoire, individual writers can create meaning by varying and modifying generic norms. Thus, any adequate theory of genre must find a middle ground between what Hans Robert Jauss calls "the Scylla of nominalist skepticism . . . and the Charybdis of regression into timeless typologies."[13] Or as Alastair Fowler points out in an excellent recent study of the problem, adjustments are continually required "to mediate between the flux of history and the canons of art."[14] According to Jauss and Fowler, then, genres are not instruments for prescribing meaning before the fact or classifying it afterward, but for interpreting and producing meaning in the moment, for a specific work and a specific historical time.¹⁵ Their observations will serve as a useful guide.

How, though, do readers actually mediate between the individual work and the ever-changing type? How do we identify the most appropriate or relevant genre? Or can a work simultaneously represent two or more genres? Here, with his close attention to the formal constituents of genres, Fowler points the way. For a work to be comprehensible, according to Fowler, it normally belongs primarily to a single genre. We do not first ask ourselves what *kinds* of work we are reading, but what *kind*. This does not mean that a text cannot exhibit traits from more than one literary genre, merely that one type will dominate, for a work will have only one of what Fowler calls its "external form." Thus, a work is first of all a drama, a novel, a lyric poem, and so on. In this way genres are distinguished from modes, which are adjectival modifications of genres in the direction of the tragic, satiric, novelistic, and so on. Modes have to do with shifts in a genre's content, its point of view, or its technique rather than with the determination of its overall external structure.

As Fowler points out, however, such classifications as drama or lyric are so broad that they tell us little that is interpretively significant about a work. Thus we need a narrower category, though still one large enough to have heuristic force. In Fowler's terminology, this is the "subgenre," made up of a group of texts characterized not only by a common "external form," but also by some limiting "genre-linked motifs or topics," sometimes modal in nature, that they commonly adopt.¹⁶ Indeed, as historical rather than universal categories, subgenres are like genres in that they can be subdivided themselves as long as the level of activity seems to demand it. The only criterion is the profoundly historical and interpretive one that the subgenre serve to assist the reader in understanding the aims of a group of works that adhere to a set of relatively precise and limited norms.

On the other hand, identifying a work's subgenre is different from studying a work's sources.¹⁷ According to Fowler, a subgenre has a distinctive kind of intertextuality, richer and more complex than that uncovered by source study, because the relationship between works in a subgenre is one of cross fertilization or mutual influence. For example, the many *Gulliver*s, *Alice*s, and *Hamlet*s do not constitute a true subgenre, for, though they are each related to a common source, they do not significantly comment on each other. As Fowler puts it, "Elaborations of an original have the latter as their context, rather than each other";[18] they radiate out from their prototype like spokes on a wheel. In contrast, works in a subgenre are related "circumferentially"; their lines of descent cross over each other and mesh in a complex web.

The literary vision, then, is properly a genre, defined by the external form of the dream or vision that provides its structure. Within this larger context, however, the philosophical vision becomes a subgenre. It shares an external form with the larger genre but is limited by subject matter—by topics, issues, motifs that it habitually takes up. It also has the kind of intertextuality that Fowler describes as typical of subgenres. Boethius's *De consolatione philosophiae* is the paradigmatic "source" for a series of medieval imitations, but not as Tom Stoppard's play *Rosencrantz and Guildenstern Are Dead* imitates *Hamlet*, directly and without mediation. Boethian ectypes engage in a process of mutual influence, with, for example, Alain de Lille modifying Lady Philosophy's character in his Lady Nature, and Jean de Meun satirically mediating between the late classical author and the twelfth-century one. Gower draws to some extent on all members of the subgenre that precede him, synthesizing, modifying, correcting when necessary. Because of this complicated pattern of influence, I prefer the term "philosophical vision" to "Boethian vision" to denote the subgenre, which I believe is characterized as much in terms of its discursive function as by its relationship to a specific literary text. In short, the works I treat in this book share not simply the common external form of a vision but also a community of interests that they express through a set of repeating allegorical characters—Nature, Genius, Reason—and arguments about sex, love, the limits of human knowledge, and the use and status of poetic fictions. Analysis by subgenre, then, provides an advantage for discussing both these texts and others in the tradition. First, it provides a way to treat a manageable group of works and thus to avoid the difficulties that the unwieldy body of the medieval vision taken as a whole has presented. Second, insights into one subgenre, the philosophical vision, may help those who study other subgenres, like the courtly love vision, by indicating the meaning and value of philosophical or Boethian elements when they appear in the generic mixtures that are an inevitable feature of literary evolution.

To identify that meaning and value, though, I will need to do more than simply compare similar texts and describe their common elements. To bring to light those features that would have been truly functional, that would have had the most organizing force for an original audience, and to begin to understand the origins of their power, I will need also to construct a historical context for the genre. Fowler's more formal approach is not adequate for this purpose, and I must turn again to Jauss. Although Fowler acknowledges the role historical studies must have in writings on the formation and change of genres, he frankly admits to a much stronger interest in the "*literary* laws of change . . . governing the formation and interaction of genres" (emphasis mine). In part, Fowler focuses on formal considerations because he believes that historical factors such as "external causation" are "not in danger of neglect at present."[19] To the contrary, I think that the current emphasis in American literary theory and practice—under the influence of the New Criticism and recent poststructuralist theory—falls so heavily on the formal, self-contained features of texts that it is now more crucial than ever to try to rehistoricize genres, to recover not just their internal laws but the mechanics by which historical developments exert pressure on those laws.

The kind of reception theory proposed by Hans Robert Jauss and his followers at the University of Constance can, I think, fill this need. Jauss, to be sure, has attracted his critics from various corners, who attack him for everything from his politics to inconsistencies in his methodology. The most incisive of these critics object to a contradiction between Jauss's acknowledgment of our "historical situatedness" as modern readers and his recourse to observations made as if from a neutral position.[20] Without wishing to diminish or ignore the problem here, I would suggest that this contradiction is almost universally characteristic of any theorist who takes his own historicity seriously and at the same time seeks to penetrate the "alterity" of an earlier time period. Jauss's focus on the reader of a text gives him at least a way to describe his own historical bias, even if he is not theoretically able to transcend it. He accomplishes this measure of objectivity through his concept of the "horizon of expectations," the pre-aesthetic and historically conditioned background of assumptions and expectations that every reader brings to a text. In his desire to reconstruct this "horizon," Jauss suggests an analysis that combines a synchronic and diachronic approach, both of which he sees as profoundly historical.[21] The first analyzes the systems of discourse that characterize literature in a cross section, the second the way a sequence of texts is received and exerts influence on other texts and readers. As Jauss explains,

> The basic principle of a historicization of the concept of form demands not only that one relinquish the substantialist notion of a constant number of unchangeable essential characteristics for the individual genres. It also demands that one dismantle the correlative notion of a sequence of literary genres closed within themselves, encapsulated from one another, and inquire into the reciprocal relations that make up the literary system of a given historical moment.[22]

Unfortunately, as Jauss also points out, older literatures rarely testify directly about their literary relations, nor does medieval social history offer much clear evidence about reception.[23] Instead, Jauss argues, the modern reader must mediate between a formalistic or aesthetic approach and a hermeneutic one by studying a whole structure or system of literary discourse, including how works fit into a "literary series," answering each other, solving formal and substantive problems left behind by previous works in their "family" or, as Fowler would say, "subgenre," and suggesting new ones of their own.[24] A thorough historical reading must also locate the genre's hierarchical position in that larger structure in order to define what issues and techniques it could profitably take up. Finally, Jauss acknowledges the power of literature not just to reflect its historical situation but also to influence it; he grants literary works, then, a socially formative role.

These approaches seem promising for the study of the vision genre, which, as I suggested before, had become one of the dominating genres of its time and, at least in its role as the philosophical vision, was occupied in exploring a definite group of aesthetic and philosophical questions. Jauss's theory, then, calls for a yoking of form and function; he would have us ask not just what are the features of this genre, but what purpose do they serve and how might their reception actually affect extraliterary historical conditions. My study is an attempt to respond to this call, especially my first two chapters. These treat the philosophical vision first synchronically, by placing the literary vision in the context of contemporary philosophical discourse, and then diachronically, by studying how philosophical change influenced the reception of the late classical visionary dialogue into the medieval tradition and how that dialogue in its turn sought to speak to its own time.

I have only one serious disagreement with Jauss, and that is when he brings questions of aesthetic value into his historical framework, positing generic innovation as the main criterion for a work's excellence. "The more stereotypically a text repeats the generic," Jauss states rather dogmatically, "the more inferior is its artistic character and its degree of historicity."[25] This position has obvious problems, especially, as Robert C. Holub has noted, in describing the relations between texts in the Middle Ages: "While most of the Formalists were influenced by current literary practices that stressed the destruction of conventions, many past eras, as Jauss surely knows, appear to have appreciated works as much for their similarity with, as their difference from, traditional norms."[26] Unfortunately, Jauss does not seem to be alone in his prejudice. Many contemporary theorists share the bias against the merely conventional, even those like Jauss who are specialists in medieval or Renaissance studies.

In contemporary theory, the words most often used to describe relations between a poet and his predecessors are adversarial—such relations are disruptions, contests, denials, negations, at best triumphs. Even John Fleming, more hospitable than most to cooperative relations between texts, sees these mainly as "fruitful literary competitions," in which a Christian text is invoked to "correct" a pagan one.[27] And Fowler, while tolerantly praising "paradigmatic" as well as "innovative" values, still asserts that "at the level of subgenre, innovation is life."[28] It seems hard to escape the modern idea that the poet's real work is to be original in the modern sense of that word, to blaze a trail or to find the novel, fresh phrase or tactic, rather than to return to origins.

Certainly, no work constitutes an exact replica of its predecessors—it would be meaningless if it did—but adherence to convention can supply a kind of meaning too. In the case of the medieval vision poem, in fact, a bias against conventionality, as I will show, can prove a serious barrier not simply to appreciation but to the very act of understanding the conservative and defensive literary maneuver in which these poets were engaged. To clarify this last point, I need now to formulate briefly my larger argument about the philosophical vision's literary significance within a wider field of discourse, in which assumptions not only about poetry but about human knowledge itself differed dramatically from the modern. By providing an overview, this exercise will also introduce the reader to many of the key concepts and historical movements I will be discussing later in the book.

Poetry and Philosophy: Models of Diachronic Change

In *The Dissolution of the Medieval Outlook*, Gordon Leff has suggested a predictable sequence for intellectual change that has great relevance to my discussion of the parallel evolution of medieval poetry and philosophy.[29] As long as a paradigm can be manipulated to account for new empirical data, Leff argues, change will occur by accommodation, as it does in philosophy until the late thirteenth century, during which time, despite shifts in focus to assimilate new evidence, there was general assent to a philosophically "realist" paradigm—one holding that truth was revealed twice, in scripture and in the book of nature as it could be understood by human reason. Because the paradigm was accepted more or less universally, such change as occurs within it Leff terms "continuous." But when evidence begins to displace presuppositions, change becomes "discontinuous," as it did according to most historians in 1277 when the condemnation of 219 Aristotelian and Averroistic Propositions in some way permanently altered the character of medieval philosophy.[30] Discontinuous change is characterized by a greater pluralism in philosophical approaches, because there occurs "a shift back in the order of discourse from what can be said in the light of certain accepted first principles to those principles considered for themselves."[31] This shift occurs in two stages: first, to reaffirm assumptions by redefining terms; only later, when this strategy becomes ineffective, to replace them. Thus, Leff's sequence includes a total of three steps, only the first two of which took place during the medieval period. These were as follows: (1) the accommodation of new evidence with relative ease into the existing paradigm; (2) the attempt to salvage a difficult paradigm by reconsidering and restructuring its first principles; and (3) the abandonment of the paradigm as no longer consistent with empirical evidence.

Leff's model of late medieval intellectual change applies directly to the poems I will be discussing, which are striking and important expressions of a period in intellectual history when continuous change was just about to become discontinuous. In terms of twelfth- and thirteenth-century philosophy, they are basically conservative; they express continuous change by extending the scope of the realist paradigm to include more and more of experience. In this, they are like the philosophy of their time—like the great *summae* of Thomas Aquinas or Albertus Magnus or the spiritual itinerary of Bonaventure. But in terms of their own poetic ontology, they are already beginning to show strain, expressing discomfort with the paradigm as it is stretched to a point of maximum tension.

No less than prose tracts, then, philosophical poetry may begin to examine not only the principles of philosophy but also its own first principles. Indeed, these poems do both. The disquiet in the high medieval vision poem thus takes the form of self-defensiveness, as art seeks to protect and define the premises that supply its own theoretical basis and the basis of the world it communicates. More than anything else, readers expected to find this sort of paradoxical concern with issues of poetic and philosophic authority in their visionary literature, each poet blending elements of unease, defensiveness, and affirmation in his own way. But in the works from the high medieval period treated here—even those not examined directly, such as Godfrey of St. Victor's *Fons philosophiae* or Brunetto Latini's *Il Tesoretto*—the emphasis falls on affirmation. In contrast, studies of later works show a changed emphasis. Lisa Kiser, in a recent book on Chaucer's *Legend of Good Women*, has demonstrated that this self-reflexive poem is at its most basic level about the uneasy marriage of pagan and Christian motifs, which Chaucer parodies in the character of the God of Love, as at the same time he defends—only by radically redefining them—the roles of art and author as purveyors of truth.[32] Sheila Delany has done similar work on *The House of Fame*, revealing the "skeptical fideism" that restructures Chaucer's attitude toward poetic truth in this work.[33] These fourteenth-century poems thus demonstrate the second step within Leff's series, marking the beginning of discontinuous change.

Although the philosophical contextualizing of this process of literary change gives it a historical basis, the shift from unproblematic acceptance to self-conscious redefinition is interestingly similar to a formal shift that Fowler proposes literary forms normally go through as they become increasingly self-aware and sophisticated. Primary literary kinds, Fowler argues, though not necessarily primitive, come at the beginning of a form's evolution, when a writer is not conscious of the system of conventions within which he is working, or at least not conscious of them *as* a system. Boethius might be seen as primary in respect to the Middle Ages, though of course he comes at the end of another highly sophisticated tradition. Secondary kinds—Alain de Lille's *De planctu naturae*, the *Roman de la rose*, Gower's *Confessio Amantis*—are more deliberate, distanced, conscious of using conventions as such, capable of generating new subgenres like the love vision. Finally, a tertiary kind "takes up a kind already secondary, and applies it in quite a new way," perhaps allegorizing, interiorizing or making burlesque of it, as Kiser and Delany have shown Chaucer's dream visions to do.[34] I am, then, suggesting two ways of regarding the works treated in this book. Historically, in the context of contemporary philosophy, they are works that function largely within a model of change I have designated as "continuous," since they expand an existing paradigm to account for new evidence rather than challenge the paradigm itself. Formally, analyzed as detached structures in a calculated sequence of literary evolution, they are primary or secondary forms of the philosophical vision, for while they may be quite deliberate in their use of conventions, they do not invert or fundamentally question their basic formal paradigm. Both approaches suggest a fundamental unity within the high medieval tradition.

Indeed, the perspective of this period did have a real consistency, which was threatened by the discontinuous change of the later Middle Ages. The difference will emerge, I think, from a comparison of two passages by Thomas Aquinas and Geoffrey of Vinsauf, exemplars of the high medieval perspective, with a discussion by the fourteenth-century philosopher William of Ockham. All three excerpts concern creation, the fundamental basis of all artistic activity within a "realist" paradigm; all use the comparison of artist to architect to describe a special relation between human and divine creative activity. In his *Poetria nova*, the most widely circulated medieval *ars poetica*, Geoffrey of Vinsauf makes use of the comparison in the famous passage that leads off his discussion of invention: "If a man has a house to build, his impetuous hand does not rush into action. The measuring line of his mind first lays out the work, and he mentally outlines the successive steps in a definite order before it is actual."[35]

The metaphor of an architect was also a commonplace in discussions of divine creation. Aquinas used it to explain how the multiplicity of created matter could have issued from the simplicity of divine conception: "The form of the house in the mind of the architect is something understood by him to the likeness of which he produces the form of the house in matter."[36] The comparison survived into the fourteenth century, but with a distinctive shift in emphasis. As William of Ockham puts it,

> For just as the artist who sees a house or building outside the mind first pictures in the mind a similar house and later produces a similar house in reality which is only numerically distinct from the first, so in our case the picture in the mind that we get from seeing something outside would act as a pattern. ... [But] works of art do not seem to inhere in the mind of the craftsman as independent subjects any more than the creatures did in the divine mind before creation.[37]

Similarities here are more immediately apparent than differences: like Aquinas and Geoffrey before him, Ockham supposes that artifacts exist as plans before they become actualities. He even uses the same metaphor for the divine craftsman popularized for centuries before him and appropriated by Geoffrey to describe the poet's activity as well. But he does introduce an important variation here. In the twelfth and thirteenth centuries, the exemplar or universal *would have* inhered in the mind of the craftsman; the pattern *would have* had a reality that existed prior to its appearance as a singular and was also an inherent part of that appearance, as Poetry came to "clothe" matter with words. The universal in high medieval philosophy had done more than just "stand for,"[38] as Ockham says, the singular; singular and universal—finished product and blueprint—had been two phases of the same manifestation. For the poet, this had meant that the actual words and images of his craft had borne a *real* relation to an idea about them that he and his reader might share, a real power to lead the reader beyond the poem to the apprehension of an intended divine truth. Like the *divina pagina* or god-created world, humanly created texts had also been truly sacramental in a way that for a nominalist like Ockham they could not be. For the nominalist, no matter how broadly or pluralistically his activity is construed, there would always be something slightly arbitrary, slightly undependable, about the relation of *significans* to *significatum*.

In noting this shift in thought as the Middle Ages drew to their close, I do not want to give the impression that the High Middle Ages were a static time philosophically. Because the twelfth and thirteenth centuries were a period of intense social, political, and cultural development, thinkers of the age continually had to accommodate new evidence into the paradigm, the philosophical theory that sought to come to terms with the whole. Poets were very sensitive to these accommodations, and so poetry did come to subvert and criticize, offering, for example, what Winthrop Wetherbee has called a critique of philosophy's "failure adequately to reconcile physics with metaphysics, divine immanence with divine transcendence."[39] But, and this is a very important point, we must also keep our eye on the way that poets sought to rise above that failure, to neutralize or contain its threats, especially in an art whose very premises, I will show, rested on that reconciliation. As Theodore Silverstein has observed, "What philosophy could not do poetry might." The special ability he referred to was not, as recent scholars have construed it, poetry's freedom to *explore* philosophical conflicts, but its capacity to *resolve* them by exploiting the special strengths of metaphor and myth.[40]

To return to an earlier point, adherence to convention—the recreation of past models—is a far from disinterested literary activity. It is now a commonplace to point out literature's subversive power when it violates normative patterns; but poems can have an equally significant effect by their profound compliance with accepted patterns, by their position in a carefully worked-out harmony of ideas. In a history of poetic reception, they can even have a special and important meaning to succeeding generations of poets in the force and comprehensiveness with which they articulate the very beliefs that would later demand reformulation. For later poets, looking backward and forward at the same time, the visionary subgenre generated by Boethius and extended by Alain de Lille, Jean de Meun, John Gower, and others would have such a meaning. These poems would embody the authority and conservatism for which later poets yearned as much as they did for change.

Using the terminology introduced here, I will be arguing that the philosophical vision poem in the High Middle Ages had as one of its governing ideas or purposes the defense of a philosophically realist paradigm within a framework of continuous change. I provide the background necessary to prove this thesis by exploring in Chapter 1 the specific characteristics of that high medieval paradigm or world view, stressing particularly the similarity between thought in the twelfth and thirteenth centuries, both of which sought to preserve a humanistic synthesis of disciplines based on the dignity of man and the intelligibility of the natural order. To uncover the presuppositions of this humanism, I describe the epistemology that permitted a rapprochement between natural philosophy and received theology; this epistemology rested on man's ability to use the faculties of reason and imagination to ascend through and beyond naturally obtained knowledge, rising from image to divine significance in a process known as "abstraction."

Based on a similar theory of poetic creation, which put "abstraction" into reverse, many medieval writers argued that poetic images, like the images of created nature, could also represent a higher truth. This time *ingenium*, or the poetic imagination, became the mediating term between the natural world and the divine one. With the proper disciplining activity, the artist could tame his subject matter, as God tamed matter in His creation of the world when He made the created world a mirror of truth. Thus, just as in the commonplace metaphor of the world as a book, poetry works like nature. What is more, in response to the tensions between higher and lower truths poets began to thematize the relation between the two by making the spiritual journey a common narrative pattern in their poetry. The order of knowing, in which a man moves from image to interpretation, from nature to grace, became one of the central, stable poetic structures of the time.

In Chapter 2, I offer some reasons for the literary vision's special hospitality to this kind of narrative pattern, suggesting why it might thereby have gained in the twelfth century a secure position in the hierarchy of genres. For one thing, dreams and visions naturally raise questions of ontology, of how the flesh and spirit can interpenetrate. Because dreams, being neither physical nor spiritual, have a liminal status, they provoked much speculation about their psychology or epistemology in Latin Arabic commentary on Aristotle. Avicenna, for example, describes them in terms of a medical psychology that makes the central drama of vision the same confrontation between imagination and reason upon which rested the high medieval synthesis of reason and revelation. This psychology is then projected onto Boethius's *De consolatione philosophiae* by twelfth-century writers, who register the primarily Platonic epistemology of the *De consolatione* now in a more Aristotelian key, as the vision becomes more explicitly an interior journey from literal to abstract understanding. The form thus allowed poets to offer a defense of high medieval humanism, which included defending poetry's right to purvey truth, for medieval dream theory frequently insisted on the equation between dream images and the fabulous imagery of the poets.

All of these inherent advantages of the form are capitalized upon by Alain de Lille in his *De planctu naturae*, modeled largely on Boethius's poem. Previous scholars have not focused sufficiently closely on the precise ways that Alain both borrows from and also changes the *De consolatione*. In Chapter 3, I concentrate on the narrative structure that I have identified as central to the genre's defensive function, the order of knowing or the visionary's spiritual journey toward truth. In such a journey, many of the poem's allegorical characters become reflections of the Dreamer's evolving consciousness of his own sin and how he may overcome it. Natura, for example, is related both to the created world over which she is a goddess and also to the mode of knowing proper to assist an individual in knowing himself through that world. Genius becomes a figure for the Dreamer's imagination. By thus tracing the interchange between the narrator and his allegorical guides, I show that the Dreamer gains in knowledge throughout the poem, following the natural order of knowing. His progress culminates in the final narrative pageant, when Genius's anathema represents not only a pessimistic banishment of evil individuals but also an Augustinian solution to the problem of evil; we come to realize that the wicked, in being only *semiplena*, literally, half full or half completed, cease finally to exist at all. Thus, this poem is ultimately more humanistic or optimistic about the possibility of uniting nature and grace than either Boethius's work, which ends on a more ambiguous note, or than Alain's other spiritual journey, the *Anticlaudianus*, which he does not frame as a vision.

A similar optimism is demonstrated by Jean de Meun, whose continuation of the *Roman de la rose* juxtaposes the spiritual failure of the Lover's lustful imagination to the wholesome advice promoted by Reason. The tension between the visionary pilgrim and his guide reflects a growing thirteenth-century tension within the Church about naturalistic study, which I relate in Chapter 4 to such events as the condemnation in 1277 of the 219 Aristotelian and Averroistic Propositions. Such tensions, however, did not create radical or discontinuous change but served more frequently to cause a tightening of defenses among poets and philosophers. The bite of Jean's satire is directed at those who would deny Reason her proper precedence in the soul, not at Reason herself. The controversial doctrines espoused by many of the allegorical characters—in particular, Nature and Genius—are thus attributable to the Lover, not to the poet, who seeks to distance himself from their beliefs. Still, he does seem more self-conscious, less secure in his role as an artist imitating nature's truth; he thus anticipates the dislocations of the coming century, suggesting that for the poet these occur first as a reexamination of his art's own basic principles.

In Dante, however, writing at the beginning of the next century, these dislocations are far less troubling. Though like Jean's poem in its comprehensiveness, Dante's *Commedia* differs from the *Roman de la rose* in putting the resources of an encyclopedic form into the defense of a conservative, realist world view. The pilgrim in this poem successfully negotiates the passage from literal to figural and absolute meaning, especially in the *Purgatorio*, where his mental journey takes center stage. Here Virgil plays Reason to the pilgrim's literalizing imagination, whose conversion to truth is articulated in stages, partly through two dreams dramatizing the visionary's failure to abstract truth and then in a final dream when he achieves wholeness and order in both the intellectual and affective parts of his soul. His progress is confirmed as he successfully uses the image of Beatrice to pass through a wall of fire and two rivers that purge and rehabilitate his memory. Dante thus draws upon the deepest liminal possibilities of the vision, which lies between flesh and spirit as Purgatory lies metaphorically between heaven and earth. But Dante is not only interested in the progress of his pilgrim as spiritual everyman, but with his role as the poet's persona as well. The pilgrim's success affirms both the possibility of visionary sight and also the value of the poetic imagery that this sight apprehends.

The final poet I treat belongs to a time period that extends past the High Middle Ages, and yet he demonstrates the genre's essential continuity by reaching back in time. John Gower's *Confessio Amantis*, written in the late fourteenth century, adopts both the frame structure and many of the characters and approaches of the Boethian or philosophical vision. Though his narrator hestitates and makes false turns in his progress and though his guide "Genius" more closely resembles imagination than the traditional Reason, finally Gower's Amans does translate the lessons provided by his earthly experience into spiritual growth. In the tradition, the *Confessio Amantis* therefore affirms a metaphysics based on the harmony of scripture and scientific authority. Still, Gower is a transitional figure, both reaching back and pointing forward to another poet whose most avidly expressed hope was a skeptical "God turne us every drem to goode!" As not only the moral philosopher but also the friend and contemporary of Chaucer, Gower's delicately poised and self-conscious use of the form provides evidence that fourteenth-century writers still found in the subgenre of the philosophical vision a means for expressing their wonder about how the divine is made manifest. It is this unique possibility of the form that, I contend, gave it a continuing power to make demands on its readers' imaginations and to excite renewed controversy. This study is one more testimony to the lasting strength of that power.

CHAPTER I

The Marriage of Matter and Form in High Medieval Philosophy and Poetics

In the *De nuptiis Philologiae et Mercurii*, the fifth-century poet Martianus Capella had sanctified the intimacy between Philology and Mercury—wisdom and eloquence, philosophy and poetry—in an allegorical marriage. This work exercised an unusually powerful command over the high medieval imagination because it harmonized with that period's ideal of marrying and reconciling expression with understanding, and, by extension, learning with truth, natural with supernatural. In a way not intended by either Martianus or his medieval commentators, marriage seems an apt metaphor for the union we are discussing. Like most marriages, it was not a match made wholly in heaven, but complicated and impelled by squabbles, contradictions, tensions. These tensions, however, did not lead to absolute rupture.

During the entire period between the late eleventh century and the late thirteenth, no thinker or school of philosophy seems seriously to have entertained the notion that naturalism should be pursued for its own sake. Science did not mean, as it now does, the study of the laws that govern the physical world for themselves alone. It meant the study of God's creatures and phenomena for His sake. As one commentator puts it, "Magis enim cognoscere est ad deum accedere" ("For to know more is to approach God.")[1] Nor in discovering physical laws did natural philosophers primarily use the modern scientific method of closely observing empirical data; instead they relied upon the work of the ancients, whose observations they sought to interpret in accordance with divine truth. Thus, though there were tensions, even times when groups or individuals faced charges of heresy for their interpretations of an antique doctrine such as that of the world soul, these tensions were controlled by a shared subscription to a common paradigm; that is, a commitment to the marriage of learning and truth. Thus, philosophical change happened in what we have designated as a continuous rather than a discontinuous way.

This is not to say, though, that changes of many kinds were not profound. As Marc Bloch, and more recently Lester Little, make clear, a major historical shift began in the middle of the eleventh century; the great invasions of Europe were over, and a new age of prosperity, urban development, population growth, increased mobility, and accelerated commerce was made possible.[2] These alterations in the social fabric in turn encouraged greater individualism and personalism in human life and a new love of nature and detail for their own sakes, new outlooks that were reflected in the art and literature of the age. But change had its darker side too, for the years in question witnessed political problems caused by quarrels over the limits of jurisdictions and a spiritual crisis engendered in large part by the difficulty of adapting older forms of monastic spirituality to the new profit economy. The results, as Little points out, were disturbing strains, for example, "between morality and behaviour, between theology and society, between religion and life itself."[3]

With social and spiritual tension, though, comes accommodation and attempts at resolution. Resolution might even draw creatively on the revival of ancient philosophy to meet changing institutional needs. The claims of the world and its Creator had to be balanced and justified in new ways, and thinkers—some of whom I will be discussing here—were not lacking to achieve the needed harmony. For example, stress within the institution of the Church caused the reforming of the sacrament of penance to allow for greater emphasis on the intentional state of the sinner (identified in Aristotelian terms with matter) while still honoring the necessity of priestly absolution (identified with form).[4] Even the development of correspondences between microcosm and macrocosm had at base a civic or political purpose. Among the greatest achievements of the twelfth and thirteenth centuries, then, were the means these times developed for coping with crisis.

Certainly, different ways of adapting to change would create differences in institutions, in the various generations, and of course between the twelfth and thirteenth centuries as a whole. R. W. Southern, for example, has recently shown that the deinstitutionalization of the cathedral school in the twelfth century freed individual masters to teach new subjects. Correspondingly, the powerful and highly institutionalized thirteenth-century universities would have had a directive and perhaps inhibiting effect on scholarship. But no historian of the age has been as adamant as Southern in asserting the basic unity and humanism of the High Middle Ages taken as a whole.[5] The characteristics of this humanism he names as follows: (1) a sense of man's dignity, (2) a recognition of the dignity and order of nature, and (3) the intelligibility of this order to human reason. These attitudes provided the context within which friction and change could be fruitful. Thus, though many writers of the thirteenth century may seem less poetic and mythically compelling to us now than those of the twelfth-century "renaissance," they are no less humanistic, for they persist maybe even more indefatigably and vehemently than ever to assert the dignity of man and nature and the intelligibility of God's universe.

It is important to note, however, that though the course of poetry as a humanistic discipline was tied to the other sciences, it was not exactly parallel. As a field of art that made its appeal primarily through affect and not intellect, its fate would not necessarily follow that of the other reasoning sciences.[6] Indeed, even in the twelfth century poetry had its serious detractors. John of Salisbury, for example, attacks a certain Cornificius, whose attempt to deny the verbal arts their place in the medieval curriculum—"[to wrest] from Philology's arms her beloved Mercury"—is so heinous, John believes, as to "[assail] the whole structure of philosophy" and to lead to the disintegration of "all civilization."[7] But, by and large, the twelfth century, with its theories of *fabula, integumentum,* and *involucrum,* allowed poetry the right to veil high mystery and truth.[8] It offered an environment more hospitable to the philosopher-poet than that environment would be again during the Middle Ages. The poetic works of Bernardus Silvestris, Alain de Lille, Jean de Hanville, and twelfth-century commentary on the poetry of Boethius and Virgil give remarkable testimony to the authority the poets had in leading their readers to some manner of philosophic understanding. Thus, we must acknowledge some break between the twelfth century and the thirteenth, when Henri d'Andeli, in chronicling the victory of logic and philosophy over grammar and the poets, writes despairingly, "Sirs, the times are given to emptiness."[9] Some of that age's appreciation for the classics was necessarily sacrificed to the huge task of assimilating the exploding body of Aristotelian natural science newly available in translation and commentary. This task of assimilation naturally changed the tone of discourse, making it more rationalistic and, one might say, systematic.

On the other hand, the arts were not totally banished in the thirteenth century. Poetry was suspect because it depended on the less certain affective or imaginative knowledge, which had to be submitted to reasonable analysis before it could be trusted. But insofar as it was susceptible to such analysis, poetry could still provide a valid insight. John of Garland pleaded eloquently for authors in the thirteenth century, and the practice of thirteenth-century poets themselves indicates, as I will show, their hope of representing not only moral instruction but also some image of truth. To be sure, attitudes toward poetry seem to have embodied more tension—to have shifted to a focus on first principles—rather earlier than those toward philosophy; one result was an earlier loss of nerve in extending the art's speculative range, such as is evidenced, for example, by Averroes's translation of the *Poetics*, which makes poetry a faculty without content and denies works of poetry proper access to scientific or philosophical subjects. Yet even in this work, there is a special attentiveness to the structure of the human soul and the way that poets give birth to an imaginative universe whose poetic decorum requires it to resemble the natural universe ordained by God.[10] The shift that was to revolutionize later medieval poetic art was not really complete until the fourteenth century, when the distance between exemplar and appearance, which I earlier located in Ockham, would also have its full effect on poetic practice in more closely circumscribing its subject matters and ambitions and gathering them in to earth.

However, so continuous a description of the art's evolution requires a certain tolerance for reading between the lines, because most of the available evidence does not address the status of poetry directly or theoretically, as we expect our own literary criticism to do. Winthrop Wetherbee notes that "before Dante, it is difficult to talk about medieval attitudes toward poetry. There is little discussion of its function as anything but a pedagogical device." But, as Wetherbee also observes, these pedagogical discussions and the poetry itself hide many "attitudes" that have gone largely unexplored until now.[11] By studying here the idea of imagination and the expectations for order in poetry that informed high medieval aesthetics, I will attempt to show the overall coherence in attitudes toward the subject during the twelfth and thirteenth centuries. In fact, their shared subscription to a notion of the poetic imagination made it possible for poets ranging from Bernardus Silvestris to Dante to build into their works a particular kind of defense of man's capacity to express in his poetry a legitimate imaginative truth, one that stands below but not separate from the truth of philosophy and scripture. It is in this context that Etienne Gilson calls Aquinas the "greatest poet of the Latin tongue of the whole Middle Ages,"[12] while Dante is the greatest philosopher in the vernacular. Both poet and philosopher engage the high medieval humanistic tradition; both adhere most strenuously to the realist synthesis of reason and revelation, one that implies as well a meeting ground between poetic and discursive modes of expression.

In the chapters that follow, I will not minimize the tensions that made this union interesting or the variety of approaches to reconciliation when problems seemed to threaten it. Even so, as Southern has demonstrated, the many different approaches that have gone under such opposing labels as humanist and scholastic, Chartrian and Victorine, rationalist and symbolist, empirical and mystical are not so much fully developed schools as individual differences in achieving the commonly held goal of opening the works of the past and the great book of nature to Christian truth. My first task, however, will be to show the underlying humanistic paradigm that made change in the High Middle Ages continuous rather than discontinuous. I will be looking specifically at the way that paradigm rested on a special epistemology, and the way that this epistemology in turn informed the age's spoken and unspoken assumptions about poetry. This focus will make possible fidelity to the syncretism of the age, to the union of twelfth-century poetry and philosophy. I will focus here on the attempt in both fields to harmonize the abstract and the concrete, to discipline their subject matters by defining the special relationship of imaginative to intellectual truth. These two poles—intellect and imagination—mirror the poles of heaven and earth. For the High Middle Ages, then, an understanding of their relationship could become an understanding of the difficult relationship of divine to earthly truth, of limited human understanding to the limitless comprehension of the Creator—and thus could become as well a means for protecting the world view that relied on unity between the two.

The Epistemological Model

Philosophy's task in sustaining the marriage of natural and divine was to help convince man of the integrity of this world, to make him conscious of the ways in which divinity was revealed in and through matter. Although educational theorists frequently divided knowledge into two kinds—science and wisdom, practical and theoretical—the ultimate task of all learning was the bringing of man to God, a fact that was significant precisely because all learning originated in the physical world. The belief that the ascent to God begins in apprehension of the material caused thinkers during this period to maintain what M.-D. Chenu has called a "symbolist mentality"; that is, they believed that by the forming of analogies between the material and the divine, the spirit could journey home to God.[13] The tenor of the age is thus Aristotelian as opposed to Platonic—or at least Platonic with heavy Aristotelian coloring even before much of Aristotle's philosophy was available to the Latin West—for it held that spiritual ascent begins in study of the natural world. As Aristotle had stated, "The soul never thinks without an image."

A kind of Platonic dualism may have lain behind the synthesis, giving it energy and urgency. Indeed, a tension between the actual and the many as against the ideal or the one can be seen as the reflection in philosophical terms of the social, political, and economic tensions I have already mentioned. But such strain is inevitable in any culture or body of thought that tries to honor the world and its Creator at the same time—whether that culture borrows its dualism directly from Plato and Aristotle or from Boethius or Augustine. As Chenu observes, "The Christian contemplating the world is torn by a double attraction: to attain God through the world, the order of which reveals its creator, or to renounce the world, from which God is radically distinct."¹⁴ But in our period—the years of the twelfth and thirteenth centuries—the tension was resolved largely in favor of the first option, namely, attaining God through a world whose order reveals its creator. Or as Gordon Leff puts it, "The overwhelming tendency was to interpret reality in terms of universal natures or essences or forms as the created expression of the universal archetypes or divine ideas in God. That held whether the particular inspiration of a thinker was Neoplatonist or Aristotelian."¹⁵

The age's ideal of harmonizing natural philosophy and received theology grew inevitably from this tendency. This goal could only be achieved if philosophers could demonstrate that reason's inductions from nature—most clearly represented in the works of the ancient philosophers—were consistent with truth as revealed in the Bible. Thus, the harmony required a psychology that would define the basis for such inductions. To affirm the unity of divine spirit with its physical expression in matter depended ultimately on the capacity of the human spirit to know both, to know the second through the first. This affirmation depended on man's ability to live as a spirit in a body, the talent of his *anima* to contain within itself the faculties capable of apprehension of the particular in material objects as well as knowledge of the universal, which participated in divinity. The psychological theory that described these faculties would thus constitute the cornerstone of the whole synthesis. Though in the Latin West it would receive its fullest and most elaborated treatment in the works of the thirteenth century, in Albertus Magnus and Thomas Aquinas, theirs would be essentially the same psychology that had succeeded in resolving the tensions implicit in high medieval thought over two hundred years. A part of the dignity, natural order, and intelligibility Southern claims as features of medieval humanism was a psychology of knowing that would give the whole system a rational basis.

Predictably, this psychology would be comparatively mechanical and descriptive, seeking as it did to explain logically the means by which the soul attains an increasingly rational and abstract knowledge. Not until the generation after Aquinas would any thinker begin to talk of an integral wholeness to the act, or of "intuition" as initiating knowledge—a revival of the Augustinian concept of illumination.¹⁶ The psychologies of the twelfth and thirteenth centuries built upon a doctrine of the faculties inherited from classical writers such as Aristotle, Galen, and Nemesius, transmitted and interpreted by earlier medieval Arabic commentators. This doctrine conceived of knowing as a procession of steps, each performed by a different faculty, each with its specific object of analysis.[17] There was considerable diversity of opinion on how many faculties the human soul possessed, or exactly what names and functions ought to be attributed to the various powers, even differences on how "rational" the process of knowing was. But like the differences between Victorine symbolism and Chartrian rationalism, the divergences are not as significant as the similarities, as least for my purposes. Nearly all schemes, whether they had their origins in Paris or Chartres, in the twelfth century or the thirteenth, held that a series of faculties, beginning with "common sense" and ending with "reason" or "intellect," in one way or another progressively "abstracted"[18] immaterial forms, the objects of rational judgment, from material substances, the objects of sense.

Since the purpose of the psychology was to define the relationship of material to immaterial—of body to soul—it necessarily had to be a physical system as well. Indeed, in its Galenic roots, it primarily supplied a medical description, and the discreteness of mental powers in part may have been derived by analogy with the discreteness of bodily organs. Inextricably linked, then, with philosophical discussion of cognitive process was a medical theory that localized mental functions and assigned them each an area in the mind. Medieval diagrams of brain function divided the brain into a varying number of cells or lobes, usually three or five. In the simpler model, the first was termed the imagination or fantasy, a receptacle for storing and combining images called forth from the *sensus communis* or common sense, responsible for coordinating the evidence provided by the five senses. The second cell was labeled *estimativa, cogitativa, ratio,* or *intelligentia,* and this was the residence of reason, which discriminated among imaginative perceptions. The third and final lobe at the rear of the brain contained memory. The model was often complicated to varying degrees. In some schemes *sensus communis* occupied its own cell, and a higher form of imagination or lower sort of estimation took a place between fantasy and reason. The Latin Arabic writer Avicenna, whose dream theory I will draw upon in the next chapter, even conflates these two in a faculty he calls—though not totally consistently—*imaginativa* in animals and *cogitans* in man. But complications and inconsistencies abound in all versions. What is important for us here is that all schemes seem to have had in common at least some version of the crucial powers of imagination, reason, and memory.[19]

The faculties, indeed, were so physiologically determined that the act of imagining or remembering required the inclining of the head forward or back to allow the flow of the vital or animal spirits (also called *pneuma*) produced in the heart to collect in the anterior or posterior ventricles of the brain.[20] The very hairs of the head were thought to be cilia that allowed for the discharge of these spirits produced by cognitive exercise. Even so, the mechanistic outlines of this model ought not to obscure the essentially critical and valuative uses to which I am arguing medieval philosophers put it. The central problem of reconciling heaven and earth, or defining the relations of matter and form, became for the High Middle Ages primarily a problem of understanding the union of mind and body. Their world view depended on overcoming the problem of how an immortal and immaterial soul could inhabit a mortal and physical body. In solving the problem, they necessarily had to give much attention to the dignity and importance of the body.

At its most elevated in the High Middle Ages, then, the body was granted a special eminence. It was not the soul's prison, but its servant and instrument. In determining spiritual progress, it provided man his bridge between an earthly habitat and a divine home. As medieval writers from Haly Abbas to Thomas Aquinas emphasize repeatedly, soundness of mind and body was a necessary prerequisite to spiritual health.[21] Proper subordination of mental faculties in the hierarchy would ultimately stimulate the proper functioning of the will and promote the total harmony of the individual. Thus, the movement between the physical faculties on which the epistemology was based constituted an act of self-discovery and self-definition. Such a scheme had strong appeal to an age that yearned for the large, universal harmony suggested by a physical explanation of metaphysical discovery.

Attractive because of its incorporation of the physical into a theory of spiritual knowledge, the medical model still buried the tensions between two truths without putting them to death. The point of the scheme's greatest usefulness in preserving the marriage of reason and faith was also its most problematic. To perform the acts of judgment necessary to spiritual progress, a faculty higher than cogitation or simple discrimination was necessary, a faculty capable of apprehending the universals essential to a knowledge of God. This higher reason or understanding was commonly held to be itself immaterial, for how could a purely physical attribute be responsible for metaphysical awareness? As Bonaventure explains, "It abstracts, therefore, from place and time and motion, and for this reason it cannot change, nor can it have any limits in space and time but is absolutely spiritual."[22] Yet this elevated reason was ambiguously related to the lower faculties; it depended on them for the images from which it could abstract universal truths. Learning necessarily began as a physical process, though at some point it moved beyond the limits of a body.

As the faculty whose judgments bore not only upon the material but also on the transcendent realm, reason partook of both worlds. In performing certain acts it was part of the sensible soul, in others the rational soul. Although Aquinas carefully differentiates the *ratio particularis*, "to which medical scientists assign a fixed part of the body, the middle of the head," from the *ratio intellectiva*,[23] many writers are not so rigorous in observing such distinctions. Many, indeed, seem to conflate the two roles, as in the following example by John of Salisbury. The confusion is inherited with the doctrine of faculty psychology itself, which had developed in two traditions—a Galenic one that localized intellect and an Aristotelian one that did not.[24] The ambiguity is both the native weakness and the strength of the system, for, though capable of lifting man above the world of sense and images, reason must also rely on images provided by its neighbors, imagination and memory. It might be thought of as occupying a physical space itself, yet somehow it is greater than that space: "Reason serves as a sort of supreme senate in the soul's Capitoline Hill, where it is centrally situated between the chambers of imagination and memory, so that from its watchtower, it may pass upon the judgments of sensation and imagination. Reason, although divine, is, as it were, set into motion by the winnowing fan of sensory perceptions and acts of the imagination."[25]

In other words, reason participates in both divinity and biology. The conflation of the two reasons—the immaterial and the material—points to the scheme's deepest purpose: a soul that lives daily in the body, subjected to the pressures of sensation and desire, requires, even as part of its bodily function, some capacity to discriminate among and also to pass judgment on sensations, some way to rise above them as an integral part of knowing them. Like a polis, man as microcosm needs a government, and the soul needs a certain power of abstraction.

Not surprisingly, the workings of this power generate the most intense discussion and cause the most persistent problems for medieval descriptive psychology—of which disagreements about the status of reason are representative. Predictably, when the model began to break down, it did so here, where the tensions had been buried, in the assimilation of "phantasms," particular and concrete images, by reason, which was bodiless and unerring. Philosophical resources were marshalled most insistently to devise structures that would defend the world view at this point. As Gilson remarks, abstraction was the "principle of which the Thomistic system is largely the metaphysical justification and consistent application."[26] Indeed, the failure of the theory of abstraction, explored in the works of later medieval philosophers like John Duns Scotus and William of Ockham, complicated the status of imaginative truth and led to the dislocations I have noted in late medieval poetry and poetic theory. It was this failure that would cause philosophical as well as literary change to become discontinuous.

The problem comes in defining precisely the relationship between reason and imagination. In the psychological tradition represented by Aquinas and his predecessors, abstraction—the operation of intellect or reason that I have been discussing—was sharply differentiated from imaginative knowing but intimately bound up with it as well. The imagination apprehended singular individuals in the disembodied images or phantasms that it stored. But the act of knowing was incomplete until the reason appropriated the image or its inherent universal idea to itself, "and this cannot happen until it is disengaged from phantasms by abstraction."[27] Abstraction, then, was the proper completion of the process toward which the human soul had been straining all along in its urge to know: "As all sensible objects find a common terminus in the common sense, so do all phantasms in the intellect."[28] In disentangling the intelligible idea from its sensible coverings and in assimilating to itself the unintelligible form, reason came to universal knowledge.

Furthermore, in thus assimilating or "actualizing" the universal form, the species of its object known, reason constructed for itself certain concepts or *intentiones* that would govern its relationship to that object. Aquinas suggests that this activity is a more exalted version of what an animal does when, using its *vis aestimativa*, it perceives *intentiones* as principles of benefit or harm in the world and so seeks or shuns certain things—as a lamb flees its enemy the wolf or as a bird collects straw for its nest. In man, the intellectual activity of the soul shaded here even into the affective, for the proper use of reason—the proper formation of *intentiones*—went part way toward curing him of his impulse toward the spiritually harmful, worked to heal his wrongful love. The final act of will in regard to these *intentiones*, an act through which the individual was blessed or not, thus depended on the discipline of his reason.[29]

On the other hand, reason was not alone responsible for this act. Because imagination provided the phantasms necessary for knowledge, this faculty was potentially the wellspring of the most profound self-awareness that reason could attain. Imagination provided the first crucial step in the soul's journey toward truth. Unlike reason, however, it was also the origin of the most destructive error. In the marriage of human knowledge and divine truth, reason or intellect did the work, imagination caused the problems. The intellect participated in the essence of divinity; imagination was part of the variable world of sense. Consequently, reason misjudged only when imagination was in error, and imagination was often dangerously inaccurate. In Aquinas's words, "Thus, just because effects, as such, are weaker than their causes, and the power and impress of an agent is less and less evident the further away are its effects, therefore imagination is even more liable than are the senses to fall into the error which arises from a dissimilarity between the sense and its object."[30] Or as Hugh of Saint Victor puts it, "Understanding is pure and certain knowledge of the sole principles of things—namely, of God, of ideas, and of prime matter, and of incorporeal substances. Imagination, however, is sensuous memory made up of the traces of corporeal objects inhering in the mind; it possesses in itself nothing certain as a source of knowledge."[31]

The perils posed by the imagination were a necessary part of the soul's itinerary in its journey toward truth, for knowledge of God must begin with knowledge of the world; insight with sight. As Murray Wright Bundy points out, the attempt to reconcile the mystic's impulse to transcendent vision with the naturalist's urge to science "resulted in an appreciation of the imagination not for many years to be again achieved."[32] In being limited by imagination, the intellect was also inspired by it. According to Hugh, judgment was "excited" by imagination; reason could "confirm" only what imagination had already "suggested."[33] This was a cause for sorrow in Dante's *Convivio*, where he laments

> that our intellect for lack of that virtue by which it draws to itself that which it perceives (I mean an organic virtue, namely, imagination), cannot rise to certain things because the imagination cannot help it, as it has not wherewithal. Such, for example, are substances separate from matter, which, although we may to some extent speculate about them, we cannot understand or apprehend perfectly.[34]

But it was this very limitation of the intellect which later, when he was speculating as best he could about these ineffables, caused Dante to elevate the imagination in his *Commedia*, to see in it the receptacle of divine inspiration. How else could God inform human reason, finally so dependent upon images for truth, than through the imagination: "O imagination, that do sometimes so snatch us from outward things that we give no heed, though a thousand trumpets sound around us, who moves you if the sense affords you naught? A light moves you which takes form in heaven, of itself, or by a will that downward guides it."[35]

Such a prophetic dimension in the imagination was implicit in the body of psychological theory with which Dante was familiar. It provided the very foundation of his world view, which was in its most essential elements also the world view of a poet like Bernardus Silvestris or Alain de Lille. Fully as important to Dante as the job of balancing the claims of earthly monarchy with those of heavenly rule was the task of harmonizing the new science with revelation. For the century and a half between Alain and Dante, philosophy had accomplished this feat when it showed its respect for the Creator by honoring the material image He had created; the greatest thinkers of the age, men whom Dante particularly admired, like Thomas Aquinas, had directed their strongest energies to the effort of preserving the harmony between natural reason and divine law, which meant above all to the effort of developing an epistemology of vision adequate to that task.

Central to this epistemology was a special relation of imagination and intellect, a grounding of human reason in the facts of this world, but also a raising of those facts by abstraction to a higher dignity that enabled the individual to make order of a life whose confusions and allurements might otherwise be threatening. One of those allurements was the imaginative world offered by the poets. Not surprisingly—since the border between poetry and philosophy was a blurred rather than a distinct line—a look at high medieval poetic theory and practice suggests that a similar epistemology also informed the synthesis of poetic imagery and higher truth.

Imagination, 'Ingenium,' and a Realist Poetics

The medieval artist gained authority, as I noted in my Introduction, from the association of his own "makings" with divine acts of creation. Correspondences between the three levels of creation—God's, nature's, man's—were commonplace, as was the metaphor of the world as a book, which implies its opposite, the book as a kind of little world. Thus, just as philosophers dedicated to the discovery of holy truth in a "sacramental" world required a psychology to find and communicate images embodying at once physical and spiritual truth, so poets of that world needed a psychology to express sacramental images. According to Averroes, for example, the "first cause" for the origin of poetry was the soul's need for images in understanding.[36] That the medieval writer did not share our post-Romantic concept of the imagination, then, does not mean, as some have argued, that he lacked a concept of any creative poetic imagination.[37] Even among classical rhetoricians, fantasy had held potential to explain how poems get created.[38] But in response to the special need of twelfth- and thirteenth-century philosophic and poetic theory—a need to define the basis of the realist paradigm and man's place within it—imagination's role grew in scope and power.

Imagination had never been simply a power of apprehension. It had always possessed other, creative resources, and these were now called upon with increasing frequency. As Morton Bloomfield points out, this faculty not only governed the retention and interpretation of images referred to the mind by the senses. It was also an "internal sense," capable of creating images by "combining or recalling them without any stimulation from the external senses."[39] Its new role in poetry called upon all its inherent abilities: its capacity to retain pictures from physical matter, to create new pictures by combining old ones, and to present those pictures, in a necessary first step of poetic creation, to other faculties of the mind capable of judgment. These faculties would then order the poet's imaginative world so that it could imitate a divine truth, thus mimicking in art the realist synthesis of reason and revelation.

Imagination's central role in knowing thus implied a role in making known. Suggestively, high medieval texts also name another faculty with this double role, *ingenium*, whose implications for poetry we may trace as well. At times, indeed, imagination and *ingenium* are explicitly linked, suggesting that an investigation of *ingenium* as a faculty can help illuminate imagination and the task of expression that human artists felt they had to fulfill in this sacramental world. The conflation of the two terms seems to have occurred as early as the opening of the twelfth century, in the teachings of Bernard of Chartres as described by John of Salisbury:

> Nature first evokes our natural capacity [*ingenium*] to perceive things, and then, as it were, deposits these perceptions in the secure treasury of our memory. Reason then examines, with its careful study, those things which have been perceived, and which are to be, or have been, commended to memory's custody. . . . Nature has provided beforehand these three factors as both the foundations and the instruments of all the arts.[40]

Other writers also pick up on the connection between imagination and *ingenium*. Frequently, for example, as part of the psychological theory I discussed in the first half of the chapter, the two are assigned the same location in the anterior ventricle of the brain. Both Guillaume de Conches and the *Aeneid* commentator make this connection by locating the two faculties in the same lobe, where, according to Guillaume in his glosses on Boethius, resides "the power of understanding which is called fantastical."[41] Adelard of Bath also locates the three powers of imagining, reasoning, and remembering "in cerebro," associating the first explicitly with *ingenium*.[42] But not only does *ingenium* in this passage and elsewhere fill roughly the same space in the epistemological scheme occupied earlier by imagination; in initiating the process that leads to the establishment of the arts and study, it also serves as the same sort of bridge between matter and spirit that we have seen to be so important in effecting a synthesis between the two realms.

This bridging function emerges in many discussions of the faculty that stress not only its native power but its human limits as well.

Although Macrobius had said of Virgil that he wrote "non mortali sed divino ingenio," in our period the power of human wit or *ingenium* could not extend so far.[43] As a cousin of imagination, this faculty must, like imagination, be ordered to reason or intellect, which provides man the access he has to truth. Because *ingenium* shares with imagination the capacity of knowing the physical world and the function of referring its sensory knowledge to man's higher faculties, it shares imagination's visionary and some of its delusive potential as well. Bernard of Chartres had pointed the way to something like this formulation in a lecture reported by John of Salisbury; there are three sorts of *ingenium*, he says: "The first flies, the second creeps, the third takes the intermediate course of walking." The third prepares the way for true knowledge because "it has its feet on the ground so it can firmly stand, and because it can climb, provides prospect of progress, and is admirably suited for philosophizing."[44] The divisions remind one of the various possibilities for awareness or delusion that imagination offered. Any natural power that sparks supernatural awareness will not only have its head in the clouds but have its feet on the ground as well, so that in the *Anticlaudianus* Alain de Lille attributes not only human strength but also human limitation to *humani ingenii scintilla*, the glimmer or trace of human *ingenium*.[45] As Winthrop Wetherbee explains, "The imagination implied by *ingenium* will be capable of expressing our impulse to participation in the natural order but at the same time of confounding reason with carnal fantasy through its involvement with the senses."[46] So also in Dante, *ingenium* inspires the greatest art, but only when subjected to "assiduous study" and "a disposition for learning."[47]

Yet it is significant for the dignity of human art and cognition that, although dangers are present, authors quite frequently mention the native insight and ability of the faculty called *ingenium*. At times, *ingenium* is clearly distinguished from imagination, and in such cases comes higher on the scale of faculties that participate in the epistemological ascent. Alcher de Clairvaux, for example, names *ingenium* as the power or intention that searches things out or investigates them. Using *ingenium*, the soul exercises or trains itself "to know unknowables."[48] In the ascent from inferior to superior apprehension, its action follows that of imagination and cogitation, and directly precedes that of intellect. Likewise, Guillaume de Conches in his *Glosae super Timeum* puts *ingenium* in a different class altogether from imagination, a power in man that merely figures absent things. *Ingenium* becomes, along with memory and opinion, "the servant" of reason and intellect: "*Ingenium* is a natural power for speedily understanding something, and *ingenium* is as if to say innerly begotten."[49]

In some ways, then, *ingenium* comes closer to resembling reason or intellect than imagination, though it never attains to quite this level. Or one might say that it has a special relevancy to a philosophy concerned with defining the relations between matter and form, for it occupies an ambiguous space between the two, between the realms of material and metaphysical, bringing man to the threshold of a higher awareness. In many writers, the faculty serves as the foundation for logic, which makes possible natural philosophy. But its powers go even further. In one twelfth-century text, it is even credited with vatic foresight: "For *ingenium* has the ability to apprehend that which is to come."[50] An *ingenium* whose sight is trained firmly on this world, but whose vision extends upwards and beyond it, will make discoveries capable of moving the soul closer to God.

Although the links are hard to draw and probably should not be insisted upon too strenuously, *ingenium*, with all its special abilities and associations, seems also to have been especially associated with man's ability to create, and especially to create poetically. Petrarch was to call Apollo, god of the poets, *deus ingenii*,[51] and Isidore of Seville says the man who has the faculty is capable of bringing forth much art.[52] A study of the word in Dante shows that for him at least *ingenium* is an especially creative source: *imaginatio* denotes man's passive faculty of comprehending images, *ingenium* his expressive power of fashioning them. In *Paradiso* XIV.103–5, for instance, Dante laments the deficiency of wit or imagination which prevents him from making Christ manifest: "Here my memory outstrips my wit [*ingegno*], for that Cross so flashed forth Christ that I can find for it no fit comparison." This, and many similar references, indicate that, as Dante understood the term, *ingegno* denoted the poetic power of fashioning comparisons or embodying ineffable ideas.[53] This was a power implied by the Latin usage and poetic theory to which Dante and his audience were heir.

The *Commentary on the Aeneid*, for instance, supports this reading of *ingenium*, for its writer seems to have identified explicitly the discovery of meaning with the invention of images to embody meaning, attributing both acts to the faculty of *ingenium*; *ingenium* becomes not only a power for discovery and interpretation, *vis inveniendi*, but also an aspect of invention, *inventio ingenii*.[54] Theodore Silverstein traces both to an ancient theory of cognition by similitudes, which suggests for *ingenium* its role as mediator between form and matter.[55] Because of its powers of divine insight, then, *ingenium* is not really that far from its modern translation, genius. Art gained legitimacy and force because readers felt it was inspired by a faculty itself informed by an ability to interpret both material and immaterial reality. In this, it is like the faculty of imagination considered in its highest sense, as it comes closest to offering authoritative images to the other powers of the soul and so to embodying the purest image of a harmonious universe. Thus, in Dante, most confident of poets, the boat—metaphor for poetic imagination from Synesius of Cyrene to James I of Scotland—becomes "la navicella del mia ingegno" (*Purgatorio*, I.1–2).

Interestingly, the *artes poeticae* and *rhetoricae* also reflect this concept of *ingenium* as a faculty that gives material shape to abstractions, though their pedagogical function as manuals of grammatical and compositional instruction preclude much specific development of philosophical topics. Although *ingenium* had been associated with invention in Quintilian and Horace, in most of the classical rhetorics available to the Middle Ages the concept was largely ignored.[56] However, *ingenium* began to take on new extensions of meaning in the twelfth-century rhetorical tradition. Geoffrey of Vinsauf's *Poetria nova*—which, as its title suggests, conceived of itself as complementing Horace's *Ars poetica*—revised the old notion of *ingenium*: "The form of the material, as if it were a lump of wax, at first is hard to the touch; if diligent care ignites the imagination [*ingenium*] suddenly the material softens under the fire of imagination [*ingenium*] and then follows it wherever the hand summons, docile to anything. The hand of the inner man leads that it may amplify or compress the material."[57]

We find out fifty lines later that this ingenious hand is responsible for the mode of comparison, for the joining together of image and idea, indeed for imagining in the fullest sense of the word.[58] As Douglas Kelly notes, "Only those capable of inventing images that accurately represent ineffable ideas possess the quality termed *In-*

genium in rhetoric."⁵⁹ If man was to imitate the divine Creator, he would need a faculty to clothe the ineffable in matter. One might say that, to fill the need, *ingenium* borrowed from imagination a facility for the dressing up of spiritual truths and hired herself out to Poetry.

To the discussions of *ingenium* in the *ars poetica* tradition and in philosophical prose, we can also add its treatment in poetry itself. A work seminal in setting the program for twelfth-century poetry, Bernardus Silvestris's *Cosmographia* is, among other things, a comprehensive analysis of its own creativity, and every significant creative act in this poem also requires an initial use of *ingenium*. *Divina Providentia*, before impressing order on Silva, calls upon her *ingenium*. It is *ingenium* that Nous must use to create a cosmic soul, and Physis, Urania, and Natura are competent craftsmen only insofar as their *ingenia* are capable.⁶⁰ *Ingenium*, then, for Bernardus, as for Dante and Geoffrey of Vinsauf, denotes the interior faculty necessary for creation. But the role of art is not just creation or expression. Grammar, the discipline under which the poets were studied, must "tame," as Alain de Lille says, and "overcome the instability of her material."⁶¹ It is not enough to have genius, insight, a facility for seeing more or saying more than others. Like the philosopher, the poet must also be able to order or discipline his subject matter. For no matter how authoritative a power of art or discovery we believe *ingenium* to be, it moves the individual only to the threshold of abstract knowledge, not to the center of that knowledge itself. To order images to a higher significance requires the reason or the intellect, which has the specific job of mastering and arranging imaginative material; this disciplining activity is often conveyed through the metaphor of the poet's or creator's hand. As Geoffrey observes above, the hand summons the material, amplifies, compresses it.

Hands provide the perfect image for this final step in harmonious creative activity. In the *De anima*, Aristotle had called the hand "the instrument that includes other instruments" ("organum organorum") just as "the intellect is the form that includes other forms" ("intellectus species specierum").⁶² The hand's perfection is thus like that of the soul: one provides, as Aquinas indicates in his commentary on this passage, for all man's needs; the other "assimilate[s] all the forms of being."⁶³ The same analogy is at the base of Aquinas's argument in the *Summa theologiae* that the hands and brain together dignify the human body and distinguish it from the bodies of other animals. Brain and hands are, in the Aristotelian phrasing of the matter, *organa organorum*, "for with them man can make a limitless range of tools with a limitless range of activities."[64] The hand, then, becomes the natural vehicle for man's most noble creative aspirations, which realize themselves most perfectly in the extension between heaven and earth. One thinks, among other works, of Michelangelo's moving painting of God making Adam, in which the touch of fingers signifies the creative transfer of life and power from Creator to created.

It is with this background in mind, which links the hand with the total informative soul and the highest creative impulses, that we must regard references to hands in discussions of man's artistic ingenuity. Frequently, the invocation of imagination or *ingenium* must be followed by another step, carried out by *manus*, the shaping hand. In Geoffrey, the hand executes what the mind conceives. The persistence of the trio—archetype, imagination, hand—is indicated by a passage, probably in imitation of the *Poetria nova*, from a late medieval commentary on the fourteenth-century French *Les Echecs amoureux*; in this commentary, the workman's plan is followed by the action of "fantasy" (the translation indicating again *ingenium*'s closeness to imagination), an action whose final step is performed by the "hand," which "moves in the similitude of the fancy."[65] In Alain de Lille's *Anticlaudianus*, the process is oddly reversed, but *manus* and *ingenium* still represent two steps in the movement from archetype to embodiment. As Logic creates the axle for the chariot to bear Prudence through the heavens, she calls first upon her hand, which in turn activates that spark of creative ability, *ingenium*.[66] In Bernardus's poem again, Providence's *manus* removes the roughness from Silva, and the "hand" of God produces the first actual creations.[67]

As Physis notes with misgivings about her own capacity, the creation of man requires both a keen *ingenium* and an informed and learned hand. The drama of the poem lies in the difficulty of creation, the near impossibility of mastering and ordering Silva—intractable, formless, hostile, "a mass discordant with itself."[68] Here we find again the tension that formed an inevitable component in the marriage of knowledge and truth, matter and form. This tension, which to some critics suggests a basic dualism underlying Bernardus's thought, has caused them to read the poem's end as essentially ambiguous, to claim that it calls attention as much to a breach as to a unity between world and God.⁶⁹ But we have seen that the age's most profound need was to resolve tension, to bridge rather than break apart. True to its time, the *Cosmographia*, I believe, more forcefully celebrates the work of creation that culminates in the forming of man than it asks us to ponder his alienation from that creation; man's survival as an individual is tenuous, his bodily existence perpetual rather than eternal. But he is given a capacity to participate in divinity by acts of his own creativity, not only through his two reproductive *genii*, but also through his inner genius, his *ingenium*, with its will to create. The imperfect, material world becomes a means to achieve greater perfection, and harmony is preserved. As Bernardus tells us, when her *ingenium* is aligned with heaven, the human soul can live as a queen within her earthly vessel.⁷⁰

The final lines help illuminate the importance of this idea in the poem: "In creating man Physis had to bestow limbs of which the universe has no need: eyes to keep watch in the head, ears for sound, feet to bear him and all-capable hands."⁷¹ Surely these hands do not, as Wetherbee argues, help man "exploit" nature's secrets "in the interests of human life."⁷² Of course, they do suggest man's insufficiency when he is compared to the universe in its wholeness; yet hands become a means to that measure of transcendence and completeness possible to humanity. One guesses that these hands will be valuable to man in the same way that hands have been of use to the other characters in the poem and as they are in the larger tradition—to enable man to participate in the divinity of creation through creative acts of his own.

Words, like hands, are also given to man alone among all creatures for his expression and self-definition. As Dante was to write, angels do not need them; animals would have no use for them. But man, whose nature is more "to make himself felt than to feel sensations,"⁷³ becomes something of a god when he creates. The Hermetic texts, known and valued by many writers of the High Middle Ages and particularly by Bernardus, make a similar point. Man alone has a double nature, one formed of elements, one of divinity. In his imitation of divine creation, one aspect of which is his use of God's gift of the word, he realizes the potential of his first and higher nature and, above all, asserts the unity of both.⁷⁴

Implicit in the whole body of theory was a notion of allegory quite different from our own. Readers delighted in the discovery of truth in a sacramental world, in a divinely inspired book, and in the fictional recreation of that truth. Allegorical meaning was not generated by a distinctness of literal and referential, by "pitting," as Angus Fletcher says, "one ideal . . . against another." The mode was not "hierarchical in essence,"[75] although no period has been so prone as the High Middle Ages to recognize hierarchies in allegiances of the will. But in the process of discovering those allegiances, man felt no need to compare and distinguish between truths, living as he did in a world where the only truth was distributed among the realms of spirit and matter, known by the human spirit first through matter. At least in the twelfth and thirteenth centuries, poetic allegory made its revelations in the same way. Poetry's job, like Nature's, was to embody images of ideal truth—in Alain de Lille's words, "she produced vocally [and] in actual fact archetypal language ideally preconceived."[76] "The excitement," Rosemond Tuve writes, "comes when we conceive the idea, the person [embodying an abstraction] suddenly then becoming charged with meaning of very great depth and extension."[77] Indeed, this depth and extension could be poetry's own contribution to the harmony of reason and revelation, a harmony which the ending of Bernardus's poem achieves by revealing creative man at one with his universe.

The Epistemological Journey and the Form of High Medieval Poetry

Within this system, though, the High Middle Ages does not present a completely uniform face; different writers accommodated tensions in different ways. In the *De planctu naturae*, written only a few years after the *Cosmographia*, the poet's focus seems to have widened. The deepening tensions between spirit and matter that had caused philosophy to focus attention on epistemology have their impact more forcefully here as well, for here is a poetry whose structure not only imitates and reflects upon the act of imagining but upon the total act of knowing. As Wetherbee notes, the archetypal pattern of twelfth-century allegory is "what may be called intellectual pilgrimage, the experience of the spirit in its attempts to rise above its earthly situation through an understanding of *naturalia* and attain a vision of truth."[78] The difficulties of this pilgrimage, rather than the problems of creation, began to engage writers more urgently as the distance between world and God seemed in danger of widening. But we must remember that we are still in a framework of continuous change; no matter how insistently problems and distance laid their claim, the basic unity of creation, the marriage of matter and form, went uncontested.

It is as part of a process of accommodation, of expanding the marriage's foundations, then, that poets like philosophers began to consider more and more explicitly the precise phenomenology of this epistemological ascent. To be sure, they did value the experience of the philosophizing mind and not just its stable goal, even as they appreciated poetry partly, as Wetherbee says, for its "capacity to reveal complex and ambiguous experience,"[79] for its narrative and not just for its moral. But we must not go too far in universalizing modern assumptions about poetry. For the Middle Ages, there are two halves of artistic achievement: the experience of a diverse *materia* as threatening and the construction of a poetic architecture capable of containing that threat. A human art that found its model in the divine act of taming matter, itself sought to discipline and give shape to imaginative *materia*. We do not have to ignore art's special imaginative power to say also that the narrative of spiritual ascent became one way, and a particularly happy one for the times, of providing that discipline and shape.

We find this focus on order in writers from Geoffrey of Vinsauf to Petrarch, from commentators on philosophical texts to contributors to the *accessus ad auctores*, all of whom place a tremendous emphasis on sequence, the proper ordering of words and narrative units, though work is only beginning in contemporary scholarship to uncover the basis of this ordering impulse or the many forms it takes.[80] Alain again calls attention to the importance of such ordering when he notes how his own verses on Cupid in the middle of the *De planctu naturae* have moved away from the "fixed sequence of the narration previously planned" or when he exiles Pacuvius from the ranks of legitimate authors because he ignorantly inverted the true order of his narrative.[81] The concern extends even to theology. Peter Damian, famous for his opposition to literary studies in general, claims that in scripture "the very sequence of the narrative and order of the words contain a great sacrament."[82] Any author interested in establishing the legitimate grounds of poetic art in such a world would have to take great care that he also ordered his narrative in a way conducive to truth as revealed in the great book of nature.

Again, the poet works analogously to the Creator. As Boethius had observed, the relation of Providence to Fate was like the relation of the artisan's formal conception in his mind to the "successive temporal acts" of his making.[83] Such a theory of the whole was implicit in Augustine's famous passage on reading a psalm in *Confessions* XI.28 or in the Latin sentence itself—both of which ask the reader to withhold his interpretation of the whole until he has integrated each of its parts in a sequence which thus forms an important part of the artist's ideal plan as it is realized in his matter. The ending of a work, Dante points out in the *Convivio*, is the most important part in casting meaning back over the whole.[84] Indeed, poetry's achievement grows not only out of the poet's intention to create discrete images of truth but also by the capacity of his narrative to create an *order* or sequence of experience that will allow the reader by the end of the work to abstract God's truth from poetic images as he does also from images in nature.

Of course, on the most general level, such organization is presupposed by a poetry whose duty is to lead its audience through a process of obtaining knowledge. But not only is this a development the poem should cause in the reader; it becomes part of a poem's manifest structure itself through a new possibility for a work's modus agendi, its mode of writing. Like medieval theorists, classical rhetoric had also been devoted to setting out categories of narrative order; but the Middle Ages extended this preoccupation by advancing two sorts of order for narrative: natural and artificial.[85] Natural order indicated the sequence in which events really happened, from first to last; a poet used the superior, artificial order when in some way he inverted or reordered this sequence. During our period there could be even another sort of natural order, and one that clearly describes how the kind of poetry I have discussed in this chapter could serve the philosophical system also outlined. This was the natural sequence of knowing, an order that might lie beneath all others—and especially, as I will show, in poems that call up an association with dream and vision. In discussing the ascent from practical to theoretical knowledge in Boethius's *De consolatione*, Guillaume de Conches calls it the "ordo philosophie."[86] The commentator on the *Aeneid*, whose sixth book also had a visionary association, puts it this way: "[Virgil's] procedure is to describe allegorically by means of an integument what the human spirit does and endures while temporarily placed in the human body. Virgil uses natural order when writing about this, and thus he observes the double order of narration—as the poet, the artificial order; as philosopher, the natural order."[87]

When they wrote about what man endures in his pilgrimage home to God—when they developed a natural order for poetry from psychology—medieval poets followed Virgil's lead here rather than Cicero, or even Geoffrey of Vinsauf, who far preferred the artificial to the natural order. Such an order of knowing, of spiritual ascent, could inform even explicitly philosophical or theological texts, for Peter Abelard claimed to imitate Moses in pursuing this kind of *ordo naturalis* in his *Expositio in Hexaemeron*.[88]

By articulating in poetic form the epistemological process that might join heaven and earth as two poles of an individual's spiritual journey, poetry could thus borrow from philosophy and begin to make a statement about that experience's grounds and possibilities. In this way it could perform the role of defending the world view, which I described earlier, even as it redefined the powers and limits of its own contribution. Even poems that are not, then, strictly speaking, "vision" poems are often about this process of vision, these cognitive stages that in the theory of abstraction lead to spiritual knowledge. At the most simplistic level, in fact, a diagram of many high medieval philosophical poems resembles in broad outline the medieval diagram of brain function discussed earlier in this chapter, charting a journey through imagination, reason, and memory, involving will and intentionality, as the poet "personifies the levels of cognition one travels in order to come to the knowledge of God."[89] But especially in vision poems, this movement from image to abstraction is one of epistemology's greatest contributions to poetic structure, as the dreamer becomes a reader of images within the poem who shows the reader proper how to benefit from the enlightening seductions offered in the poet's imitation of nature.

CHAPTER 2

A Grammar of Dream and Vision for Medieval Poetry

The Vision as a Liminal Phenomenon

The twelfth and thirteenth centuries may have been the Age of the Dream Vision, the period of this genre's most active flowering, but they were not the years of its inception. There had been an energetic tradition of fictional and nonfictional visions even before 1100. Already in works like the ninth-century *Vision of Bernoldus* or *The Voyage of Saint Brendan*, found in manuscripts from the tenth century, the motif of the otherworldly journey had begun to catch hold of the medieval fancy.[1] To an age concerned with converting pagans and warning Christians away from sin, the sort of vision that could portray graphically and energetically the terrors of the afterlife was an attractive form. Such a motive no doubt partly accounts for the genre's overall appeal and more particularly for the extensive popularity throughout the Middle Ages of the fourth-century apocryphal *Vision of Saint Paul*, found in more than one hundred manuscripts and clearly told to convert the sinful by means of the ingenious and elaborate tortures they would suffer if damned.[2] Even to Aquinas, fear of God was a necessary prerequisite to love of God, and Dante himself would capitalize on this inherent power of the genre. I would like, then, before considering the vision as it was given literary shape by such writers as Alain de Lille, Jean de Meun, or Dante, first to look carefully at one of these earlier, less sophisticated medieval visions to see what it can reveal about the form's underlying structure.

The vision of Drycthelm, as recounted by Bede in the eighth century, can provide us with a narrative containing the essential features of the simple embedded vision that would later evolve into the philosophical vision.[3] In this story the devout but prosperous patriarch Drycthelm falls ill and dies in the middle of night. To the consternation of those present, he returns to life at daybreak, having had a visionary experience that will permanently change him. What follows is the narrative of that experience. Guided by an angel, Drycthelm has viewed the fire and ice that mark the tempestuous approach to Hell, the darkness and horror of Hell's pit, and last, though he is not permitted to enter Heaven proper, the Earthly Paradise, where many of the blessed await entry. The angel, who knows Drycthelm's future, has also instructed him that he may one day merit this bliss if he changes his habit of life. Already a devout man, Drycthelm is moved by his visionary experience to an even deeper spiritual conviction. It prompts him to distribute his wealth to members of his family and to the poor, and to become himself a monk. Indeed, Drycthelm is now so ascetic that, when his fellows marvel at his discipline in submerging himself into icy, wintry streams, he responds blandly, "I have known it colder."

Though Bede's focus on the response of the uninitiated requires that the narrative be told as a kind of flashback, the Dreamer's experience can easily be analyzed into three parts—his existence before the vision, the vision itself, and his life afterward. In this way, the vision is like any rite of passage, in which, according to anthropologists Victor and Edith Turner, the initiate travels through three different stages: separation, when he is detached from his stable cultural group, in this case Drycthelm's family; limen or margin, when as in Drycthelm's vision he "passes through a realm or dimension that has few or none of the attributes of the coming state"; and aggregation, when he returns to normal life with a newly defined role and in a "new settled state," as Drycthelm does when he joins the monastic community.[4] It is the middle, unsettled state I am most concerned with here, for this transitional area is the realm of the vision proper. Anthropologists, who call this state "liminal" or "liminoid," now argue that understanding its constituents can also help us understand the more settled, secure states that enfold it: "Liminality is now seen to apply to all phases of decisive cultural change, in which previous orderings of thought and behavior are subject to revision and criticism, when hitherto unprecedented modes of ordering relations between ideas and people become possible and desirable."[5]

Thus, as a liminal state, a vision like that experienced by Drycthelm can offer a comment on the social organizations from which the visionary emerges and to which he returns. In this case, the visionary experience puts pressure on Drycthelm to become more spiritual, ascetic, less concerned with the grievances and rewards of his previously stable domestic existence. The vision has the power, then, to call into question, even to "reformulate," as the Turners put it, "the social structure and the paradigms which program it."[6]

The Turners' interest is in pilgrimage as a "liminoid" phenomenon, but as they point out, the liminality of pilgrimage is similar to that of mysticism, for "if mysticism is an interior pilgrimage, pilgrimage is exteriorized mysticism"; both are purgatorial or salvific journeys that release an individual from the irritations, rewards, and pressures of normal life while initiating him into "a new, deeper level of existence."[7] The frequent use in visionary poems of pilgrimage and exile as a motif seems to me to grow out of an awareness of this connection. Jean de Meun's, Dante's, and Guillaume de Deguileville's visionaries are all repeatedly and explicitly named as pilgrims too, though of course of widely diverging sorts, and Boethius's Lady Philosophy is concerned to reformulate pilgrimage for the narrator, redefining the poet's interior life as central and relegating his earthly existence to the marginal or liminal by identifying *it* as an exile from or pilgrimage toward the divine.

Similarly, the naming of the visionary at a key moment in his instruction also calls to mind the structure of a rite of passage, which may include at its conclusion the reassimilation of the individual by a "naming ceremony," especially in rites where "politico-legal and generally social elements are more important."[8] The granting of a new identity is implicit in the *De consolatione philosophiae*, when Philosophy teaches Boethius anew that he is a man and what that means. In this case, however, rather than giving him a new identity, she reminds him of one he already had. Even more suggestively, Dante breaks the rule he set forth in the *Convivio* against using his own name, when "necessity" forces Beatrice's use of it in *Purgatorio* XXX just as the pilgrim converts from a more literal and earthly love to a new heavenly one and as he exchanges one teacher for another. Likewise, we will see, the Lover in Gower's *Confessio Amantis* is first named at the end of his visionary conversion, when he recognizes and accepts a new identity.

But such a concept of vision as initiation was not merely implicit in the Middle Ages; through Macrobius's *Commentary on the Dream of Scipio*, it entered the medieval consciousness of vision quite directly. According to this commentary, the secrets of Nature, offered to dreamers during prophetic visions, are veiled in enigmatic shapes, images, and fictions, so that she will be able to conceal them from all but the "more prudent individuals": "Her sacred rites are veiled in mysterious representations so that she may not have to show herself even to initiates. Only eminent men of superior intelligence gain a revelation of her truths; the others must satisfy their desire for worship with a ritual drama which prevents her secrets from becoming common."[9] Thus, dreams for Macrobius become occasions for a liminal experience, an experience of being initiated into sacred truths that, perhaps partly because they may subvert social organization, bear finally a marginal relationship to society and should thus be known only by the initiated and especially wise.

Vision, like pilgrimage, is liminal in being "betwixt and between all familiar lines of classification."[10] It is an experience that happens to a man when he is between stable physical states—neither of the body nor removed from it. This transitional quality is clearly a feature of Drycthelm's vision, for during his initiation into the truths of Heaven and Hell, he seems to exist in a state between life and death so horrifying to the members of his own family that all but his wife run away at his awakening—and she remains with him only through great love, while she is herself "trembling and fearful."[11]

Not all visions, of course, occur in so resoundingly sacred and unnatural a way. Most take place when the visionary still clearly inhabits his body, though Jean de Meun's Nature refers to the "horrible folly" of those who believe that the soul can depart from the body on spiritual journeys without leaving the body, "thus denuded," a permanently lifeless corpse.[12] In fact, the medievals were quite interested in the marginal relationship of body and soul during vision; it was this aspect of the dream or vision's liminality that seems to have occupied their thought and commentary more than any other, thus making the fictional vision the perfect literary form for poets seeking to explore the philosophical issues that were so urgent to this age, with its need to unite the spirituality of Christian faith with the naturalism of Aristotelian reason. Also, because the function of liminal experience is not simply to reflect the paradigms that govern mainstream thought, but also to reflect *on* them—to reformulate them, as it were—we will also find, within the stories of philosophical vision narrators, many more sophisticated attempts than Drycthelm's to comprehend and structure their experience so that it casts light on the relationship between nature and revelation.

Indeed, close study of high medieval writings on the subject of dreams and visions suggests that the capacity of these states to body forth what in fact has no body was especially puzzling and intriguing. "For while your body lies down," writes Alcher de Clairvaux, "the soul walks. The tongue of your body is silent, the soul speaks. Your eyes are closed, she sees. And so in herself complete and entire she is perceived as the similitude of your flesh."[13] The interpenetration of spirit and flesh is likewise important to Alcher, who demonstrates the soul's essential spirituality from its power to evoke the absent world. About his own vision of the third heaven, Saint Paul wrote that it occurred "whether still in the body, or out of the body, I do not know; God knows."[14] Thus marked from the outset by ambiguity, the Pauline discussion attracted to itself a lengthy commentary tradition in authors from Augustine to Aquinas, not to mention the many visions in Latin and the vernacular elaborating on the heavenly and infernal sights that Paul witnessed.

In his attempt to understand Paul's vision and to identify the different varieties of visionary experience, Augustine in the *De Genesi ad litteram* isolates three categories of knowing or sight: the *visio intellectualis*, a sort of vision unmediated by images; the *visio spiritualis*, the type most characterized by the ambiguous connection of body and spirit, in which a man sees the disembodied image of the object perceived; and the *visio corporalis*, the vision of bodies directly.[15] Alain de Lille seems to be drawing upon this triad when he asserts that there are three sorts of sleep: the first—corresponding to intellectual vision—occurs without aid of bodily powers, the second uses the body's natural powers to ascend, the third is enslaved by them. "Primus somnus fit supra hominem; secundus secundum hominem; tertius infra hominem. Primus miraculosus, secundus imaginarius, tertius monstruosus."[16] Here I am not concerned so much with the first, miraculous and above man, nor the third, monstrous and below his state. Being wholly incorporeal or corporeal, these would not evoke the kind of mind/body ambiguity or liminality that would yield the most interesting high medieval speculation on man's natural ascent to sacred truth.

Instead, I will focus on the *visio spiritualis*, in which a man, being still bound to a body, sees, as Saint Paul says, the truth as "a dim reflection in a mirror" which later he may know more fully and directly (1 Corinthians 13:12). As Alain de Lille writes about this passage, "To see enigmatically through a mirror is, through visible creation, to comprehend God as if through certain images."[17] Such is the kind of knowing we have found to be so central in the thought of the High Middle Ages. This variety of sight significantly includes dreams and visions, which may be treated as a special instance of the category of the *visio spiritualis*, especially as visions are discussed in the works of Arabic writers like Avicenna and Averroes, who attempted to formulate the process of vision and particularly of dream in a newly evolving philosophical terminology.[18]

An approach from this perspective will make it possible for me to study the psychology or mechanics of vision instead of concentrating on how Macrobius classifies the *products* of vision, as most modern students of theory popular in the Middle Ages have done. I will primarily be studying the vision *process* and structure as it was conceived by Macrobius and others widely read in the High Middle Ages. Because the systems I will be exploring focus on process, they will be seen to embody a real generative theory of vision; they will also indicate the most fundamental assumptions held by twelfth- and thirteenth-century poets about vision as these poets created the literary works that thereby gained a special power to address the age's philosophical and poetic concerns.

Besides studying the visionary process and structure, I will also investigate the literary models that medieval poets appropriated for their own visions, which quickly went beyond the model provided by Bede's vision of Drycthelm. In the twelfth and thirteenth centuries, commentators and imitators of the vision form turned not simply to the poetry of their own recent past, not only to the otherworldly visions already briefly described, but back to the classical period, where they also looked for intellectual nourishment in the works of Greek and Roman philosophy. Cicero's *Somnium Scipionis*, Augustine's *Soliloquia*, and Boethius's *De consolatione philosophiae* all suggested fruitful possibilities for vision poetry—and especially the last, with its focus on the healing power of vision and on vision psychology.[19] The genre of the philosophical vision—my subject in this book—comes from a synthesis of these different traditions. In the process of making this synthesis or mixture, though, the high medieval writers reinterpreted old structures and topics in characteristic and suggestive ways, which we must study now.

Literary Models

Like Martianus's *De nuptiis*, Boethius's *De consolatione* dominated the high medieval awareness of late classical personification allegory because it provided a way to talk about issues central to that age. Like the *De nuptiis*, the *De consolatione* is intensely concerned with unity and reconciliation, and especially with defining the terms of the collaboration between nature and grace. More specifically, it explores the role of man's psyche in bringing this collaboration about, and so brings fresh insight to an old problem of cognition and the relation of human experience to ineffable truth. It is still difficult to talk about the relationship of the *De consolatione* to specific literature of its own era, though Boethius clearly drew upon many literary and philosophical traditions, including apocalypse and Menippean satire. But the poet seems to have found a special precedent for the focus and structure of his work in two previous dialogues, also known to the Middle Ages, that can illuminate some of the emphasis and shape of his unique synthesis—Cicero's *Somnium Scipionis* and Augustine's *Soliloquia*.[20]

Indeed, to medieval vision poets as far back as Boethius, Scipio's vision was probably as important a literary influence as Macrobius's commentary on it, though the commentary has received far more attention in literary scholarship. In his dream Scipio is initiated into the secrets of the universe, secrets of life and death, through the oracular wisdom of his grandfather Africanus. His experience, related in the last book of Cicero's *De re publica*, incorporates a surprising number of elements that would later become necessary to the vision form: notably, the dumbfounded dreamer, the ambition to present an encyclopedic or comprehensive survey of knowledge, and most centrally the concern with establishing in the dreamer a proper understanding of the relationship between his corporeal and spiritual natures. Yet the precise character of that relationship betrays the author's Platonic inspiration—the prototype of this vision is, of course, Plato's vision of Er—which leads him away from a focus on the Dreamer's experience as earthly being. From his position high in the spheres "the earth appeared so small [to Scipio that he] was ashamed of our empire which is, so to speak, but a point on its surface." Like Troilus at the end of Chaucer's epic romance, the Dreamer is made to see the smallness and insignificance of his planet. As he gazes down, his grandfather demands, "How long will your thoughts continue to dwell upon earth? Do you not behold the regions to which you have come?"[21] He is asked ultimately to see earthly fame in opposition to heavenly glory, time contrasted to eternity, this life as a distraction from rather than as a reflection of the next.

In his *Soliloquia*, Augustine adopts an attitude even more overtly contemptuous of earthly glory. According to Augustine, the soul that wishes to know its true, immortal nature should pay no regard to fleeting mortal experience. Like Cicero's, the work was valuable to Boethius in suggesting that lessons in such a Platonic truth could provide the basis of a dramatically satisfying dialogue. More than this, though, the *Soliloquia* presents the conversation of the soul with itself, a device extremely suggestive for Boethius and later writers. In this little treatise, which along with the *De consolatione* would later be translated and interpreted by King Alfred, the narrator's physician Reason takes on the job of turning the truth-seeker's eyes away from earthly distractions and toward God. Again and again Reason tells Augustine: Flee the senses. The body is a trap, a snare that keeps the soul from flying into its own free air.[22]

Along with the work's general strategy, the metaphor of captivity suggests some of the value Boethius may have found in the *Soliloquia*: Augustine is a precise observer of his own psychology, and his treatise is filled with nice insights into the difficulties of the struggling soul. More than once the pilgrim cries out, sheds tears, shows eagerness, impatience, is confronted with the evidence of his own backsliding. He claims one attitude toward the caresses of women during the light of day, Reason points out, and realizes another in his nighttime musings. This kind of fine self-observation must have proved an inspiration to Boethius, whose insights into the nature of truth and humanity bear much similarity to Augustine's. But there is little that is visionary about the *Soliloquia*. Reason does not "appear," as Lady Philosophy does, embodied as it were. The method of the work is sternly Platonic and deductive, with appeals to sense or emotion forming no part of the "order" that may lead a man to truth.[23] For Lady Philosophy's disciple, on the other hand—and those who succeeded him—insight occurs as a matter of sight, revelation, or showing; spiritual healing became a precisely embodied event.

Boethius's genius lay in realizing the dramatic potential of the synthesis of vision and philosophical dialogue structures. He was the first to combine the main features of Scipio's dream, features that would become increasingly important to writers of vision poems, with the idea of the soul's soliloquy borrowed from Augustine. And along with Cicero's dumbfounded dreamer and the widely ranging universal instruction of that work, he also appropriated the Platonism that had lain at the heart of both dialogues, though with some modification, which I will examine now. Scipio's ascent had occurred as an immediate translation. There was no gradual achievement of greater and greater awareness on the Dreamer's part, and the human condition with its needs and hungers did not play a large role in stimulating or shaping the kind of guidance Africanus provided his descendant. Even for Augustine, appeals to psychology were something to be avoided, not exploited. For Boethius, however, personal need—a need that went beyond any previous writer's, to bring both human psychological reality and earthly experience in accord with grace—played a great part in the vision experience. To find the structures that would enable him to address that need, Boethius had to draw upon another tradition, and again one descriptive of dreams—the tradition of Neoplatonic dream theory, which is represented in the *De insomniis* of Synesius of Cyrene.[24]

Synesius, an early Christian Neoplatonist who wrote about a hundred years before Boethius, shows an interest not just in the regenerative power of dreaming and hence in the force of human need in conditioning dreams, but also in the importance of human psychology for determining their structure and direction. It is this attempt to relate a psychology of the soul to a theory of dreaming as divination that marks his work as innovative.[25] Careful psychological description of the dream had begun with Aristotle, who had outlined the physiology of unreliable dreaming. But now it was invoked to explain prophecy, a use that was to become more and more prevalent during the High Middle Ages. Drawing upon Aristotelian and Galenic psychological categories and faculties like those I described in

Chapter 1, Synesius especially praises the power of imaginative experience in dreaming, which he feels can raise us to the contemplation of the highest things; indeed, he recommends that such dreams might provide new challenges and new subject matters for a poetry that would explore these: "So new and so extensive a wealth of subjects is there," he writes, "for one who has the courage to let loose his language upon them."[26] Although they would not have been known to the writers of the twelfth and thirteenth centuries, these remarks or similar ones were likely read by Boethius, who was in a position to take up their poetic challenge.[27]

The *De consolatione* never announces itself as the narrator's dream or vision. But the relationship of this work to Scipio's dream alone might have caused its early audiences to read it as a kind of dream poem, if the work itself had not suggested associations with vision and particularly with dream—such as, for example, the poet's location of himself in bed, which was insisted upon by many medieval manuscript illuminators;[28] Lady Philosophy's dreamlike changes in size and appearance; or the healing function of the experience as a whole. This last recalls not only the Platonic view of philosophy as physician, but also rituals quite common in both the classical and medieval periods in which a god or later a saint provided healing ministrations to an initiate wounded either in body or spirit, and did so within a dream.[29] One unmistakable sign of the work's connection with dream is the number of medieval poets—from Alain to Chaucer—who would read it as one and cast their own imitations in the form of dreams.[30] But although it is clear that the *De consolatione* is the chronicle of some sort of visionary experience whose conventional shape would have conditioned the original reader's response to the work, this fact is not believed to have had much significance for interpretation. It is generally held that in Boethius and in his imitators, the vision frame is a mere "convention more or less blindly adhered to."[31] Therefore, the precise structural relation between Boethius's poem and vision poetry as a genre has not been given the clarification it needs and deserves.

In Boethius's case, a psychology of vision like that described by Synesius became inextricably bound up with his poem's thematic purpose and appeal; because of this fusion of perspectives, later writers in the philosophical tradition would perceive interest in a psychology or epistemology of vision as necessary to the form. The dream motif itself would become a generic marker signaling to readers that the vision could evoke both physical and metaphysical realms of experience *and* that its particular psychology could make that juncture possible. In H. R. Jauss's words, "A literary event can continue to have an effect only if those who come after it still or once again respond to it—if there are readers who again appropriate the past work or authors who want to imitate, outdo, or refute it."[32] Medieval authors, I will argue, fixed upon Boethius's *De consolatione* in a remarkably self-conscious way because of the special opportunities its vision dialogue form afforded them to realize their deepest philosophical concerns and to express them with the unique affective and symbolic force of poetry.

As medieval commentators were to note with increasing emphasis, the π and the θ on Philosophy's robe represented the realms of practice and theory, of knowledge grounded in physical experience and knowledge based in metaphysical truth; and as they also observed, "One must ascend from practice to theory."[33] The stairs between the two letters represent, in the words of Paul Piehler, "the spiritual ascent the prisoner has to make."[34] Later I will suggest that the dream seemed an appropriate poetic vehicle to the High Middle Ages for this ascent because of its liminal character, its ability to combine the realms of spirit and matter in a single experiential phenomenon. But even in Synesius's writings, the dream's liminality provoked psychological and epistemological speculation. How could a man in a body come in contact with immaterial truth? Boethius's vision poem also addresses this question, thus suggesting to a later age not only that the vision form was an appropriate one for exploring in poetry man's communion with and ascent to the divine, but also for testing the epistemologies that made such ascent possible.

The central experiential problem presented by Boethius's work is one of outlining the relation between the natural and divine orders. Can this world, the poet asks, with its injustices and disappointments be a creation of the great and good Christian God? Can it be a mirror of His true, providential intention? The solution will be found when the visionary remembers the answer to the question of his identity, for he has forgotten who he is. Through Philosophy's teachings, which thus rely heavily on the Platonic epistemology of knowledge as reminiscence, we discover with the narrator that he is, as I pointed out earlier, a pilgrim exiled from his true home in God.

In her redefinition of exile for the narrator as a spiritual rather than a physical deprivation, the Lady restores to Boethius an archetypal memory of who and what he is, of the diminished meaning of worldly fortune when compared with heavenly destiny, a lesson also learned in a less subtle form by Scipio in his dream. So, though at points in her argument she describes other models of knowing and though she is more concerned than Africanus with the poet's psychic process, Lady Philosophy still instructs him primarily using the methods of Platonic dialogue, working as the pilgrim acknowledges "with what he remembers of the highest truth, using what he saw on high in order to fill in the forgotten parts."[35] "If Plato's Muse speaks truly," she explains, "whatever is learned is a recollection of something forgotten" ("Quodsi Platonis Musa personat uerum, / quod quisque discit immemor recordatur"; Book III, Meter 11, ll. 15–16).

This overriding Platonism may seem strange when we consider that Boethius's lifework was the translation, transmission, and harmonization of the philosophies of Aristotle and Plato.[36] Indeed, his appeal to the High Middle Ages as well as his historical importance now derive partly from the fact that he introduced many Aristotelian doctrines to the Middle Ages, including an Aristotelian epistemology, which he describes in the *De consolatione* (Book V, Prose 4). Indeed, both the narrator and Lady Philosophy imply at times that truth can be gained in Aristotelian fashion, by rising through a more complete understanding of the natural world to the divine order represented in the heavens: "No one wonders," sings Philosophy,

why the storms of Corus beat the shore with pounding waves. . . . The causes of such natural phenomena are quickly understood. . . . All sudden and rare events bewilder the unstable and uninformed. But if the cloudy error of ignorance is swept away, such things will seem strange no longer.

> Nemo miratur flamina Cori
> litus frementi tundere fluctu. . . .
> Hic enim causas cernere promptum est. . . .
> Cuncta quae rara prouehit aetas
> stupetque subitis mobile uulgus,
> cedat inscitiae nubilus error,
> cessent profecto mira uideri.
> (Book IV, Meter 5, ll. 13–14, 17, 19–22)

A similar impulse underlies the Boethian narrator's desire to bring the anomaly of evil down to the level of common understanding, to the experience that he and others have of the world, "because people ordinarily hold that some men suffer bad fortune" ("quia id hominum sermo communis usurpat, et quidem crebro, quorundam malam esse fortunam"; Book IV, Prose 7.6). Yet even in her response to this demand, Philosophy resorts to the Platonic method of deductively moving from general truths to their specific implications and instances, guiding the narrator from his equation of the good with the profitable to the corollary that the misfortune which tests the virtuous is also good.

As Pierre Courcelle points out, the *De consolatione* originated primarily in Neoplatonic theories, and it is as a kind of commentary on Plato, which he never had time to write, that the work constitutes its author's "véritable testament philosophique."[37] Though Boethius, like Synesius and other Alexandrian Neoplatonists, may have introduced an Aristotelian impulse and Aristotelian categories into Platonic thought, the Platonic framework took precedence in dictating the shape of his synthesis. This is seen not only in specific exchanges like the ones just described, but also in the epistemology that determined the overall external structure of the *De consolatione*: it was one that subordinated an Aristotelian epistemology to a Platonic one and that thus ultimately devalued the world. Though man's rationality includes the sensitive and imaginative modes of knowing also appropriate to beasts, his task is not to work *through* those, using sensation and imagination to help him apprehend truth, but to stand above them, erect, "despising the earth" (Book V, Meter 5, l. 11). Thus, the imagery of Nature and her creatures in the work is uniformly frightening and negative, even when the poet professes to be praising the goddess's rule. She seems a threatening force only barely held in control:

The Carthaginian lions endure their fair chains, are fed by hand, and fear the beatings they get from their masters; but if blood should smear their fierce mouths, their sluggish spirits revive, and with a roar they revert to their original nature. They shake off their chains and turn their mad fury on their masters, tearing them with bloody teeth.

> Quamuis Poeni pulchra leones
> uincula gestent manibusque datas
> captent escas metuantque trucem
> soliti uerbera ferre magistrum,
> si cruor horrida tinxerit ora,
> resides olim redeunt animi

> fremituque graui meminere sui,
> laxant nodis colla solutis
> primusque lacer dente cruento
> domitor rabidas imbuit iras.
> (Book III, Meter 2, ll. 7–16)

Given this view of the world, God's plan, according to Boethius, works itself out in this life in very mysterious ways. Despite the famous Book III, Meter 9, the world will not always reveal these ways to us, at least as long as we attempt to analyze it primarily using our inductive capacities—a method that Philosophy's Platonic dialectic largely avoids. At times, to be sure, Boethius seems to suggest the ultimate justice of this world, the participation of the limited goods found here in the self-sufficient Good of the Creator, or the relation, however imperfect, of Fate to Providence. At one point, Philosophy even suggests that the memory of his previous good earthly fortune should console the narrator and serve as a stimulus to his archetypal memory, as long as he knows that there are people worse off than he (Book II, Prose 3–4). But finally the poet condemns those who, in their blindness and ignorance, "dig the earth in search of the good which soars above the star-filled heavens" ("et quod stelliferum transabiit polum / tellure demersi petunt"; Book III, Meter 8, ll. 17–18). Ascent to God requires the visionary's careful study of the works of nature and human society, but only to compare them with a higher truth he knows by an intuition or illumination that ultimately provides the real direction and goal of his quest. Even if improvement does not come about as rapidly as she first promises, Philosophy always returns to the pedagogical method she had set up in Book I, when she predicted, "I shall quickly wipe the dark cloud of mortal things from your eyes" ("paulisper lumina eius mortalium rerum nube caligantia tergamus"; Book I, Prose 2.6).

The twelfth century, on the other hand, inaugurated an era that, though profoundly similar in its philosophical concerns to the late classical period, also differed from it in important ways. We have seen that, from the end of the eleventh century throughout most of the thirteenth, the age's greatest minds were absorbed with finding the most precise and comprehensive correspondences between the orders of nature and grace, and preoccupied with devising an epistemology that might lead one from this, most literal, world to the next, most divine, one. That epistemology, based on the theory of abstraction, was finally more Aristotelian than Platonic—even when it borrowed nothing directly from Aristotle. If Boethius's *De consolatione*, when compared to the *Somnium Scipionis* or the *Soliloquia*, balances Plato with Aristotle, it may be said that Guillaume de Conches, Alain de Lille, and certainly Dante balance Aristotle with Plato.

I am talking about a shift in emphasis only, but one no less important for being subtle. The Middle Ages chose to concentrate their most intense energies on the analysis and imitation of Boethius because of an affinity with him. But they altered him slightly in the process. During this era, commentators on Boethius's vision focused on its hymn to the divine power in charge of nature; it was an era that explicated in detail the ascent from practice to theory depicted on Philosophy's robe. Guillaume de Conches, for example, speculated on the world soul in Boethius's vision in ways that drew charges of pantheism. The editor of Guillaume's controversial commentary on the poem sums up the modern reader's impression of its bias when he remarks succinctly, "Physical explanations take a large place in the commentary on Boethius."[38]

The *De consolatione* exhibits a concern with the world, its problems and its humanity, that must have appealed to writers of the twelfth-century renaissance and that must have felt different from Plato, Cicero, or Augustine even to the work's earliest reader. Despite the poem's Platonic bias, the Boethian narrator, we have seen, repeatedly asserts the claim of his own experience. When the author of the twelfth-century *Commentary on the First Six Books of the Aeneid* tells us that both Boethius and Aeneas began their spiritual ascents in an investigation of the fragility of earthly matters, he is merely recognizing this aspect of the poem. Yet we feel also a change in *his* emphasis from that of Boethius, for the Sybil, Aeneas's guide, requires of her charge a fierce and rigorous descent into the physical unlike what I think a more objective reading must see as Philosophy's gentle though firm abnegation of the world. The *Aeneid* commentary, then, projects into Boethius's vision that natural order which we have found to exert such organizing force in the literary theory of the day: "Hunc ordinem Boetius observavit."[39]

High medieval interpretations of Boethius, thus, indicate what I have already noted about this age—its belief in the interpenetration of the realms of spirit and matter and with the possibility of knowing spirit through matter, not as something separate from it that merely casts its shadow back over this world, giving it a kind of incidental value. In their reception and imitation of Boethius's dream vision, medieval authors would examine the problems that had urgently engaged the classical poet, but in a new light. The Boethian Dreamer's desire to discover in the order of nature a mirror of God's plan, a desire that had played a counterpoint to Philosophy's stoic guidance, would assume greater importance as poets established a new patterning of experience to function as the norm in their poems, for in the medieval system the dependence of spiritual awareness on physical perfection, of knowing on physical function, was of the highest importance. This shift in focus would bring to prominence different elements of structure from those that had given shape and coherence to the earliest readings of the *De consolatione*.

The *Commentary on the First Six Books of the Aeneid* can suggest something of the same revisionary process acting upon Virgil as on Boethius. There had been a rich late classical tradition of allegorizing Virgil, preserved mainly in the comments of Servius and Macrobius on the classical poet. But it has been noted repeatedly how much the twelfth-century commentary differs, for example, from Servius's scheme, which was taken up by John of Salisbury in the *Metalogicon*, or even from Fulgentius's widely known interpretation of the Latin epic. Servius had seen in the *Aeneid* an allegory of the six ages of man; Fulgentius, whom our commentator follows more closely, discerned the progress of a human life as it is revealed through the etymologies of names.[40] In David Thompson's words, when the twelfth-century commentary takes up the epic, it "becomes a Platonic allegory, the story of the human soul imprisoned in its mortal body."[41]

Yet this commentator does not, as Thompson declares, write "as though he were a late-antique Platonist, closer in spirit to Maurius Victorinus than to Hugh of Saint Victor."[42] Indeed, one of the features that most decidedly distinguishes the twelfth-century writer's work from its predecessors is its incorporation of a relatively new medical psychology borrowed, as Daniel Meerson has demonstrated, from Constantine the African and Guillaume de Conches.[43] Increments of spiritual advancement in the commentary are insistently measured by the animal soul's capacity to receive knowledge. As the commentary indicates in its opening section, the human mind in its infancy is impeded by vapors caused by "the ingestions and eliminations of the body."[44] Progress through human life to its culmination in heavenly ascent is achieved only as one conquers these impediments, as a person comes to transform the body's prison into a vehicle of ascent. The brothers Castor and Pollux represent the soul and the body, writes the mythographer, and Pollux descended to the underworld so that Castor might rise: "The soul endures the death of the body for a time so that the body may then share the immortality of the spirit."[45] "On this view," writes Meerson, "virtue is contingent upon knowledge; the educational problem thus posed is basically physiological."[46]

It is little wonder that the commentator found philosophical truth declared "more profoundly" in Book VI than in any other section of Virgil's epic. As the commentary's most recent editors write, he seems "mesmerized by it."[47] Fulgentius had noted that in the sixth book, Aeneas gives himself over to the pursuit of wisdom; by contemplation, he comes to a knowledge of "the secret mysteries of nature."[48] But for Fulgentius, this was but one phase only in the whole of a lifetime's development. Though less important to Fulgentius than Book VI, the last part of his commentary traces briefly Aeneas's progress in Books VI through XII, which "show the good man, having acquired wisdom, actively struggling against vice."[49] The twelfth-century writer leaves a consideration of these books off altogether. It was the mental journey, the contemplative movement of the soul to its Creator "by a cognition of creatures"[50] that dominated his imagination almost exclusively. More precisely, our commentator reads this book as a journey through the faculties, a journey that signals Aeneas's advancement past his early attachment to *inanes picturae*, at a time when he was clearly defective in respect to his imagination, to his purification by the rigors of study in Book VI.[51] His apprenticeship to the Sybil is explicitly a discipline of reason. The Sybil, like Lady Philosophy, the commentary tells us, represents reason, both human in that aspect of her being which she shares with Aeneas and divine in the dimensions of understanding that exceed earthly comprehension.[52]

Significantly, Aeneas's journey reaches a kind of completion just as he is about to enter Elysium, for here the commentary breaks off as Aeneas lays the bough of philosophy, previously identified as theoretical intellect, across the threshold before him, which we learn is the chamber of human memory.⁵³ The vault leading from the underworld—the world of *visibilia*—to Elysium—that of *invisibilia*—is named here as the human brain with its three chambers: "We come to heavenly contemplation through these (as we said before) by exercising wit [*ingenium*], reason [*ratio*], and memory [*memoria*]."⁵⁴ Thus, the epic journey is interpreted as a voyage through the faculties, the "natural order" as the order of apprehension. This is the same order that I noted is also found by this commentator in the *De consolatione*, for he makes clear by innumerable references that the epic hero's education in its basic form will involve an order of experience similar to that found in Boethius.⁵⁵

But why this similarity between the *De consolatione* and the *Aeneid*? Why this concentration on Book VI as a chronicle of spiritual ascent? Surely no modern reader of the two works would remark on their likeness considered in isolation from the medieval tradition. "We are left," writes Winthrop Wetherbee, "with the sense that almost any meaningful narrative could be reduced and 'translated' in a similar way."⁵⁶ But why *not* just any narrative? One way that these two works became bound together in the medieval framework, I submit, was by their shared generic status as visions. What Aeneas had in common with Boethius is that, like the experience of the narrator in the *De consolatione*, his is not simply any act of mental discovery. It is affiliated by the commentator not only with man's natural descent into a body but with his artificial one as well, and hence as Jane Chance Nitzsche has shown, with the *daemones*, divine intermediaries, and figments of dreams.⁵⁷ Part of the appeal of Aeneas's contemplative journey lay in this association with dream and vision, reinforced by the tree of dreams that marks the beginning of Aeneas's descent in Book VI and the gates of ivory and horn that signal its close—not to mention the Sybil whose oracular guidance recalls Philosophy's.

What was it, though, about dreams that made them the appropriate vehicle for the high medieval spiritual ascent? A partial answer might be that because in both the medieval and modern periods dreams have been felt to be educative, to be capable of imparting knowledge, their psychologies have reflected some of the central epistemological assumptions of their times. Historical changes in such assumptions have always been registered as profound changes in dream theory. Yet some similarity between dream theory in the

Middle Ages and Freudian and Jungian analyses has led many readers of the medieval dream poem to apply, rather indiscriminately, modern psychological theories to these older poems. I would not deny that the method is potentially fruitful, but it requires a thorough and rigorous analysis of the similarities and differences between the categories and assumptions presupposed by the two bodies of theory, a kind of analysis no critic has yet been fully prepared to perform.[58] Thus, the results of the approach have been disappointing. Since the Middle Ages itself produced a full set of observations of dreams, this tactic has also been unnecessary. For the remainder of this chapter, my method will be to reconstruct those epistemological structures that conditioned the genres used by the poets we are studying.

A New Psychology of Dreaming

According to medieval theory, dreams and visions—both, as I have said, varieties of Augustine's *visio spiritualis*—begin with the appearance of phantasms to the imagination. In this, they are not unlike any epistemological phenomenon. But dreams speak more personally and authoritatively to man than does his daily experience. Because dreams occur while man is in the body and yet seem to lead him to a knowledge that transcends bodily limitations, they have a special relevance to the thinker who seeks to explore the threshold between body and spirit. As the *Aeneid* commentator puts it, "A dream is the resting of the animal powers, the repose of the five senses. Its house is the human body, and an elm tree properly figures it. For just as the elm does not bear fruit but nevertheless sustains fruitful vines, so too the flesh is spiritually sterile but nevertheless is the fruitful home of virtues and knowledge."[59]

Yet the metaphor hides the complexity of the role dreams thus play in knowing. In John of Salisbury's treatment of dreams, as in his location of reason discussed in Chapter 1, we see the confusion that sometimes arises when a phenomenon felt on some level to be primarily spiritual is given a new physical interpretation. First John tells us that the animal powers or senses ("animales uirtutes, scilicet sensus") are quiescent—but only so that other physical or natural powers ("naturales") can intervene. In this state, between body and soul, the spirit, relieved of the exertions of the body ("animus corporis exercitio releuatus"), returns to its own sphere (presumably a noncorporeal one), where it contemplates truth in Pauline terms, now enigmatically and now face to face ("nunc per figuras et enigmata nunc immediata facie"). But, strangely, we discover that for John even this most direct variety of visionary experience is not purely intellectual or bodiless, but "is seen by the eyes fully and in its own true form" ("plena et uera specie sui oculis uideatur").[60]

Fortunately, though, John's mixing of visionary modes was not universal. Others tackled more rigorously the task of distinguishing "intellectual" from "spiritual" vision and of explaining the processes of the *visio spiritualis*. As dreams present a kind of archetypal example of this latter category, many of the new physicians and scientists worked at carefully defining their way of delivering truth. A complex theory was devised to account for dreaming, which described the effects on brain physiology of changes in the bodily humors and in the natural and animal spirits during sleep. Natural philosophers thus began to analyze dreams in terms of their relationship to the dominant epistemological model and the dominant physical model of brain function, which I described at length in Chapter 1. The most significant difference between waking and dreaming cognition in this analysis lay in the increased independence, activity, and visionary power of the imagination. Aristotle had identified imagination's role in a physiology of dreaming that precluded prophecy; Synesius had suggested its power to initiate prophetic vision. But now natural philosophy came to appreciate imagination in both these aspects. More than ever before, the mechanics of heavenly vision were rigorously defined; physics and metaphysics merged in the natural philosophers' explanation of the dream. In a remarkable application of the natural to the supernatural, medieval science tells us that imagination's increased visionary potency during dreams comes about because certain faculties (common sense, reason, memory) doze so that the soul can concentrate its energy in another lobe of the brain, imagination.

Except for this change, knowing proceeds normally in dreams: "At that time that which appears internally is of the same kind as that which appears from the outside," writes Avicenna in his *Liber de anima*, which made such a dream psychology available to the Latin West by at least the second half of the twelfth century.[61] The psychology was to remain relatively intact for the remainder of the Middle Ages—resurfacing, for example, in the Thomistic analysis of dream.[62] In this description of dreaming, the common sense lay, for all purposes, dead to the external world; yet imagination stimulated it to present images to the mind as though they were physically present. These images could embody either the residue of waking life or inspiration from some divine source. Depending on the state of the dreamer's soul, they could thus for some men represent the most meaningless illusion or for others, in whom the "virtus imaginativa" was "most powerful and established," the highest truth.[63]

Although no one claimed that all dreams were true, those valued most highly as subjects for poetry *were* the ones that seemed divinely informed—at least during the twelfth century when the first philosophical vision poems were being composed. If a dream conveyed truth, it could represent the purest experience of a world of images suffused with meaning, as twelfth-century man wished and believed his real world to be. Haphazard dream images in this early period were not worth writing about, nor, as Macrobius argues, even worth interpreting.[64] Rather, dreams were to be regarded as highly organized allegories whose interpretations might yield profound truths. As one modern analyst of the dream poem observes, "The form certifies the presence of allegory."[65]

But how could a person tell when his dream was true and when false? When would a man's imagination be divinely inspired and when would his dream be mere illusion prompted by waking preoccupation? This was a vexed question for the Middle Ages. The age did, however, provide a theory to explain the generation and mechanism of dreams and to differentiate the psychology of a true from a false dream, though it had more trouble finding a method of distinguishing between them after the fact. Significant dreams required both man's inspiration by God and the proper subordination of his imagination to his reason or estimation. This last was a requirement for any act of reliable knowing, but as Avicenna makes clear, the ordering of imagination to the reasoning or estimative faculty was especially important to the soul that must evaluate the rich and ambiguous images provided to it during a dream.[66] Or as John of Salisbury points out in his discussion of biblical dreams in the *Policraticus*, "The light of truth shines out more frequently in the case of certain personalities inasmuch as they possess well ordered minds; others are more prone to be led astray."[67]

In his Prologue to the *Anticlaudianus*, Alain de Lille suggests a similar distinction when he requests that his poem be read only by those who do not allow their reasons to dwell in the *turpes imagines*, the "foul images," of dreams.[68] The dreamer ought, he says, to remember more than simply what he has seen. He ought, the poet implies, to remember an interpretation capable of giving abstract and reasonable significance to dream images. The reasoning necessary for this interpretation might occur inside or outside the dream proper, for though high medieval psychology held that the ordering of imagination to reason normally occurred as preparation for inspired dreaming, the dream itself might incorporate the experience of such ordering. If a man's cogitative powers are quick and acute and he is able to draw on his memory, he might, in Avicenna's words, "see the interpretation of his dream within his own dream."[69]

Avicenna's testimony suggests that a model of dreaming as confrontation between imaginative and reasoning faculties emerged during the high medieval period. This confrontation is very like the encounter between dreamer and oracle, which had already been combined with a psychology of knowing by Boethius and which thus provided the deep structure of the dream vision as it was taken up as a genre by twelfth-century poets. Medieval theories of dreaming would reinforce classical ones, but their differences would also become part of the working of new upon old from which poetry would benefit. The new science and medicine caused the kind of spiritual growth and self-definition that had informed the *De consolatione* to be articulated in a certain way. Faculty psychology had demonstrated that the active faculty in dreaming was imagination, so inevitably the dreamer himself would be identified with this faculty. Reason had already been personified as an interior guide by Augustine. But also because of its privileged access to unerring, bodiless truth and its role in raising and informing imagination by means of that truth, reason's role as healer in the dream encounter between the two faculties had a special rightness.

Poets of the age thus naturally transferred the ordering of imagination by reason, which Avicenna described, to the encounter between wounded dreamer and philosophical therapy that lay at the center of the *De consolatione*. This sort of vision—one that actually served to define for an individual the right relation between reason and imagination—had rhetorical potential. In its instructions of imagination, a figure representing the viewpoint of reason, standing in for the dreamer's sleeping reason, might show dreamer and reader alike the map of ascent from matter to spirit, an ascent whose charting, as I demonstrated in Chapter 1, was a matter of considerable urgency to the period. Difficulty or failure in correctly understanding the relationship between world and God might constitute a serious spiritual crisis, to which the dream, both physical and metaphysical in nature, was ideally capable of responding.

The *De consolatione* itself, with its basis in Platonic dialogue and its subtle personification allegory, had suggested equations between the actors in the poem and psychic powers. Philosophy embodies through her teachings a kind of Augustinian blend of dialectic reason and Platonic memory, while Boethius's Wounded Muses indicate that he may be, in part, a figure of misguided poetic imagination. But these identifications are left largely implicit. Medieval translations and imitations of the *De consolatione* indicate the degree to which later writers regarded such equations as fundamental to the allegory. Lady Philosophy's role is frequently taken by a character named Understanding or Reason; Boethius's role becomes that of the human mind.[70] The equations are not rigid, and no one actually names the dreamer "Imagination." But vision poems from the twelfth century onward come to represent the dreamer as something close to this faculty; for example, in *Piers Plowman* or in the *Commedia*, the Dreamer becomes something like the Will in its imaginative aspect. In any case, as the dream came to be seen by the natural sciences more explicitly as part of a mental journey, marking a specific stage in a psychological itinerary, the dream poem itself came to imitate that journey in its poetic progress more self-consciously than even Boethius's poem had done. Indeed, because it demanded a psychology specially devised to bridge the chasm between the physical and metaphysical, the dream when used as a device in poetry came to invoke that "natural order" of knowing that I have suggested was so important to the poetics of the age. But it is now an order made dynamic by the drama of a reason figure's attempts to inform and cure a diseased imagination.

In the pages that follow, close study of individual dream visions will show that they tend to open with the presentation of a luxuriance of images to a dreamer who does not seem to have the strength of reason necessary to interpret them. These are what Paul Piehler, in applying modern psychological theory to these poems, calls "seminal images."[71] Their meaning will be clarified and explicated as the doctrine offered in the course of the poem gradually gives the dreamer the required knowledge, or more exactly, as it stimulates the growth of knowledge from the seeds of awareness represented by the images themselves. In a large sense, Piehler identifies just those gross structural units my own, more historically based analysis also brings to light. But on a more precise level, it does not suggest what stages in this process would have been most clearly articulated for a medieval audience of these poems, or how a dreamer's spiritual progress would have been evaluated as he achieved new levels of awareness.

From the beginning, physical features of the landscape in a dream poem, dimly perceived, suggest a level of abstraction the dreamer cannot achieve; but subsequent dialogue with a figure more capable than he of intellectual analysis who "explicates" the allegory's "imagistic elements" serves as his means to this level.[72] Simply put, in terms consistent with medieval psychology, what happens in these poems goes something like this: reason's dialogue with the dreamer's imagination prepares it to receive the truths that can be abstracted from images, truths that at the end of the dream or immediately after waking can finally be deposited in memory. The dreamer's initial sickness is thus located by the poet in the relationship between imagination and reason. Because they have not properly ordered the first to the second, these literary dreamers suffer from an illness that necessarily renders them incapable of abstracting truth from the images of the dream. Though at the outset of the poem they do not possess the well-ordered soul described by Avicenna as a precondition for the true dream, the kinds of visionary images produced by their fertile imaginations indicate that they are somehow ripe for a revelation, a liminal experience, that will lead to moral and psychic wholeness.

It is clear from medieval accounts of dreaming not only that the *oraculum* might be combined with the enigmatic *somnium*, but also that it was the most highly valued of the various classes of dreams. Our modern supposition that the impetus and energy for a dream comes from within ourselves was not shared by the medieval writer, for whom a crucial part of learning involves acquiescence in a higher truth.[73] Thus, a dream physician, a figure of reason, provides remedies that lead to a reordering of the mind, preparing the dreamer finally for the reception of this abstract truth. Ultimately, the strength of reason, originally perceived as something extrinsic to the dreamer, is absorbed by the dreamer's own reason itself, and he is able to reformulate his view of the world to include a new awareness of the wholeness of natural and divine truth. This is a much less stern truth than that gained by Drycthelm, reflecting the greater optimism of the later age.

Though the first significant medieval vision poems formed part of a movement to revive Platonism, their interpretation of that philosophy, like that of the *Aeneid* commentary, was thus materialistic in important ways. In their verse, a Platonic epistemology of knowledge as reminiscence came to be supplemented by an Aristotelian one based on sense-mediated images. Like the narrator in the *De consolatione*, the dreamers I will be examining have lost a sense of their true identities, knowledge they can regain in part from an archetypal memory. But Platonic dialogue is synthesized with other structures of discourse, which ultimately become more important—structures derived from an epistemology based on abstraction. This kind of synthesis was appropriately effected by a dream or vision in which knowing might at each point be impelled forward by a dialogue that presumes some native knowledge in the human soul of its divine home, but in which knowing might also proceed in a natural sequence of increasing abstraction. "Why do dreams occur?" asks Averroes. "They take place because of [divine] solicitude for man . . . since man is defective in the knowledge and comprehension of the rational, cogitative faculty."[74] Human science is only possible, Alain de Lille writes, "when divine excellence descends so that human excellence may ascend."[75] God's generosity to man might be conveyed by His healing power extended in a dream, and a dream also allowed for the human response required by such generosity. In terms of contemporary theology, this human response corresponds to what Aquinas would call "medicinal grace," in being natural and internal to a man; the divine descent to "elevated grace," inspired and external.[76] The dream form thus embodies perfectly the paradox of a God whose force can be simultaneously immanent and supramundane. It becomes the ideal metaphorical vehicle to convey the fine collaboration between nature, whose revelations the psyche must strive after, and grace, whose revelations are as freely given as the dream itself.

Dreams and Art

We are now in a position to see that the dream had another, not incidental, appeal to the poets, for it was ideally suited not only to defend the possibility of knowing God's truth in nature but also to "thematize" ways that truth might be known and revealed by poetry. This capacity made it an appropriate mode for poetic self-reflection, for that shift back in discourse that I have suggested occurred both in philosophy and also in a poetry that sought to redefine the bases of a legitimate art. In the fourteenth century, two hundred years after the period I have been discussing, the philosopher-poet would be rare. Now, few limits were placed on what sorts of philosophical issues an audience might expect him to explore. Even so, the age was already experiencing difficulties in defining the precise relation between the trivium and the quadrivium—or between poetry and either of these. The difficulties suggest how vexed the problem of poetic authority was already becoming and point to reasons a poet might well feel slightly insecure and threatened.

In Book III of the *Didascalicon*, Hugh of Saint Victor discusses the relation of poetry to philosophy and expresses the kind of attitude poets of this age must have felt they had to combat. There are the "arts," he says, and there are the "appendages of the arts." In the last category fall all types of poetry with their "verbal detours" and "confused discourses." The man who pursues these "appendages," he goes on, will find only "exceedingly great pains and meagre fruit."[77] But in its capacity to represent the relations between imagination and reason, the dream poem could suggest an antidote to this view of poetry. The dreaming imagination's presentations might seem at first "confused discourses," but nature provided them that they might be ordered and clarified by reason's analysis. As we read and try to understand the images of the poem, we are implicated in the struggle for understanding that the dreamer undertakes. Worthy fruit would not only reward the reader's and dreamer's "exceedingly great pains," but that fruit would mean more, taste better as it were, because of the trouble in its gathering.[78] With its special psychology of ascent, the dream provided an ideal framing device for an art whose narrative sought in part to defend the possibility of ascent and clarification, a poetry that partly by invoking the reader's participation in an epistemological experience drew upon formal strengths not available to philosophy.

Like acts of artistic creation, dreams began in the imagination, an ambiguous power. Imagination could reflect superficial and mundane desires or it could represent to other mental faculties images susceptible to the most detailed and profound philosophical explication. Even when divinely inspired, the imagination was a kind of prerational realm of consciousness, and as such, its vision was suggestive rather than conclusive, chaotic rather than controlled. After imagination's activities, it remained still for reason to judge, analyze, and give shape to those prerational, "seminal" images. In this effort, reason involved itself in the kind of activity we have seen attributed to poets of the age—the effort to control the implications of a subject matter, in this case of one provided by the dreaming imagination. An artist's first step was to attend to his *ingenium*, his poetic imagination, that he might bring forth imagery which would be capable of accurately representing an idea or experience. But his next step, if he was a legitimate poet, was to order that imagery, to submit it to the disciplines of rhetoric that it might yield to its readers an abstract truth. Reason, thus, took the role of the shaping hand and became a maker of allegories, for the ordering and shaping of *sententia* through narrative and image was the task of intellect, whether in dreams or art.

For poet as for dreamer, then, neither reason nor imagination alone was sufficient. Imagination gives physical substance to a conception that has value and significance only when all the poet's faculties are properly aligned. Thus, his ability to produce an art with some spiritual validity becomes a sign of a dreamer's psychic wholeness; as artifacts themselves, increasingly complex and luminous dream images serve as indicators of a dreamer's spiritual progress, just as his capacity to absorb increasingly complex doctrine also signals his advancement. Boethius and Alain de Lille draw on this notion of poetic validity in their use of the *satura*, with its mixture of poetry and prose: the Dreamer's poetry comes to stand for his spiritual state. A study of the verse sections of the *De consolatione* or the *De planctu* shows that a legitimate poetry—one which grows out of and stimulates psychic wholeness—becomes more and more possible as the Dreamer's will becomes aligned with God's. The last of four poems attributed to the narrator in the *De consolatione* (Book V, Meter 3) can serve as an example. This meter takes advantage of poetry's special capacities, for unlike philosophy, poetry as a mode of discourse is able to pose nondiscursive questions, questions that have a purely emotive or rhetorical force: "Why does the mind burn with such desire to discover the hidden aspects of truth?" ("Sed cur tanto flagrat amore / ueri tectas reperire notas?"; ll. 11–12.) "Why does it go on laboriously trying to discover what it already knows?" ("Sed quis nota scire laborat?"; l. 14.)

Yet the philosopher indulges in poetry here not simply to give vent to emotional problems, as he did in Book I, Meter 1, but to indicate his deeply confirmed awareness of a truth that to him, if not to his later commentators, was more profound than any other he could offer. The human urge to question, implies Boethius, is a sacred proof of man's divine origin, an earnest of his safe passage home to God. His point is like Dante's "questioning springs up like a shoot, at the foot of truth" (*Paradiso* IV.130–31). Though shrouded in clouds of flesh, "whoever seeks the truth," he sings, "knows something" (ll. 25–26).

In contrast, Lady Philosophy's conclusion to the book's argument (Book V, Prose 4–6) works strictly logically and discursively, distinguishing among the levels of knowing appropriate to man, beast, and divinity, and demonstrating the incommensurability of human and divine knowing, a distinction that explains the narrator's continuing need to question, his failure to grasp the ultimate compatibility of two truths, of human freedom with divine foreknowledge. The problem, she reveals, lies not in the "thing which is known" but in "the capacity of the knower" (Prose 4.25). In this case, the most elevated capacity of the Boethian knower or visionary seems not finally to come in the use of his reason, which she also recommends, but in the way he employs poetry to offer an emotional equivalent to reason. Significantly, even the visionary's poetic voice more or less drops out of the final, difficult discourse on predestination and free will, as his formal objections are here taken up by Philosophy: "But you will say," she anticipates, "that even though foreknowledge does not impose a necessity of future events, it is still a sign that they will necessarily happen" ("Sed praescientia, inquies, tametsi futuris eueniendi necessitas non est, signum tamen est necessario ea esse uentura"; Book V, Prose 4.10; see also Book V, Prose 6.25). Meter 3, then, constitutes the narrator's last full statement of his position, making it possible to say that Boethius offers nondiscursive poetry as the most plausible alternative for the mortal whose "human reason cannot comprehend the simplicity of divine foreknowledge" (Book V, Prose 4.2)—perhaps the only alternative. It is only here in song or poetry that Platonic memory has, to some degree, redeemed imagination; that the Wounded Muses—those "whores from the theater"—have given way to the inspirations of psychic health and verity.[79]

Sensing the power of art when thus reclaimed by a higher "rational" vision, classical and medieval commentators both focus on the kinds of statements dreams can make about art, perhaps more so than on nearly any other aspect of dreaming. The parallel between inspired art and the divinely informed dream fascinated them. Significantly, the subject of poetry comes up near the beginning of Macrobius's commentary on the *Somnium Scipionis*, when, just before introducing his famous classification of dreams into five types, the commentator draws a distinction between fabulous narrative (*narratio fabulosa*) and fable, comparing them implicitly to true and false dreams. Scipio's dream is a *narratio fabulosa*, "a decent and dignified conception of holy truths . . . presented beneath a modest veil of allegory."[80] In a remarkable adaptation of this impulse to classification, Pascalis Romanus attributes a separate sort of literary type to each of the five Macrobian classes of *somnium, visio, oraculum, insomnium*, and *visum*. In dealing with the three prophetic varieties, Pascalis writes that depending on the degree of liberty the soul achieves from the body, it may apprehend the future allegorically as in a *somnium*, historically as in a *visio*, or prophetically as in an *oraculum*.[81]

Other twelfth-century writers also extended Macrobius's literary theory with its application to dream by proposing adaptations frequently more subtle and flexible than those of either Pascalis or Macrobius. As Peter Dronke has demonstrated, Guillaume de Conches attempts to provide a justification for certain less respectable sorts of *fabula* by admitting to the class of *narratio fabulosa* a wider range of fictional material than Macrobius had allowed.[82] In thus strengthening the ties that had bound philosophy to poetry, the twelfth century stays true to the central idea that Scipio's dream is an allegory that gracefully conceals a philosophical truth, and the connection between dream and legitimate poetry remains intact. The diction itself used to describe the dreaming experience in medieval writings also works to enforce the equation. Dreams and poems are both "polysemous"; at times, writes Pascalis Romanus, the future is seen "sine aliquo integumento" in dreams, but at other times, he goes on, integument, allegory, and figure are all necessary.[83] The dream, writes John of Salisbury, "stretches before the body of truth a curtain, as it were, of allegory."[84] From Macrobius on, the gate of horn has an opacity seen to be like the veil of allegory.[85]

The connection between dream and allegory, insisted upon by the age, suggests a way to move beyond the usual medieval comments on dream and art, which can seem at times superficial and even contradictory. Take, for example, John of Salisbury's evaluation of dreams in the *Policraticus*. This passage has been called "one of the most baffling collections of statements on the subject that we can find in medieval writing."[86] The modern reader's difficulty rises from the fact that John never makes clear whether he values and respects dreams for the profound truths they can convey or whether he detests them as meaningless and deceptive. He seems to hold both views simultaneously, for he spends three chapters describing true dreams, then begins a fourth with the statement, "Whoever involves himself in the deception of dreams is not sufficiently awake to the law of God, suffers a loss of faith, and drowses to his own ruin."[87] Though, as in other matters, John himself never resolves the contradictions in his discussion of dreams, perhaps we can see the form such a resolution might have taken.

What bothers John is the difficulty of interpreting the profuse, often unclear, signs offered by dreams. His problem is not unlike Hugh's difficulty with a poetic art whose images and fictions Hugh also found confusing. John himself points out the similarity: "As the work of artists who imitate nature is surpassed by the works of nature herself, so the significance of events, which is much more intricate than meaning conveyed by words, requires much shrewdness for the interpretation of dreams and the elucidation of riddles and signs."[88]

The key to the reader's problem in the *Policraticus* and indeed to the relationship between dream theory, epistemology, and poetry in general lies in this distinction between the "meaning conveyed by words" (*vocum*) and its significance (*significatio*). "In the multitude of dreams," Pascalis Romanus reports Solomon as saying, "there is vanity and too many words, and dreams and vain illusions make many to err." Solomon does not mean by this, offers Pascalis, that we ought to condemn dreams, but rather that we must recognize in their interpretation, as in all things, that "the letter kills, the spirit however gives life." We must use reason "and investigate the truth signified."[89] It is extremely hard, argue the Middle Ages, to move from the image to its significance; few of us have the rectitude of soul to make the crossing. But for those whose souls are so "ordered," the journey will be worth the trouble. In his discussion of dreams, John of Salisbury can stand as a kind of symbol for his age. He displays a discomfort we have seen before at the confusion and seductive beauty of sensuous reality—whether experienced directly or recorded as images in dreams and poems. But as in philosophy, man's increasing awareness of his natural world leads to a need for synthesis of heavenly and earthly. John also shows this characteristic need to transform worldly confusion to order or *significatio*—to find, in beauty, truth.

Because it pits imagination against reason, image against significance, the dream provides the perfect vehicle to call forth John's ambivalence about the world and its images. But consequently the resolution of that ambivalence—the act of dream interpretation and clarification—clearly gave him profound satisfaction. We see here the mode's appeal. As a writer two hundred years later was to demonstrate, the landscape of a dream includes the field of folk and the castle of Truth. For Alain or Dante, it might also include the path of knowing that led between the two—a path, though difficult and strenuous, they mapped out with a clarity that Langland by the end of the fourteenth century had lost. As we will see now, their vision poems could thus assert, in the face of worldly ambiguity and diversity, that art, life, and God's truth can be reconciled.

CHAPTER 3

Myth and Vision in the 'De planctu naturae'

Critical Perspectives

When C. S. Lewis compared Alain de Lille's two great poems—the *De planctu naturae* and the *Anticlaudianus*—he ruled the first superior to the second, but only because, as he put it, it is blessed by "the enormous advantage of being comparatively short." Even in the briefer work, Lewis found the poet "cold" and "disinterested."[1] We might be able to pass over Lewis's exuberant distaste were it not for the fact that in modern times Lewis's evaluation has been typical. Alain has usually been regarded, even by sympathetic readers, as "pedantic." The most recent translator of the two poems departs from Lewis only in preferring the later *Anticlaudianus* to that youthful "display piece," the *De planctu*, which he complains "tortures the Latin language to such an extent that one is reminded of some of Joyce's English."[2] The *De planctu*'s previous translator remarks in his introduction to the work that "the importance of Alain's work lies wholly in what it prompted; by itself it would have long since been justly forgotten."[3] This formulation, however, should be a clue to us, for what the *De planctu* in fact prompted was the *Roman de la rose*, *The Parliament of Fowls*, the *Confessio Amantis*, and the profoundest appreciation of its age. It is, in part, the work's influence on the poetic tradition, which I believe to be nearly equal to that of Dante, Guillaume de Lorris, or Jean de Meun, that justifies devoting an entire chapter to Alain. But even though we will probably never regain a taste for the kind of poetry Alain's work represents, we can still reformulate the structural laws that gave the work some of its original meaning and appeal. The very fact that we have difficulty understanding the poem's high valuation by its contemporaries is a sign that we need to engage in such reformulating, that we need to relocate what Jauss would call an earlier "horizon of expectations."

Readers like R. H. Green, and more recently Winthrop Wetherbee and George Economou, have done much to make the poem accessible again.[4] Yet their attempts to recreate the grounds for an appreciation of the poet's achievement have focused primarily on the intellectual traditions brought to bear in the poem and not on its relations to the past literary models that, as current genre theory demonstrates, would have provided a basis for literary understanding. Chapter 2's discussion of the ways in which classical and medieval vision theory shaped early visionary literature should help us approximate the high medieval reader's coherent experience of this poem. As a corollary, it will also make possible a more clearsighted evaluation than we have had before of the *De planctu*'s relationship to its poetic sister, the *Anticlaudianus*, for the two works differ formally or generically in significant ways.

The *De planctu* may be, as Wetherbee argues, a kind of allegory of poetry's failure perfectly to disclose truth;[5] or it may be as others argue, an allegorical attack on sexual indulgence, perhaps as practiced by the Catharists.[6] These significances, however, would have been organized by a reader whose experience of the philosophical vision would have caused him to see the poem first, and very literally, as an allegorical vision presented to a Dreamer whose psychic condition and development would itself assume thematic importance. Modern readers have not, by and large, found this Dreamer to be of much interest;[7] consequently, we have lost track of the one structural element that a medieval reader trained in Augustinian and Boethian dialogue would have interpreted first—the Dreamer's movement from confusion to spiritual health. By reattending to the poem's narrator, I hope to show the poet's skill and inventiveness, the ingenuity in his uses and transformations of sources. Alain does tend to overload the form he works in, just as he pushes to their limits the resources of Latin syntax and diction, so much so that at times the most primary levels of meaning may be rendered obscure to us. To recover these levels, let us look now at how the poem takes up and alters the most basic conventions of its genre.

The *De planctu* clearly sees itself as a vision poem on the model of Boethius's *De consolatione*. The similarities between the two works have been frequently noted, and correspondences are so obvious that they hardly seem worth repeating: the opening lament; the appearance to a stuporous dreamer of a female wisdom figure who wears a decorated gown that has been ripped by man; that dreamer's "illness," which comes from a failure to recognize his mistress, and so on. But these likenesses only signal the profound changes and continuities that make Alain's use of Boethius so fruitful. The real power and originality in Alain's poetry rise from its dazzling ability to hold together in a simple structure the expanses of his age's vision, to suggest by a single symbol the multiple valences of his meaning. Still, this power can be fully appreciated only by noting first the way that the poet's new broader perspectives are made possible by a more conventional focus on a single character's growth, stereotyped though that character may be. Though my study will thus be obliged to assume a limited viewpoint on the poem, one that may at times seem perverse in the context of Alain's larger intention, it is only in this way I can redress the general critical neglect of the Dreamer's controlling role in the poem. On the level of what I will call psychological or moral allegory—more than on any other—Alain took his lead from Boethius, for the twelfth-century poet made the healing power of Lady Philosophy's wisdom flow from Lady Nature, causing that power to work upon the faculties of one Dreamer's psyche and strengthening him to move through the world of *visibilia* to a divine truth.[8] It is this generic continuity with which I am primarily concerned.

Alain does not develop the character of his Dreamer nearly as fully as Boethius did—perspective is a more occasional or localized technique in his work—but his use of the Boethian vision, as I have suggested, does signal to his audience that the reader of the *De planctu* ought to pay some attention to the Dreamer's psychological development. There is no dearth of other evidence in the poem to support this idea. The Dreamer's laments open the work; his delirium provokes the teachings that make up the poem's bulk. Indeed, the narrator's lament can be seen as a kind of prospectus for the rest of the poem, beginning as it does with the disorders of nature and concluding with a reference to the anathema of Genius. This structure may suggest that the narrator's disturbance about these things is what the poem, first of all, seeks to resolve.

The advent of Natura occurs, in fact, as a clear response to a deficiency in the Dreamer's psyche. We might almost call her, in modern terms, a projection of some unconscious principle in the Dreamer. In medieval terms, the metaphor of physician provides a useful vehicle to describe the way that her arrival, like the beneficence of grace, answers his special needs. She appears as physician to a Dreamer who, although his speaking part is not dominant, is at least never forgotten. He continues to interrupt Natura throughout the whole of her presentation, either to ask questions or to beg for the examples that will provide him with moral strength. Even in the final movement of the poem Alain reminds us subtly but continuously, by his concentration on just those sights and sounds available to the narrator, that we are still seeing the action—in this case an allegorical pageant—through his eyes. Hymen's appearance, for example, is primarily noted for the "amazement" it causes in the Dreamer, and the detailed description of this character focuses on just those details that appear most impressive to the poem's narrator. Only when Natura calls him by name does the Dreamer, or the reader, realize who Hymen is.[9]

Thus, Alain seems to be in some control of the narrative perspective of his Dreamer. Even if he does not call attention to it at every point in the unfolding drama, we must imagine that the narrator's development qualifies the other levels of meaning in the poem. Alain may, in part, as Paul Piehler suggests, "depict man as seen through the eyes of the *potentia*,"[10] in this case Natura. But the poet also shows the goddess Natura as seen through the eyes of a man, and a man whose changing perspectives are reflected, just as Boethius's had been, in the kinds of learning vouchsafed to him by his mentor. Natura's methods of explication thus take on, as Wetherbee has so aptly pointed out, "a thematic significance."[11] This focus, however, does not imply that we are meant in the early stages of Natura's argument to concern ourselves primarily with the limitations of her doctrine, as Wetherbee does. Even in the first half of the poem the reader is not asked to see, in Natura's identification with earthly rather than heavenly knowing, "a powerful criticism of . . . Chartrian 'natural philosophy' and the pursuit of wisdom in secular literature,"[12] any more than Philosophy in Boethius's poem might be called into question on the same grounds.

Natura is not ignorant of her counterpart, theology. She fully recognizes the authority that supersedes her own. Although Natura knows she cannot approach the mysteries of faith, she does point out that "in many things, we are aware of diversities, but not enmities" ("in plerisque non aduersa sed diuersa sentimus"; VI.152–53, p. 829). That these diversities are not fully harmonized in the first two-thirds of the poem is a problem that reflects on the Dreamer, not on the principles of explication that Natura invokes, as both Wetherbee and Economou seem to assume.[13] To absorb fully the importance of this fact, we must postpone as long as possible in our reading a precise identification of the themes embodied in each character's discourse. In this way we ensure that our interpretations will take place at the highest and most formal level demanded by the poem—the level, I will argue, that is organized by the Dreamer's full experience of the vision, lived through in sequence to the end. Particularly in the first part of the poem, instead of merely providing information, Natura is engaged in restructuring the Dreamer's soul. As she herself makes clear, only in the prolonged and significant confrontation of her doctrine with the Dreamer's imaginative response, confirmed in his experience, will true learning take place.[14] The kinds of "statements" the reader will take away from the work—whether about poetry or about the social and philosophical issues of his day—will thus only emerge in the formal play and development of motifs and themes, and not in a single character's discursive act.

I make this last point even though the *De planctu* has been repeatedly attacked for its formlessness, for its lack of any but the most arbitrary rhetorical structure provided by Natura's whim.[15] Close study of the Dreamer's progress will suggest the contrary: that the order of the poem is not, as most critics would have it, merely repetitive. Read as an example of the philosophical vision, the work details a profoundly meaningful progression of experience, an experience of inspired vision, which in the twelfth century begins first in a dreamer's imagination and culminates in the strengthening of his reason and memory. In this healing process, Natura comes not only to represent the "principle," to use Piehler's phrasing, on which the final resolution of the Dreamer's problem is based, but she is also, like Lady Philosophy, the "mode of thinking" by which such a resolution can be achieved.[16]

The literal-minded Dreamer, we will see, thus speaks as imagination, initially cut off from the sources of its redemption. Genius, that most enigmatic of characters, becomes imagination reconfirmed in the sources of its strength and ordained by Natura as *ratio* to a truly marvelous natural priesthood, one which, by its seeming authority to speak to so many of the poem's most central concerns, brings into a meaningful relation all of the diversities and hesitations that critics have found so puzzling in the poem. As in another work by Alain, the *Sermo de sphaera intelligibili*, the philosopher seeks to find a means of uniting the most disparate approaches of his age to the cosmos. In this treatise, the sphere whose center is everywhere, whose circumference is nowhere, becomes the image that, as Peter Dronke has pointed out, can hold together "the two ways of thinking—naturalistic and dualizing—that coexist in all [Alain's] work."[17] He is, in the words of G. R. Evans, "preoccupied" with the threshold between theology and natural science.[18] Does God stand above the world, cradling it in His hand perhaps, but radically separate from it? Or is He at its center, infusing it with meaning? Transcendence or Immanence? We have seen already that the sequence of abstraction was the narrative line generated by this pattern of oppositions. By playing a key part in this narrative, Natura comes to lead the Dreamer, and us with him, to a solution of the teasing puzzle that absorbed Alain. To see precisely how, let us now look more closely at the "natural order of knowing" that the dream sequence in the poem embodies.

The Dreamer in Alain's Fabulous Narrative

The work opens, it seems, in the midst of a dream.[19] The narrator is lamenting the destruction of nature by those who pursue sensual rather than reasonable love. Like Boethius, he is deeply troubled by the existence of evil, which he can recognize but cannot understand. His acuteness of perception seems to earn him the visitation of the goddess Natura. But then social disorder becomes suddenly personal, for Natura's appearance throws him into a spiritual lethargy. He falls to his face, his mind wounded by astonishment or stupor ("stupore uulneratus"; VI.5, p. 824); he suffers from a condition that

Natura diagnoses as an "infirmatio rationis" (VI.14, p. 825). Like Lady Philosophy, Lady Nature must cure the Dreamer of this infirmity. In doing so, she partly substitutes for the Dreamer's *ratio*, his reason, which has been injured specifically in its ability to abstract truth from created nature and to realize that truth in his humanity.

Of course, Natura never ceases from engaging in her larger part as goddess of all nature; there are times, in fact, when she must be read as a cosmological principle and nothing else.[20] But when she, with her "ratio nature," interacts with man, she brings forth what his nature most uniquely and essentially is, a reasoning one also.[21] Reason was a role Alain might expect his readers to recognize Natura playing from the practice of other contemporary poets, from the term's philosophical background, and from specific characteristics of his own description of the goddess. In his own dictionary of theological and philosophical terms, Alain had defined nature, among other things, as "naturalis ratio," which dictates natural law.[22] Jean de Meun, in attributing to "Reson" many of the details Alain gives to Natura's teaching, also testifies to the functional equivalence of the two characters in the earlier poem. Indeed, it is as a mode of knowing that Alain differentiates Natura from Faith in the *De planctu* (VI.151–58, pp. 826–27), just as later in the *Anticlaudianus* he was similarly to oppose Reason to Faith (VI.6–23). But the mode of knowing by which the Dreamer will be healed in the *De planctu* is not exactly philosophical reason, as it had been in the *De consolatione*; it is that reason which permits man to abstract truth from created nature. Her way of apprehending truth is like Philosophy's, of course, but by her nomination the poet chooses to emphasize the fact that the ascent to the divine begins in the natural world. In *Il Tesoretto*, a dream vision from the next century, Brunetto Latini would exploit this same emphasis by beginning the encyclopedic and worldly instruction of his own naive pilgrim with a vision of the goddess Nature that borrows both from Alain and Boethius, stressing as Alain does the unity and complementarity of natural knowledge and received truth.

In Alain's poem, as in Brunetto's, the arrival of Natura in response to the Dreamer's impasse leads to a long, detailed, and luxuriant description of the images of the created universe that appear on her gown, a description more than ten times as long as Boethius's introduction of Philosophy and constituting over one-quarter of the poem. The sheer bulk of this passage suggests the importance of the changes Alain has made in the earlier poet's guide. The illness that plagues his narrator is thus, near the beginning of the work, located precisely in his use of Natura and the images of her world. The pictures that decorate her gown call to mind the whole of the natural universe, which in one of her aspects she embodies allegorically. Though the jewels of her crown signify the stars and planets of the firmament, we see on her garment the entire parliament of living creation, from eagle to eel, including man, who is depicted on a torn section. He has damaged Natura's gown, the poet tells us, by his failure to follow *ratio*, to pierce through to heavenly *archana* (II.233–34, p. 817). The vision is a *speculum*, we learn, a mirror that ought to reflect divine essence to mortals who cannot look upon it directly.[23] The Dreamer's folly, his stupor in the face of the images reflected here, is a failure he shares with the rest of humanity who are responsible for the tear in Natura's gown. As a *speculum*, the whole vision is provided "sub picture ingenio" (II.291, p. 819); it is an imaginative presentation, requiring for its penetration the proper ordering of the imaginative faculty to reason, necessary for proper abstraction. Even our Dreamer, with his intuitions of what is wrong in nature, does not possess this psychic order completely, at least not at the outset of the vision.

The precise terms of the Dreamer's loss are made even clearer throughout the second section of the poem, which begins in Prose III and continues through Meter XIII, and during which we overhear "an exchange of short questions and long answers between Alain and his august visitor."[24] In the specific lines we will be considering now, however, the Dreamer is struck dumb, and Natura both asks the question—"Why has the memory of my face wandered from your memory?" (VI.14, p. 825)—and suggests the answer, as she describes the powers of discernment with which she has endowed man to counteract those bodily appetites that seem now to be challenging the sovereignty of intellect and so causing the loss of archetypal memory:

Your spirit, also, I have distinguished by vital powers, lest it, poorer than the body, envy the body's successes. And in it I have appointed a power of *ingenium*, which is a huntress of subtle things in the search of knowledge, and brings them to intelligibility. On it also I have impressed the sign of reason, which separates, by winnowing, empty falsehoods from serious matters of truth. Through me also the power of memory serves you, which hoards in the chest of its recollection the noble treasure of knowledge.

Tuum etiam spiritum uirtualibus insigniui potentiis, ne corpore pauperior eius successibus inuideret. Cui ingenialis uirtutis destinaui potentiam, que rerum uenatrix subtilium in noticie indagine easdem intellectas concluderet. Cui etiam rationis impressi signaculum, que sue discretionis uentilabro falsitatis inania a seriis ueritatis secernat. Per me etiam tibi memorialis ancillatur potentia, que in sue recordationis armario nobilem censum scientie thesaurizat. (VI.33–39, pp. 825–26)[25]

This passage recalls the one from John of Salisbury quoted in Chapter 1. In both, reason, although participating in the divine, is described as a winnowing faculty. Real insight into the natures of things can potentially be achieved first by the imagination, or here *ingenium*, which can have, as writers ranging from Hugh of Saint Victor to Avicenna demonstrate, a kind of direct access to truth. When reason properly disciplines the lusts of the body, the darkness of the mind becomes illumined, and *ingenium*, as Alain's nonpoetic writings indicate, becomes capable of a kind of penetration through the substantial natures of things to their exemplars or archetypes.[26]

But it is just this penetration that Alain's Dreamer lacks, with his infirmity of the reason that ought to rule in the hierarchy of the soul. Only this deficiency can account for the sorts of questions he asks in the first half of the poem: Why have you come? Why is your cloak torn? And those literary questions: Why are unnatural acts imputed to the gods? These queries illustrate the weakness of the Dreamer's *ratio*. To the inquiry about the tear in her garment, Natura responds, "From what has been touched upon before, you should be able to deduce what is figured mystically by the splits and separations [in my gown]" ("Iam ex prelibatis potes elicere quid misticum figuret scissure figurata parenthesis"; VIII.164–65, p. 838). This answer suggests both the degree of this Dreamer's ignorance and the degree to which Natura's lore is designed to accommodate the natural limits of the Dreamer's knowing.

Natura's frustration in the lines quoted can be explained by her feeling that, despite efforts to make her reasoning accessible to him, the narrator is like all men—wayward, distractible, drawn by the sensual and prurient in poetry. He seems not to be attending to her teachings properly, for he is not using the model of exegesis that she has just provided him in her discussion of the poets to understand the images seen on her gown. If nothing else, one idea ought to have been clear from Natura's discussion of art: that true poetry discloses a philosophical referent, and that judgment is therefore a necessary component of interpretation. The goddess's ambivalence about the effects of poetic imagery, specifically in pagan works, indicates, as Wetherbee has noted, a deep ambivalence about poetry in general, though within its "elegant structures" ("elegantes suturae") and even at times within the "superficiality of its literal shell" ("in superficiali littere cortice") can be discovered the highest truths. For poetry does not deviate from its "peculiar quality" either ("a sue proprietatis genere") when it leads men away from the truth (VIII.128–38, p. 837). Thus, the failure of Natura's account to provide a special method of distinguishing between the two kinds of art is, as Wetherbee says, "a crucial omission." But it is not one that, as he argues, reflects on the possibility of rational exploration or figural interpretation in a post-Edenic world.[27] The Dreamer's confusion here, embodied in the ambiguousness of Natura's lore, no more represents Alain's final stand on poetry than her condemnation of sexual license provides a decisive judgment that legitimate human love is impossible—something her advice on Cupid can be read to imply.

At the end of Meter V, Natura advises the Dreamer, as Chaucer's Dreamer was to be similarly advised in *The Parliament of Fowls*, that "Th'eschewing is only the remedye" in matters of love; "However, you will be able to curb this madness by yourself, / If you flee, no stronger philter is given" ("Ipse tamen poteris istum frenare furorem, / Si fugias potior potio nulla datur"; IX.67–68, p. 844). This advice makes no sense in the context of her larger discussion of *Venus caelestis*; she must mean, I think, that flight is the proper response to the enticements of love for the Dreamer in his present state of mind. Thus, like her discussion of poetry, her advice on love reflects on the Dreamer as its proper subject. We need, then, to focus more directly on the Dreamer's errors in questioning, which generally rise from a puerile literalism, a lack of judgment. Natura's allegory is conceived as a response to that literalism, which it will seek gradually to correct. This reading of the moral action is confirmed by the fact that the goddess's methods of teaching and her doctrine change and develop throughout the poem. Despite moments when the Dreamer backslides and arouses her temporary frustration, Natura's method is ultimately an effective one. For example, in her first speech, portions of which I have already quoted, she describes the structure of the soul, its intended sovereignty over the body, and implies in her comments on theology her own identification as natural reason. These are the pieces of information most necessary to begin the education of a Dreamer who suffers from an indulgence in fantasy. They cause him to rise from his stupor, to throw off his delirium, for "as if by some medical potion, the nauseated stomach of my mind, as it were, vomited forth its remaining fantasies" ("uelut quodam potionis remedio omnes fantasie reliquias quasi nauseans stomachus mentis euomuit"; VI.173–74, p. 830). Immediately afterwards, in a luxuriance of metaphor and paradox so typical in Alain's writing, the Dreamer describes his spiritual famishment, his hunger, which nourishment only increases.

Such eagerness in the narrator remains his constant attitude as he continues to question the goddess. He does, however, change and grow as he comes to experience a more fully differentiated longing for Natura's doctrine, which he finally desires with his entire soul. By the middle of Prose IV, having satisfied the Dreamer's curiosity over her torn garment and the causes of man's apostasy, Natura has clearly ignited those powers of his soul that we have seen to be most essential in the movement from world to God—powers she had previously implied were dormant. Here he yearns for her teaching specifically with the hunger of *intellectus*, the sharpness of a burning *ingenium* and mind, and a stable and firm attention (VIII.196–98, p. 839). Significantly, this statement of his full desire occurs directly after Natura's appeals to just these faculties (VIII.179–82, p. 839). We may say, I think, that the Dreamer makes his journey toward truth in a continuous and carefully defined manner, for the poet calls our attention to the way that this narrator's increased receptiveness to truth is made possible by the revitalization of these specific mental faculties, *ingenium*, *intellectus*, and *mens*.

This articulation of stages in the mind's ascent to truth is not surprising when we consider that Natura adds to Philosophy's pedagogical resources the allure of the sensual reality that she embodies, the sensual reality that the Dreamer must submit to the rigors of analysis. Alain's poem, more than Boethius's, then, calls upon the psychology adopted by his own time, the theory of abstraction whose contribution to high medieval dream theory I have discussed at length. In the terms of this psychology, the Dreamer's perspective has been that of *ingenium* or imagination, whose powers of intuition and visualization are, for better or for worse, as Avicenna explains, set loose by the dream. Natura becomes both healer and reason figure, naturally provided to each man for the ordering of his soul, yet forgotten until the divine generosity of a vision. By Prose V of the *De planctu*, her reason has brought light to the dimness of the Dreamer's perception. In pointing the way to an abstract significance for the images lavishly envisioned by the poet's imagination, she places that imagination under the control of her superior power.

We can find confirmation of this summary of the psychological allegory in the fact that, to indicate the near completion of this process, Natura now briefly addresses *memoria*, the last faculty to receive knowledge and the farthest from her direct apprehension in the map of the mind: "These things, then, which I throw into your mind, affix there by the nail of tenacious memory and by the wakefulness of soul shake off slothful sleep, so that, excited by my maternal feelings, you may be compassionate and condole over the wrecks of dangerous men, and armed with the shield of early admonitions run to meet the monstrous army of vices" ("Ea igitur que disseram tue menti clauo memorie tenacis affigas animique uigilantia sompnum torporis excutias, ut mecum maternis excitatus uisceribus, periclitantium hominum naufragiis compaciendo condoleas et, preambule ammonitionis clipeo loricatus, monstruoso excercitui uiciorum occurras"; VIII.178–82, p. 850). Just as earlier the Dreamer withdrew from the goddess into a stuporous sleep, now the poet shows us that sleep can be a turning from the self-deceptions of the world, an awakening to Natura's truth; the Dreamer responds to Natura here by describing his "exhilaration" at the Lady's teachings. He moves to the end of that journey through the faculties which we have seen to exert such an ordering force on poetry. His education should be close to its perfection—at least insofar as natural knowing will permit.

I suggested earlier when discussing the *De consolatione* that the kinds of messages offered by poetry can serve as signs of a visionary's spiritual progress. Thus, in Meter VI, when the Dreamer seems to have completed a full revolution towards truth, Natura vouchsafes him, in verse for the first time, that complaint for which the poem is named. Although up to this point Natura's weeping has indicated her grief over man, the only metrical invective has been the narrator's own opening lament. The other meters have included prayers, invocations, soothing hymns on natural themes. Now the goddess seems to feel that her pupil is ready for stronger stuff, ready to have the precise evils of the world identified to him, and equipped with the rational strength to understand them. Her opinion of him seems to be justified, for his next question will earn her praise as having a "worthy aim" ("ratio emerita"; XII.5, p. 852). He wants her to abandon her general mode of speaking and to address the specific evils that have prompted her visit.

If the first section of the poem is comprised of a description of Natura's appearance, and the second part includes dialogue for the purpose of restructuring the Dreamer's soul, the work can be said to begin a third movement after Prose V. For the more than four hundred lines that follow, Natura fires the Dreamer's soul with those particulars he finally has a context for understanding. As an indication of the new level of his cognitive awareness, the Dreamer no longer asks his excessively literal questions. From now on, he will desire only further images and exempla to establish Natura's lessons more firmly in his mind and to enable him to follow through their implications. Indeed, toward the end of this part of the dialogue, he takes the role—previously assigned to Natura—of ordering and disciplining the course of the narrative: "Then I, restraining the speed of her continuous narration, said, 'I wish that you would strengthen with the ramparts of your rational teachings the forts of my mind against the furious armies of these vices'" ("Tunc ego continue narrationis aurigationem refrenans dixi: 'Vellem ut rationabilibus tue disciplinationis propugnaculis contra furiales istorum uiciorum exercitus mee mentis roborares oppidulum'"; XIV.141–43, p. 864).

Following this evident advance in the Dreamer's rational control, Hymen and the maidens who personify the virtues appear in the poem. From Prose VI to Meter VIII, then, particulars about the world are all that Natura provides to give the Dreamer strength and virtuous motivation. For the most part, what she reveals is fairly horrifying: a world gone bad, where Greed, Drunkenness, and Pride, along with numerous other vices, lead to a general perversion of mankind. Yet implicit in her speech—for the first time in the work—is a fully realized standard against which to judge these evils, a standard that Natura's faith in him causes us to believe that the Dreamer has internalized. Here we receive, for example, the first full description of human wisdom. We had known before that wisdom or *sapientia* existed, that it had its seat in the head, but now we hear it described at length (XII.126–48, pp. 856–57). Here at last we see Natura offering the Dreamer a perspective, like that of Cicero's Scipio, from which he can view earthly renown in its true relation to *uera fama*. Finally, at the very end of this section of the poem, Natura provides the Dreamer with the kind of practical lore about how to do well in this world that a critic such as Wetherbee has felt missing from the beginning of the poem (XV.1–40, pp. 864–65).

Why does the work not end in Meter VIII, then, with this pragmatic advice? The ordering of the Dreamer's psyche is complete; the specific ills of the world have been adduced and catalogued. Yet in rendering the world and its deficiencies more lucid, Natura has simply thrown into greater relief the terrific problems of human sin and evil in a fallen nature. Fuller knowledge and a fuller poetic solution to the problems raised by the poem are still needed. The ultimate section of the *De planctu*—the allegorical pageant that continues from Prose VIII for about 450 lines until the end of the poem—can be read as a pessimistic solution to these problems, as the poet's apocalyptic warning to sinners of their ultimate judgment. The virtues that balance the earthly vices can congregate only in the heavens. Before returning to the poem's moral or psychological allegory, I want to stress that a part of Alain's achievement in the *De planctu* lies in the multiple levels of the work's meaning. Seen from a large social and historical perspective—certainly one level of interpretation the poem demands—humankind may seem to be largely damned. But seen from a psychological perspective, man may be saved individually. The final section can thus be read as optimistic if it is interpreted as an action occurring in the Dreamer's soul that confirms in him and clarifies for us the meaning of his psychic ascent.

It may be possible to justify this psychological reading by showing how it makes sense of the allegorical pageant that ends the work, a movement in the poem that formally balances the opening presentation of Natura. Why end with such a pageant? What has justified the appearance of these virtues? The answer lies perhaps in our recognition that the Dreamer has earned this last part of his vision by his imaginative advance from the poem's beginning. If we see Natura as the Dreamer's reasonable human nature, we may logically think of the character Chastity as the Dreamer's new ability to envision the quality of chastity, as well as Generosity and Humility with his new grasp of those virtues. All these characters are described in such a way as to indicate their close relationship to Natura. If she is the gem that reflects the virtues of her Creator, they are her facets. Generosity, for example, is named by Natura as her sister. The symmetry of these two aspires even to an identity of essence ("ad idemptitatis aspiret essentiam"; XVIII.26–27, p. 874). Generosity seems to represent that part of Natura which laments for man, which cannot but be moved by man's sin. It is part of Natura's essential being to be bountiful and generous—even to a fault, for mercy must be tempered with justice. The indulgence of *largitas* is innate to our Dreamer. It is what is most distinctive about his own *natura*. Thus, with the appearance of the personification, he is confirmed in what is creditable about his sympathy and freed of what is out of balance. The Dreamer, whose lament for human sin has provoked the entire vision, is able at this point to regard his sorrow for defectors from Natura's law in a new light, finally a more rational one. The appearance of Genius signals his new attitude about mankind—in fact, a much more masculine one, a sterner one—an attitude he has been moving inexorably toward from his first lament. His new sternness, as I will show, occasions a reflection both on the immensity of sin and also on the possibility of individual redemption.

But how does the end of the work bring about or represent such a change in attitude? What are we to do in our analysis of the moral allegory with this Genius, whose appearance initiates the final action of the poem, or with Hymen, whose advent marked the beginning of the allegorical pageant? Unlike the others, these two characters seem more appropriate to the macrocosmic world than to the microcosmic. Yet I think that they too can be considered as aspects of the Dreamer's particular human nature. Let us look first at Hymen, the God of Marriage. His domain is primarily a social one; by lawful marriage men and women carry out God's will that they be fruitful, and in the rule of husband over wife put right Adam's submission of reason to imagination in the Garden of Eden. But as this last function suggests, marriage had also become a metaphor for the *conjugium spirituale* between flesh and spirit in the individual man.[28] It was as well a figure for the union of substance with matter, or of form with substance, a figure that Natura herself uses in this way earlier in the poem (VIII.217–23, p. 840), and that Alain so employs in his more philosophical works.²⁹ It is as he represents this sort of marriage that we can understand Hymen in his appearance at the end of the poem. He becomes not only the force of marriage in society; he also stands for that rule of reason over appetite through which a man can realize his nature, through which he may be able to unite the opposites of his being, to bring his material being into the proper alignment with his spiritual self.

It makes sense, then, in the moral or psychological allegory, that Hymen should be followed by Chastity. The proper marriage of form and substance should result in chastity within lawful love; the marriage of Hymen and Venus had produced Cupid, whose opposition to Mirth marks him as an ideal character. Similarly, it is logical that Temperance should follow Chastity, since chastity is a kind of temperance in love; temperance, in a sense, is chastity exercised throughout more areas of the soul. The only intemperate or excessive thing in the soul of our Dreamer as the poem draws to its close is his continuing largesse, his abiding generosity for his fellow creatures, who ought not, in fact, to be considered his spiritual comrades at all. In a sense, this quality has unmanned him, made him passive and somnolent in his dealing with vice. As a guiding angel had said to Paul when he witnessed the torments of the damned in his apocryphal vision, "Wherefore mournest thou? Art thou more merciful than God?"³⁰ Likewise, Natura has suggested to Alain's Dreamer that he needs both the compassion and the passion to meet the army of vices head on (XIV.141–43). The correction of this problem Natura signals here in her encounter with the personification Generosity, later to be associated explicitly with Prodigality (XVIII.30–56, pp. 874–75). Yet even this correction has its own spiritual danger, for the Dreamer's new condition is susceptible to the pride that any individual may feel who denies community with other men. To this danger, Humility is the proper response.³¹

The Dreamer at this point may be understood as having achieved a kind of ideal understanding, for as Natura says to the virtues gathered round her, which now represent their deeply felt unity with her by modeling their features after her own, "I understand [your grief] with a deep-rooted and mature comprehension" ("radicate cognitionis maturitate congnosco"; XVI.160, p. 870). Earlier in the poem, all of creation had celebrated Natura's advent by the sort of conformity that these personifications of human virtues achieve now: "Indeed at the virgin's coming, you would have thought that all the elements were celebrating the occasion as if renewing their own natures" ("in prefate uero uirginis aduentu, quasi suas renouando naturas omnia sollempnizare crederes elementa"; IV.18–19, p. 821). Only man had been excluded from the harmony. Now we see that even he, in the person of the Dreamer, may be reintegrated into Natura's world.

The Natural Priesthood of Genius

With the appearance of Genius, the poet's focus seems to widen again. In his main features this character is appropriated from Pantomorphos in the *Cosmographia*, whose residence in that poem was at the outer limit of the created universe. Bernardus Silvestris had named him as "that Genius devoted to the art and office of delineating and giving shape to the forms of things."[32] The outlines of Pantomorphos's character were in turn borrowed from Apuleius's *De deo Socratis* and from a tradition, possibly derived from Claudian, of scribes and *senes* who establish the laws that determine life and death in the universe.[33] But Alain's Genius is a far more complex character than Bernardus's Usiarch. His reception and growth as a literary force—in the *Roman de la rose* or in the *Confessio Amantis* after even Natura herself had dropped out—is testimony to the importance medieval readers must have assigned him when interpreting Alain's work. Perhaps sensing that the secret to the *De planctu* and later works that borrow Alain's Genius might thus be found in this enigmatic figure who is called upon to excommunicate sinners from Natura's realm, much recent scholarship has focused on his role in the literary and philosophical texts that Alain might have known.[34] In the available tradition, Genius seems to embody the principles of generation and transcendence, descent and ascent most crucial to the age, but principles that conflict, indeed that often are quite opposite in their significance. This chapter's discussion of the vision experience that Alain's poem is largely concerned with relating ought to give us a needed context for understanding how Genius's many roles come together in this work. First, though, I must carefully describe the backgrounds from which Genius is drawn, for what is remarkable about Alain is the way he manipulates the traditional mythographic character to call forth so many of his associations in all their suggestive richness.

In the earliest part of the classical period, *genius* was a spirit of male generation, a function that in slightly later times expanded as he became a general spirit of virility, then a tutelary spirit born with the individual man or provided to a whole people.[35] Yet it was not unusual throughout classical times for more than one meaning to be invoked for *genius* in the same work. As Denise Baker has shown, this occurs in Augustine, in Martianus Capella, and during the twelfth century in Bernardus Silvestris.[36] In Bernardus, four *genii* are relevant to our discussion, for they usefully summarize the crucial roles that *genius* might assume at this time: they are Pantomorphos, whose scribal office we have already noted; the intermediary *genii* of the upper air, who are responsible for watching over the generic man; directly below them "the *genius* who is joined to man from the first stages of his conception, and shows him by forebodings of mind, dreams or portentous displays of external signs, the dangers to be avoided"; and finally the twin *genii* in male sexual organs who are assigned to perpetuate humankind.[37] Indeed, with respect to man, Genius's functions are intrinsically related, as Wetherbee has pointed out, for it is the guidance of the sexual *genii* that directs man in the act of procreation.[38] But this is still a limited tutelage; it remained for Alain to suggest more comprehensively the profound ways in which a god of generation might be a moral guide as well. Whereas Bernardus took pleasure in multiplying *genii* and in distinguishing among the various functions of the classical figure, Alain was more interested in collapsing or unifying these functions.

One of the questions that has most puzzled readers of the *De planctu* is why the character of Genius needs to exist in the world of the poem at all. He is identified extremely closely with Natura, more closely than any of the other allegorical characters; she sends her greeting to him as to another self, an "alter idem" (XVI.188, p. 871). His creative actions in the world clearly mirror her own. G. Raynaud de Lage first called attention to the question: "One asks oneself immediately why Alain has taken the trouble of doubling his heroine."[39] Raynaud de Lage's answer is disappointing, however. According to his argument, the priestly function of excommunication would be unseemly if performed by a female figure: "It is then to a masculine double that the ingenuity of Alain has entrusted this role and this mission of excommunication."[40] No doubt Raynaud de Lage is right that poetic decorum is a felicitous outcome of the doubling, but one feels that the poet had a more profound reason for introducing the character of Genius and for describing man's exclusion as an excommunication. As a god of generation—one specifically responsible, as we will note shortly, for uniting form in its various aspects with matter—Genius would have been an attractive character to amend the generative world, to perform an act of anti-generation, as it were. Also, as a male principle, he could play the active agent to Natura, whose passivity is indicated by her attitude of complaint. But even after these observations, we still have not fully explained Genius's presence at just this point in the poem, for we still do not know why Natura *needs* him to perform the exile of sinners from her realm. Why can she not do this herself?

A small body of criticism has now grown up to answer this question by defining precisely how Genius's creative functions differ from those of the goddess he serves. David Brumble, for example, points out that Natura governs only the realm of perpetual or secondary forms. As he puts it, "God is the simple idea, Nature is that idea made multiform, the 'world' is a composite of those ideas ready to be, and being, imposed upon matter."[41] As governess of perpetual forms, Natura needs assistance when she comes to impose those forms individually on matter. It is to this need, the argument goes, that Genius responds, and he thus becomes an intermediary between man and nature. A similar argument is made by Jane Chance Nitzsche, who sees Natura as the goddess of natural forms and Genius as the god of form as it is specifically realized in human nature.[42] Yet other scholars, notably Economou and Wetherbee, have just as thoroughly outlined the role that Natura, not Genius, plays as an intermediary between the physical world and the realm of perpetual forms. In Economou's words, "Alan's portrait of Genius kissing Natura as the eternal ideas meet with matter through the intermediate iconiae identifies Genius' office with that of the secondary forms."[43] Evidence for both points of view is persuasive, yet they are mutually contradictory. Finally, the poem suggests no more than that Genius and Natura both mediate, in varying ways, between the earthly and the divine. They share and augment each other's efforts in interpreting pure forms, exemplars or archetypes in God, and making these manifest in the created world. In this sense, they are not distinct; Genius is truly Natura's "other self."

Let us view the problem, though, from the perspective of what I have called the poem's moral or psychological allegory. If, as I have been demonstrating, Natura plays the role of his rational faculty to the Dreamer, Genius may be seen as fulfilling the part of imagination. Like Natura as a cosmological principle, Natura as *ratio* is unambiguously a force for good. She is the *vicaria Dei*; in human nature, she is what is immaterial, immortal, infallible about man's moral sense. Reason can only be corrupted, in fact, when it allows its sovereignty to be usurped by imagination and the sensuous, concupiscent desire associated with that lower faculty—that ambiguous power of man's soul, like Genius, capable of both virtue and vice. Natura or Reason, though personal to each man, is somehow undifferentiated in her divine essence.[44] She is thus incapable of righting the sin of imagination, which is different for each individual, being determined by the circumstances of his specific surrender to the desire of sensual images. This fault may be corrected only in that part of the individual's soul which is in error. Those who sin against Natura or reason are flawed in their imaginations; it is there that they will be healed as well. Only as he works through imagination does Genius have the authority to enact the recovery of this Dreamer, or indeed to point the way toward any man's regeneration. As a sign of his ambiguous involvement with matter, of his dependence on the circumstances and complexities of personal fate, Genius brings to life more fully individuated beings than does Natura. Natura makes man; Genius makes Helen and Thersites. Natura cannot deal directly with man's perfidy; Genius can. It is as imagination, then—or as a fully individuated creative power that lies behind imagination—that Genius serves an indispensable function in the *De planctu*; he represents an aspect of the Dreamer's psyche that Natura could not represent. And it is thus that we can follow the poem's psychological allegory to its end.

Through the concept of *ingenium*, there are, in support of this reading, significant links between *genius* and imagination in the tradition outside the poem. Some of these links have been identified by Wetherbee, who sums up the connection by calling *genius* "a creative principle, responsible for uniting matter to form and ensuring that the resulting creature expresses its proper nature, pursues its *inge-*

nium."⁴⁵ But the relationship, I think, needs further and more precise elaboration. As I have suggested, it is in the new conformity of Genius, as he embodies the Dreamer's *ingenium*, with Natura, as she represents his reasonable nature, that the full meaning of the end of the *De planctu* emerges. Wetherbee has not pointed out some of the most obvious similarities between the concepts of *genius* and *ingenium*, and these are worth noting as parallels that complement the obvious lexical relationship between the two words.⁴⁶ Both began, we have seen, as creative principles that gained tutelary functions along the way. *Ingenium*, through its association with imagination in the medieval period, participated in those crucial first stages of apprehending a truth in the images of the material world, a sensuous truth that could lead a man to God; it also thus had, as I noted in Chapter 1, the creative function of expressing that truth through the images of art. Indeed, it may well have been imagination's ability to perform in both these tutelary and creative roles that suggested its identification with *ingenium* in the first place. Similarly, as Pantomorphos's scribal duties show, Genius was also treated as a maker of images.

The two concepts were related in their tutelary functions as well. Like the imagination of the philosophers that I studied in Chapter 1, *ingenium* and *genius* were both part of human nature in its corporeal existence. Genius was the guiding spirit born with, and extinct with, a body. He was, as Nitzsche puts it, "the concupiscent soul of the microcosm, whose appetites and desires typify the union of the soul with the body."⁴⁷ In like fashion, *ingenium* was that part of man's soul required by the union of physical and spiritual so that this union might be potentially beneficent; it was also, in this way, closely tied to the natural descent of the soul into its body.⁴⁸ Like imagination or *ingenium*, a man's *genius* was thus morally neutral; it might serve purposes both diabolic and divine. The Horatian definition of the god served the Middle Ages well in this respect; according to this oft-quoted passage from Horace's *Epistles*, a man's "Genius" ruled the star of his birth and was "a god of human nature, mortal in every head, mutable in aspect, white and black."⁴⁹

So Genius was a god of human nature, different for each man, mortal and morally neutral—indeed, he was the personification of a quality that we must see to be like imagination or *ingenium*. But the usage of the time suggested an even more precise and comprehensive relationship between the two sets of concepts. The identification of *genius* with concupiscence was, as Nitzsche has demonstrated, conventional among twelfth-century humanists. Taking this identification further, Wetherbee has pointed out the striking similarities between the description of *genius* and the naming of *ingenium* by medieval philosophers as an *ignis terrenus* common to all men, "a vital link in human consciousness, uniting the highest and the basest capacities of will and curiosity."[50] It seems plain, Wetherbee goes on, that this *ingenium* is "basically identifiable" with the twelfth-century concept of *genius* as a "natural desire . . . committed by nature to pursue as its proper good whatever is most pleasing."[51]

The *locus classicus* of the definition of *genius* as concupiscence is found in moralizations of the Orpheus/Eurydice myth, in which Eurydice is named as *genius* and Orpheus as man's rational nature.[52] Wetherbee's identification of *genius* with *ingenium* suggests for us a useful gloss on twelfth-century interpretations of this myth and, in effect, reinforces Wetherbee's reading of Eurydice as *ingenium*. We may, I think, see in Orpheus's attempts to redirect desire or concupiscence to the upper world—in his attempt, in fact, to rescue the soul from the sensual pleasures of untutored imagination—the age's own attempt, which I have already noted at length, to order and control by forms of artistic discipline the excesses caused by enslavement to imagination. As Orpheus's music calms beasts and urges Eurydice upwards to daylight, he becomes the poet's reason, taming his *materia* by the light of intellect. This identification finds support in the fact that *genius*, like imagination and *ingenium*, is strongly and suggestively associated with the ambiguous, artistic images of dreams, offered to man by genial spirits who provide him with a link to the divine.[53] This classical tradition, followed as we have seen by Bernardus in the *Cosmographia*, attributes dreams to tutelary *genii* of the lower air, who thus become analogous to *imaginatio* or *imaginativa*, which in the Avicennian scheme becomes fully active during prophetic vision. In both models of dream, a special force—*genius* or *ingenium*—is brought into play during vision to inform the dreamer and to deliver to him an imaginative truth.

The Third Vatican Mythographer suggestively names Genius as the god of the forehead.[54] Does he imply by this an association between the god and the imaginative faculty that resides in the forepart of the head? The idea that *genius* might have been considered as such a mental faculty, an aspect of the soul as it expresses itself in a body, finds confirmation in the closest thing we have to an explicit identification between *genius*, as part of the *anima rationalis*, and *ingenium*. In a passage from *The City of God*, Augustine transmits to the Middle Ages Varro's identification of the rational, moral *genius* in man with the universal *genius*, the *anima mundi* or Stoic world soul.[55] In other classical and medieval texts, this *anima mundi*, this *genius*, becomes *ingenium mundi*.[56] By analogy in the microcosm, *ingenium* we might expect will also be a vivifying, spiritual principle. *Genius*, *ingenium*, and *imaginatio*, then, clearly form part of a nexus of concepts that express man's participation in a universal impulse towards creation. Together they provide him access to the cosmic rationality that forms part of his own godhood, however complicated it may be by the terrestrial world of which it is also a part. I do not wish to imply that any of the three terms is exactly equivalent to any of the others, but they are close enough in their associations to make it useful for us to consider them together, just as a poet in the twelfth-century syncretic tradition might also have been tempted to do through his symbolic structure.

A comparison of two passages from Alain's nonpoetic writings on the subject—one that concerns *genius* as a "substantifying" force and one that concerns *ingenium* as a mode of perception—will point to the connections between the two concepts in Alain's mind that, I believe, made him able to enrich the character of his Genius by its possible identification with *ingenium*. In *Quoniam homines*, a tract that seeks to defend the honor of theology, Alain clearly distinguishes between two modes of revelation: theophany and natural philosophy. Knowledge of the first proceeds through a kind of direct cognition of symbols. Knowledge of the second proceeds by a more laborious and rational deductive process. It is to the second realm that the concept of *genius* belongs: "By substantifying *genii* is meant the substantial natures [of things]. For *genius* is said to be the nature [of a thing] or the god of its nature. This kind of manifestation pertains to natural philosophy that deals with the natures of things."[57] But, as Alain goes on, "Natural philosophy does not have knowledge of God through substantial natures."[58] The *genius* of a thing is the essence of its being, particularly its mode of realizing that essence in nature. *Ingenium*, on the other hand, as Alain indicates in the *Sermo de sphaera intelligibili*, seems to be a mode of perceiving the substantial natures of frail things. It is a power that resides in the fourth sphere, the realm of pure ideas, where it "circles round the properties of things, able with difficulty to dream their earthly natures," where it returns "plurality to unity."[59] It becomes the instrument of the kind of perception occurring in dreams that permits man to pierce through to an understanding of the *genius* or nature of a thing. And yet, since it inhabits the highest sphere of the universe, *ingenium* is also capable of grasping, in some way, a supernatural, transcendent, or theophanic truth.

Given Genius's identification with *ingenium* in the poem's moral allegory, this character then becomes a god in a special sense, for he is endowed—perhaps more so than any other character in the medieval mythographic tradition—with those contradictory attributes noted so frequently in the gods of religion.[60] These he unites in a most illuminating way. Genius is a god of nature, almost a chthonic deity, a god of the most reflexive, unthinking of human processes—of sex, birth, the generation of individuals and species. He is, at the same time, a god of a more rarefied sort, a god of supernature, a priest, a miracle worker, an emissary from ethereal spirits, impalpable and transcendent. In this tutelary role, which itself stands in a kind of opposition to his generative one, Genius is a god of the imagination, host as we have seen already of the age's most central contradictions. As a figure of imagination, Genius becomes capable of initiating the cognitive process that culminates in knowledge of the highest truth, a truth by its very nature transcendent. Yet at the same time, imaginative truth is, of course, the truth found in images, its beauty wholly sensuous and worldly. This paradox returns us to the central high medieval philosophical problem: the capacity of truth to lie both *in* this world and *beyond* it. The theory of abstraction had been a logical response to this paradox, attempting to explain philosophically how a single truth could coexist on two planes and be known not just on one of them, but on both.

However, this contrary may be resolved on another level, a less discursive one—the level of myth, whose structure Claude Lévi-Strauss argues is marked by the attempt to mediate between opposites.[61] And here is where our analysis of Genius will become particularly useful. But to see the significance of the resolution he effects, we must first see that even before the advent of Genius the poet has confronted his readers very insistently with the contraries most endemic to his world view. First of all, Natura herself has called attention to the limits of her narrative perspective by setting her kind of knowing in opposition to that of faith or theology. The primary metaphors of the poem have also been based upon an opposition between nature as purely sensuous and nature transcended or transformed. The lawful sexuality represented in the marriage of Venus with Hymen, a marriage whose offspring is Cupid, directly precedes in Natura's narrative the illicit fornication of Venus and Antigamus, a union whose issue is Jocus. Unlawful grammatical constructions and false poetry are contrasted with the more appropriate *translatio* as well as the forms of artistic truth represented by the images on Natura's gown or the words of her teachings (described as "archetipa uerba idealiter preconcepta"; see above, p. 42), with the musical harmonies we hear at the poem's close, and with the poetry Alain must have meant the *De planctu* itself to represent. The poem's form itself—the philosophical vision—suggests that the highest kinds of knowledge may be simultaneously divinely inspired and naturally achieved. On every level, then, Alain is extremely self-conscious of the way in which his work moves among the age's most profound conflicts. The balancing of *Venus scelesta* with *Venus caelestis* or of Hymen with Antigamus are only the more obvious examples of pessimism about the value of worldly images set in opposition to a far-reaching optimism.

Thus, there are compelling literary reasons for rejecting the currently more popular reading of Antigenius for Antigamus in favor of the manuscript tradition followed by Migne.[62] In the action of the poem, Antigamus or "Antimarriage," in his role in the allegorical action described by Natura, stands in a contrary position to Hymen, the god of Marriage; the two characters balance each other nicely, whereas there can be no Antigenius or opposite to Genius in the poem. The *genius* of a thing is what it is, whether virtuous or vicious; its integrity is self-defining.

Genius, as he is presented in the *De planctu*, represents this fact by containing within himself all opposites, which he can then body forth. With his right hand he draws figures of perfect beauty, strength, knowledge, eloquence, and wisdom. When his left hand takes over, subterfuge, perfidy, and license take shape. Even this creative power itself is represented in contrasting writing instruments; the "reed of fragile papyrus" ("calamum papiree fragilitatis";

XVIII.68, p. 875) Genius carries in his right hand suggests man's intellectual aspiration, and in his left "the hide of a dead animal that the bite of the knife had shaved completely of its hair" ("morticini pellem nouacule demorsione pilorum cesarie denudatam"; XVIII.70–71, pp. 875–76) brings to mind man's earthly transience. Indeed, every aspect of Genius's appearance evokes the worldly plenitude that comes from the embodiment of opposites or varying qualities.

> His stature, which was duly limited by the canon of the mean, neither complained of subtraction and curtailment, nor grieved at addition and excess. His head was clothed with locks of hoary whiteness and bore the marks of wintry age; yet his face was delicate with the smoothness of youth, and unfurrowed by any of the plow-marks of old age. His garments, whose workmanship followed nature, seemed now to be in flames of purple, now to be bright like hyacinth, now to burn with scarlet, now to be a clearer white than lawn, not knowing the want of any one.
>
> Cuis statura mediocritatis canone modificata decenter nec diminutionis querebatur afferesim nec de superfluitatis prothesi tristabatur, cuius caput pruinosis caniciei crinibus inuestitum, hiemalis senii gerebat signacula. Facies tamen iuuenili expolita planitie nulla fuerat senectutis exaratione sulcata.
>
> Vestes uero, opere sequente materiam, huius uel illius nescientes inopiam, uidebantur nunc inflammari purpura, nunc serenari iacinto, nunc colore succendi coccineo, nunc bisso expressius candidari.
>
> (XVIII.58–66, p. 875)[63]

Although Hymen is also a yoking principle (and Alain's description of him hence reflects the same binding of opposites found in his description of Genius), his action in the poem is limited to carrying Natura's message to Genius, a fact that diminishes his importance to us. Yet it is significant that Genius is summoned by a character who represents the marriage of the world of forms with the physical world, suggesting that it is this union that makes Genius's presence possible. He is invoked by Natura, goddess of the physical, to perform an action upon which she has determined; he is thus Natura's priest. Yet the very priestly garments that he puts on at this point in the poem evoke the contradiction that lies beneath all these clashes of ideal and real, the contradiction between two modes of knowing.

As a priest, Genius would seem to evoke faith, which takes God as its starting point and ascends directly through sacrament to His truth, indifferent finally to the earthly reality of the images it meditates upon. But as an agent of Natura, he represents natural knowing, which using reason tries to understand the relation of world to God, fate to providence, a relation in which Natura has educated our Dreamer throughout the poem. In the contrasts of his being, then, Genius calls to the surface the deepest ambivalence of his age about how one uses properly the images of this world. This tension has propelled forward the psychological action of the whole poem, as the Dreamer, with no small success, has attempted to comprehend nature rationally, not only for her own sake, but as a true mirror of her Creator. The poem celebrates his achievement here at its end, when Genius's symbolic wholeness—his liminality—clarifies just how much has been made known, through purely natural means, in the poem. The moment is thus remarkably similar to that point near the end of Alain's *Sermo de sphaera intelligibili*—a work similarly concerned with defining the relation between the purely natural and the divine—that Peter Dronke has described so well: "Suddenly there is an astonishing *peripeteia*. The climax of the fable is the reaffirmation of the physical at the centre of the divine: the midpoint of the intelligible sphere is itself the mortal world. . . . All at once there are no more higher and lower spheres: the one intelligible sphere encompasses all the apparent opposites."[64]

It is by a similar moment of reversal, a similar *peripeteia*, that the *De planctu* becomes mythic, and Genius a particularly mythic character. As Lévi-Strauss points out, "Mythical thought always progresses from the awareness of oppositions toward their resolution. . . . Two opposite terms with no intermediary always tend to be replaced by two equivalent terms which admit of a third one as mediator."[65] In Alain's philosophical vision, this structure of replacement meshes nicely with the narrative line I outlined earlier, in which a sequence of abstraction marks the visionary's attempts to eliminate tension between his earthly experience and its *telos* in God. Moreover, it is Alain's characteristic terminological maneuver to resolve seeming paradoxes by dispensing with the usual rules of language and logic, so that an understanding of a term's self-contradiction becomes an avenue to understanding the divine mystery.[66] In such a maneuver, Genius becomes, as we will see now, the mediating term that signals the experience of conflict transformed into understanding. Consider for a moment how his appearance makes this ending different from that of its literary progenitor, the *De consolatione*, a work I have suggested is more fundamentally Platonic or dualistic than Alain's poem and yet upon which his poem rested in the creation of its meaning. Although Alain's borrowings from Boethius were most profound and comprehensive, he needed at the end of his work a character like Genius whose action could make clear that he had solved central problems that Boethius had chosen to leave unresolved.

At the beginning of the *De consolatione*, as at the beginning of the *De planctu*, the horror of sin in this world is seen as incomprehensible, lacking meaning and pattern, if contemplated along with its opposite, a divine presence that ought to manifest itself in all life. This pair—Evil and Providence—are, however, replaced in their turn by others, "equivalent terms" as Lévi-Strauss would call them, more harmonious because they suggest a way to overcome the contradiction: these are pairs, like Reason and Understanding in the *De consolatione*,[67] or Nature and Theology in the *De planctu*, which seem to suggest that any view that takes the evil of matter and the goodness of God as incompatible is delusion. The contradiction, we come to understand, develops from two complementary ways of looking at the world: the perspective of eternity, which devalues earthly fortune and so is capable of comprehending sin as part of God's plan, and the perspective of time, which is deficient because it is not capable of such comprehension. Because she makes him aware of his delusion, Lady Philosophy can provide the narrator in the *De consolatione* with the principles that will facilitate his reconciliation to fate. She cannot, however, give him a full and present awareness of a truth that, after all, is not possible to one in his worldly condition. Unlike Alain's Dreamer, the narrator in the *De consolatione*, as we saw there, continues to question his mentor throughout, and his questioning conveys a residue of doubt and incomprehension that Philosophy never seems completely to remove. In her final lesson, concerning the relation of providence and fate, which ends with an exhortation to the prisoner to flee vice and follow virtue, "she elicits from him no word of assent," as Wetherbee points out, "and, for the first time, fails to cap her argument with poetry. Reason and intuition give way to faith."[68]

Alain's poem comes to a considerably different close. We have seen already that the Dreamer in this work does *not* continue to doubt and question his teacher and physician, Natura. Yet Alain is as sensitive as Boethius to the doubts and hesitations that accompany man's attempt to understand his bewildering world. The difference between the two poets, I believe, grows out of Alain's insistence that, despite its difficulties, a more complete resolution of the problem of evil is possible, and indeed possible to man, living in nature and in time, because he can use properly those powers of reason and imagination that are given to him by Natura and are represented in the poem by her allegorical presence. In imitating the sequence of a dream, the work has traced the "natural order" of the Dreamer's knowing, an order of abstraction through which the Dreamer has ascended from the images of the natural world depicted on Natura's gown to a higher truth. This progress along a temporal axis is confirmed at the poem's end by the judgment of Genius. His anathema embodies the Dreamer's comprehensive understanding and, like a culminating chord, harmonizes all at once the poem's many notes and melodies, resolving all previous discords.

In the psychological allegory, Genius represents the Dreamer's fullest insight, an insight Boethius's narrator never finally achieves. In Books III and IV of the *De consolatione*, Philosophy had demonstrated to him that evil was nonexistent, that it was merely the deficiency of good, and therefore without real power to achieve its ends: "Perhaps it may strike some as strange to say that evil men do not exist, especially since they are so numerous; but it is not so strange. For I do not deny that those who are evil are *evil*; but I do deny that they *are*, in the pure and simple sense of the term."[69] Because they are so lacking in virtue or essence, as Philosophy goes on to explain, evil men are weak, especially in the power to realize fulfillment through their lusts. But this truth is not finally sufficient for the Boethian narrator, who continues to wish that the will to do evil were punished by some more worldly justice. In the *De planctu*, however, Genius's anathema, his excommunication of sinners from Natura's realm, accomplishes precisely this justice. By their exile from Natura's orthodoxy, their segregation "from the harmonious assembly of the things of Nature" ("a naturalium rerum uniformi concilio"; XVIII.145, p. 878), sinners against Natura can be seen as simply ceasing to be.[70] Since they have no essence in God as He is interpreted to man by Natura, the wicked have no essence at all, no virtue and no power to achieve happiness. The figures drawn by Genius's left hand are sinners of this sort, images described by Alain as *semiplena* or only partly real (XVIII.85, p. 876). In imposing as the penalty for avarice the continual yearnings of poverty or as the punishment for gluttony the shame of a beggar, Genius is merely describing what is already fact: that the sinful lack being and hence the power to realize the ends they seek.

Genius's presence in the poem as the Dreamer's *ingenium*, thus, serves as a sign of the Dreamer's comprehension of the role evil plays as part of God's plan—and hence of the completion of an educational process that began in confusion about this role. As they did to Boethius's prisoner, evil and providence may seem like irreconcilable forces, but their contradiction may be understood as simply the result of two different ways of looking at things—the purely natural and the theological. Upon inspection, these two ways of regarding the world may themselves be compatible, the poem seems to say, for the insight of a properly ordered imagination can unite within itself the perspectives of material and metaphysical knowledge. The Dreamer's experience is thus a truly liminal one: by withdrawing from a state of mind or understanding ordered by its own stable principles into the gray, fluctuating, and marginal area of vision, he is able to achieve new insight and reintegration on a higher plane. Moreover, one might say, the soul accomplishes this reintegration by discovering a new way of understanding its own liminal position, betwixt earth and heaven.

In this moment of concord at the end of the *De planctu*, then, Alain accomplishes what we suggested earlier poetry in general took as its task; he resolves potential philosophical tensions by exploiting the special strengths of metaphor and myth. At first, Genius, like imagination, serves good or evil; the images he creates are ambiguous. But when assisted by Truth, who is herself born of the joyful kiss ("geniale osculum") of Eternal Mind and matter, a union that is effected by the mediation of an image, Genius celebrates a newly sacramental reality. The theme of imagination—not the theme of love as Lewis has argued, or even of poetry as Wetherbee has implied—becomes the tertium quid, the middle term, capable of giving fullness to this poet's vision, capable of mediating successfully between his desire for a truth that is of this world and one that finally transcends it.[71]

It is no wonder that these persistent sets of oppositions in the *De planctu* generate for the best and most sensitive of the poem's readers its most comprehensive meaning. Green, for example, sees the work at its end, suspended, waiting for "supernatural intervention and a new birth."[72] And Wetherbee argues that through much of the *De planctu* Alain is dismantling the Chartrian world view until we are left at the poem's end with a greater sense of "unfulfillment" than we experience in the *De consolatione*. I believe, however, that Alain does more than merely suggest "in a very oblique way," as Wetherbee writes, a possible rapprochement between the realms of nature and grace.[73] My argument indicates that the most powerful effect of this poetry develops from its ability to mediate between the contradictions implicit in a philosophical system. There is an important difference between a romantic poet—a poet like Wordsworth or Shelley—who, although he may ultimately embrace a symbolic tradition, seeks repeatedly to draw attention to the limits of its expressive powers and a medieval writer who attempts to erect a new mythic structure to contain the most central conflicts of his age, a poet who by that structure seeks from the beginning to the end of his work to vindicate the very myth-making activities of that age.

It is precisely in this respect that the *Anticlaudianus* differs from the *De planctu naturae* and can finally, I think, be seen as a retreat from the earlier poem's mythic insight. The *Anticlaudianus* leaves behind the realm of contraries whose ultimate unity yields new understanding of the relations of nature and grace.[74] Its perspective is purely cosmological and universal; it does not bother with the Boethian visionary whose personal struggle contributes so greatly to the drama of the *De planctu*. Instead of the *De consolatione*, its model is the *De nuptiis*, an allegorical ascent for the purpose of initiating a new supernatural intervention. Thus, the guidance of Reason is clearly marked off from that of Faith. At the beginning of Book VI, Phronesis, who must ascend to God to accomplish the creation of the perfect man, falls into a stupor as she approaches the throne of God. Hers is a condition of spiritual confusion not unlike that experienced by the Dreamer in Alain's earlier poem. But Reason does not have the force of Natura; she cannot restore to her charge the full powers of her mind, so she beseeches by prayers the assistance of Faith, a character who then appears as a guide to replace, not merely to complement, Reason. The position the poet holds here is, of course, fully orthodox, and one that he had also maintained in the *De planctu*. In her descent to humanity, Natura was towered over by a strange man breathing "the mystery of godhood" ("deitatis ... archanum"; IV.12–13, p. 821) who guides her approach. No one believed that unassisted reason was capable of revealing to man the most arcane secrets of God or the universe. My point is simply that, in the *Anti-*

claudianus, Alain chooses a form that will enable him to stress the ontological distance between the provinces of Reason and Faith rather than the epistemological continuity that the earlier poem had allowed him to emphasize.

The story of Abraham and Isaac that the poet quotes just after Reason has yielded to Faith in the *Anticlaudianus* will help me make this argument more dramatically. Through a detailed description of the moment of choice during which the father is faced with a decision between his God and the child of his own flesh, Alain makes this a parable of the regret and difficulty involved in overcoming the limits of the body, and also of the absolute discontinuity between man's natural urges and his higher obligation:

> In him, Nature and Faith at variance carry on a battle and draw one mind to irreconcilables. For Nature tells the father to spare the son. On the other hand, Faith takes a firm hand and orders him to spurn his son in order that Nature may show deference to the Father in heaven. The father, then, wills what he does not wish. Now trying to spare him, now willing to sacrifice him, he finally abandons the alternative he longs for. Nature, then, submits to Faith and sadly yields to the victor what it would not consent to yield under physical compulsion.[75]

The triumph, then, lies not in using the powers of the body to achieve atonement with God, but in denying the instincts of the body to please Him. Perhaps the difference between the tension we feel so strongly here and the resolution the *De planctu* moves us towards can be explained by a change in literary models. But *this* change itself seems to be a symptom of a deeper shift in the poet's intention. The ascent in the *Anticlaudianus* is more boldly and clearly drawn than the one in the *De planctu*, and there is less hesitation in Reason's tutelage than in Natura's, as she calmly yields place to Faith. Even so, in transcending Nature Alain seems to sacrifice that Boethian tolerance for ambiguity and that liberal and speculative cast of mind which caused him to look to the philosophical vision for a form capable of suggesting on a single plane multiple modalities of vision, multiple perspectives, of both nature and grace.

The Role of Poetry

It is by appreciating Alain's deep impulse in the *De planctu* to find a meeting ground for the orders of nature and grace that we can best understand the poet's many references to poetry, including what one critic has called "his peculiar grammatical metaphor."[76] There may be, as James J. Sheridan has pointed out, something inconsistent in reading the *De planctu* as an "allegory" of the failures or successes of poetry when so much of the poem makes explicit reference to the art's function and value.[77] But in a very literal way, the frequency and detail of such references do suggest that one of the things Alain was concerned with defining was the proper role of art in his world. The philosophical vision afforded him an ideal form in which to accomplish this, for, as we have seen, the vision itself was regarded as an analogue to poetry and thus, if its images were wholesome and divinely inspired, they could serve as an implicit standard against which to judge the incomplete images of a defective poetic art.

In the opening meter of the work, we are introduced to the grammatical metaphor that will recur throughout the work. It is used here to illuminate sexual perversion, which itself serves as a recurrent metaphor for the general moral confusion that overwhelms mankind:

> Having been made woman, man refuses the honor of his sex.
> Magically, the art of Venus makes him hermaphrodite.
> He is predicate and subject, likewise of two declensions.
> He liberalizes too much the laws of grammar.
> . . . Art does not please him, only artifice,
> Nor can that artifice be called true metaphor,
> For the figure falls into the category of vices.
> He is too fond of logic for whom a simple conversion
> In an art causes the laws of nature to perish.
>
> Femina uir factus sexus denigrat honorem,
> Ars magice Veneris hermafroditat eum.
> Predicat et subicit, fit duplex terminus idem.
> Gramatice leges ampliat ille nimis.
> . . . Ars illi non placet, immo tropus
> Non tamen ista tropus poterit translatio dici.
> In uicium melius ista figura cadit.
> Hic nimis est logicus per quem conuersio simplex
> Artis nature iura perire facit.   (I.17–20, 22–26, pp. 806–7)

The metaphor set up in this passage is used again and again at crucial moments to denote man's turning away from nature and God. Twice in Prose IV as she is explaining the nature of man's sin against her, Natura draws upon the comparison. Man's heinous fault is a departure from the "grammar" of love. Man alone suffers from Orphic delirium (see VIII.53–67, pp. 834–35; VIII.81–92, pp. 835–36). The passage concludes with Natura's description of her own activity as that of an artist, except that she becomes a kind of secretary to God, "so that the right hand of the supreme authority should direct my hand in action" ("ut mee actionis manum dextera supreme auctoritatis dirigeret"; VIII.233–34, p. 840). This kind of stewardship describes the ideal relationship of God to artist, whose creative hand significantly is guided by divine authority. In a later prose section, Natura announces that she has delegated part of her role to Venus by giving her a reed pen to help in the job of embodying the natures of things. Thus, Venus's betrayal of nature can accurately be designated as an abrogation of her duties as artist. Indeed, Alain pursues this point at length at the end of Prose V when he describes Venus's infidelity to Hymen, her adultery with Antigamus, as art, by false and vicious conversions, becoming mere trope (X.108–48, pp. 848–49).

Such discussions help us to understand the brief but suggestive treatment of poetry provided by Natura in Prose IV. God himself she describes as a poetic architect, a "universalis artifex," and Natura, as she tells us, receives her authority directly from Him, who directs her pen. Despite her frustration with idle poets, it is clear that a wholesome view of art lies beneath her invective. The human artist, she implies, must strive, like her and through her imitation, after a product, which, for all its labyrinthine complexity, discloses God's unity as its referent. Art, then, is an ambiguous force, whose value depends both upon the state of mind of its creator and of its reader—here the Dreamer, whose progress we are meant to emulate. Most of the poem, indeed, trains us in its dangers and abuses. But by the end we feel a change in the wind, as Alain begins to emphasize the possibility that art may reflect the dignity of truth. Meter IX recapitulates in little this larger movement in the poem. This meter opens with the horrible, thundering clang of the war trumpet, a noise that is closely followed by the discord of the horn, which does not know obedience to musical order ("nescit / Organicis parere modis artique fauere"; XVII.5–6, p. 872). These sounds, however, soon modulate to others: the clear, fair voice of the cithara, the lyre, the pipe, drums, and other instruments that join together in a new *concordia discors*, leaving far behind the cacophony that has preceded.

Such harmony is reflected in the appearance of Genius. As a scribe, Genius is an artist like Natura. Depending upon the source of his inspiration, he may create images of wholeness and virtue or images of warped and contorted sin. The figures of Ennius and Pacuvius represent the second type; they are perpetrators of the vicious art we have seen denounced throughout the poem, an art that does not bring some figurative dimension or *translatio* into play and that is therefore lacking in the power of signification. Like them, Genius draws with his left hand such Virgilian figures of vice as Paris, Sinon, Thersites. But with his right hand, he becomes a Virgil with all the authority the Middle Ages granted that poet to imitate God's beauty in nature. Helen, Turnus, Hercules, Capaneus, Ulysses are all characters taken from the *Aeneid* who represent some ideal quality, whether beauty or strength or skill. And Genius takes on, as well, the verbal authority of sober rhetoric when he calls to life Cato and Cicero, or the heights and profundities of philosophy when he forms images of Plato and Aristotle. It is significant that these figures, these forceful images, are not those created by God directly through the agency of nature. Natura's beauty had always stood as a measure of her own imagistic power. Instead, they provide evidence that man is able to bring his highest powers to bear in art, among others his ability to imitate a truth in nature that, as I demonstrated earlier, might earn poetry the right to stand just below philosophy as a vehicle of truth. The *De planctu* thus demands to be read as a kind of metapoetry, a poetry that seeks, in the tradition of the Boethian or philosophical vision, to define the terms of its own existence, to establish a true and viable basis for its authority.

Alain is not naive about the rights and powers of the mortal artist, for he recognizes time and again the temptations to sin in art, perhaps most poignantly so in the character of his Dreamer, whose progress towards truth is impeded several times by a confusion about the purposes of myth and romance. Still, a moment of unity, brief though it is, between Dreamer and Mentor confirms the insight of the poem before the lights dim and the mirror of vision is taken away. At the moment when the Dreamer and all-seeing poet become one, as it were, the moment when the Dreamer's insight approaches that made possible by Natura, the vision ends. But that moment is significant. The truth of this vision and of the art that it comes to represent is corroborated by the profound insight that the Dreamer achieves by the work's end, as he turns his *ingenium* away from artifice and "incomplete depiction" to the wholeness and peace of true vision. The story of Orpheus and Eurydice recorded only half of reality. Imaginative desire, Eurydice's *genius, may* be trained by intellect to the light of truth, although it will not always be so. We can gauge the power with which Alain endowed art by this Dreamer's ability, according to the strength of his individual soul, to turn imaginative insight to a higher good without relinquishing its unique immediacy, its special mythic power to be both sensuously and spiritually compelling.

❦ CHAPTER 4 ❦

Mirror or Mirage? Jean de Meun and the Satire of Visionary Failure

Historical Backgrounds

Compared with the twelfth century, the thirteenth was more logical, more infused with a thoroughgoing rationalism, probably simply because it confronted more logic and natural philosophy that had to be both interpreted and accommodated. Thus, as we move into the later thirteenth century, I will need to summarize, rephrase, and extend slightly my presentation of the philosophical and poetic backgrounds to vision poetry.

The difference in attitude between the two periods, as I pointed out in Chapter 1, lay neither between Platonic and Aristotelian conclusions about the nature of the universe and the human soul nor between their methodologies, but rather in the spirit in which thinkers and poets of each century embraced their task. The thirteenth century continued to progress in the humanistic directions marked out by the twelfth, if by humanism we mean with R. W. Southern a belief in the power of man to know his world and to participate in its improvement. We will find that poets of both centuries adopt the basically conservative posture of defending the realist world view that, I have argued, typifies the High Middle Ages as a whole. This is not to deny that intellectual pursuit in the thirteenth century may seem mechanistic in comparison to the twelfth, for during this period the elegant and poetic were generally eschewed in the face of the overwhelming task of assimilating a rapidly developing science; to speak on its behalf, though, the Age of Aquinas was probably more rigorous and comprehensive than the Age of Alain in its attempt to explore and to come to terms with the relation of pagan to Christian philosophy, to find a meeting ground between the truth of science and the truth of theology.[1]

Indeed, the persistence of this attempt at synthesis is, paradoxically, what ultimately led to the "dissolution" of the high medieval world view, for the efforts of philosophy to expand its area of inquiry appeared to Church officials to take on an energy and life of their own. In the eyes of the established hierarchy, those who sought philosophical truth *seemed*, at any rate, to be doing so with less and less regard for the marriage of reason and revelation. Modern scholarship has frequently asserted that after the year 1277, the year of the famous condemnation of 219 Aristotelian and Averroistic Propositions, the character of medieval thought was irreversibly and drastically altered. No doubt this is a simplification of a complex historical process. But it is fair to say that, after 1277, the spirit of scholastic inquiry which had been the hallmark of the High Middle Ages no longer prevailed. As Gordon Leff puts it, the condemnations "signaled the effective end of an independent realm of philosophy in matters which belonged to theology. . . . [They] marked the beginning of philosophy's circumscription, bounded on the one hand by the demands of faith and on the other by the growing recognition of the limits of natural reason which put revealed truth beyond its reach."[2]

Precisely what philosophy's sin had been is less clear. In the condemnations, Bishop Stephen Tempier censored an assortment of doctrines, many of which would have been threatening to theology if anyone in fact had argued for them. Certainly, selected discussions of writers like Siger of Brabant on topics such as the eternity of the world did have heterodox implications. But Siger and others like him claimed to plead only for the freedom to treat such issues as topics in their commentaries on Aristotle, arguing that discussing an idea is not the same as supporting it; stages in dialectical argument ought to be separable from conclusions.[3] This, at least, was the apology they offered. Even if such disclaimers were disingenuous, that fact does not explain Tempier's condemnation of other doctrines which it is doubtful were ever entertained even by the most radical of thinkers. Indeed, of the 219 Propositions, only fifty-eight have been securely traced to their sources, and sixty-eight seem never to have been argued in any form by anybody. Among these latter are such unlikely proposals as "that the Christian law impedes learning," "that one should not confess except for the sake of appearance," and "that simple fornication, namely, that of an unmarried man with an unmarried woman is not a sin."[4]

The so-called "doctrine of the double truth" also falls in this category. According to Tempier, proponents of the "double truth" held "that things are true according to philosophy but not according to the Catholic faith, as if there were two contradictory truths."[5] In the absence of proof that anyone ever said such a thing, I do not think, as David Knowles does, that its mere condemnation is "presumptive evidence that some, at least, were ready to exploit the phrase."[6] In Tempier's grab bag of propositions, we find some that are truly heterodox, quite a number that are perfectly orthodox, and some that would have seemed quite implausible to any medieval author. As Roland Hissette concludes, "Study of the sources of the condemnation of March 7 reveals the lack of objectivity and discernment of the commission convened by Tempier."[7]

If Tempier was not capable of bringing "objectivity" and "discernment" to his study of contemporary thought, however, he did have another perspective that *was* invaluable to his discipline. His commission was, perhaps, more sensitive than the philosophers themselves to the kinds of threats that the new Aristotelian cosmology might eventually pose to the received tenets of faith—more sensitive, it has even been suggested, than many modern scholars to what was heretical in the new learning. And it is this sensitivity that I must speculate about for a moment, in order to understand the reactions of the poets to the climate of dissent and backlash which plagued philosophy at this time. Medieval Christian metaphysics was founded on a faith that authorities differing in kind would not differ in truth, that the Bible and Aristotle could engage in meaningful and almost limitless dialogue. This faith was the system's greatest strength, also its inherent weakness. The moment inevitably came when the limits of dialogue would indeed be reached, when a metaphysics based on myth, analogy, and symbolism would reject the investigations of logic and reason. Because, as a churchman, he did not share the philosophers' commitment to reason, Tempier seems to have recognized this weakness in the system more readily and clearly than the philosophers themselves did. Ironically, it seems to have taken a greater faith in the harmony of reason and revelation for a Christian philosopher like Siger of Brabant to continue to pursue philosophical truth—despite its seeming contradictions along the way to faith—than it did for a theologian like Tempier to suppress inquiry. Indeed, many of the condemned propositions are similar to theories held by Aquinas, whose commitment to pursuing harmonies between reason and revelation is unquestionable.[8]

But the Bishop may have had other motives too. The struggle between theology and philosophy was at once over dogma and also over jurisdiction. Tempier brought to the condemnations his theological perspective and his theological vocation. He objected, I believe, to the way that a world view resting upon the assumed unity of natural and divine spheres of inquiry could afford to allow natural philosophy its separate competence. This competence was objectionable both because it might conceivably result in heresy and also because it posed a threat to the dignity and preeminence of a theology that had gained some of its authority from that reason which could be made to serve it. A strand of antischolasticism had existed within the Church at least from the time that Bernard of Clairvaux had disputed Abelard's authority. In its thirteenth-century form, it can be witnessed not only in the condemnations themselves (and in the ones that preceded them in 1270), but also in decrees such as the one passed in 1272 by the Faculty of Arts at Paris forbidding any Bachelor or Master to dispute theological questions at all.[9]

Dissonant notes were growing loud enough to disturb the harmony between reason and revelation. In 1277, Bishop Tempier merely took advantage of this fact as he moved to put philosophy formally under his dominion—where, in his view, it must have belonged. He thus bears a problematic and transitional relation to the world view that I discussed in Chapter 1, still basically supporting it, but no longer seeming to trust in it. His action heralded a new age of caution in philosophical circles, of reexamination of basic principles. Rather than redirect toward God the impulse to naturalistic inquiry, as he must have hoped to do, he merely ensured that change would become what we have called discontinuous, for now philosophers had to move back the area of inquiry, to negotiate a new settlement between the dominions of faith and reason. Though Tempier's fears may have had only a limited basis in the late thirteenth century, by the mid-fourteenth century the most important of them had been realized, for the new nominalistic epistemologies of this age truly were based on a belief in two separate truths. Only thus could the metaphysics of God's absolute power, for example, be preserved. So, because naturalistic inquiry could no longer be depended upon to serve theology, it was more or less left to pursue its own course. Ironically, then, Tempier's action, in anticipating a quarrel between science and faith, inadvertently may have helped to precipitate an estrangement.

The way that such developments were experienced in the life of the thirteenth-century university has a special relevance to us here. The two works that I will consider in this chapter and the next—the continuation of the *Roman de la rose* by Jean de Meun, a Master of Arts at Paris, and Dante's *Commedia*—were both learned poems, influenced each in its own way by a scholastic tradition that was interpreted differently at the centers of learning in France and Italy. Tempier had recognized a situation that existed primarily at Paris, where his action was made possible partly by changes in the university curriculum, changes that had particularly serious implications for poetic authority. The arts had been losing ground to theology at Paris throughout the thirteenth century, and within the School of Arts poetry especially suffered at the expense of natural philosophy.[10]

The course of study followed by the twelfth-century student in the educational institutions of northern France, which was defended by John of Salisbury in the *Metalogicon*, had prescribed frequent and close reading of the classical authors and grammarians; grammar, which includes the study of poetry, ought to be, John argues, "the cradle of all philosophy."[11] But by the end of the thirteenth century, the status of this branch of the liberal arts had grown shaky. With increasing attention in the Schools to logic and natural philosophy, the influence and authority of grammar as a liberal art gradually diminished. Grammar became relegated to the lower levels of education, reduced to more like what it remains today: rules of composition that a student must master before he can go on to "acquire" what Hastings Rashdall calls "the subtle but unliterary jargon which would enable him to hold his own in the arena of the Schools."[12]

Philosophical poetry was one of the great casualties of this reduction. Instead of being studied in its own right for the profound truths it might reveal—as it had been in the twelfth century, when understanding the *auctores* was an important part of grammatical instruction—poetry now came more frequently to be classified in the *accessus ad auctores* as part of ethics,[13] or worse, in works offering an Aristotelian classification of the sciences, as a division of logic;[14] in O. B. Hardison's words, "a technique for manipulating symbols like demonstrative logic, dialectic, and sophistic—rather than a 'science' like politics or astronomy." Even a philosopher like Thomas Aquinas, who was willing to consider poetry as an instrument of moral edification, had little sympathy finally for the way that symbolic modes of expression such as those elaborated by twelfth-century writers in their theories of *fabula* and integument could reveal spiritual truth.[15]

Although the status of poetry and grammar, then, seems to have remained fairly low in the thirteenth-century university, it suffered more at Paris than elsewhere. For example, at the University of Bologna, where Dante is believed to have followed the arts course and perhaps even to have equipped himself to become a teacher of versification and the *auctores*, some evidence exists for a "rather healthy interest" in grammar in the second half of the thirteenth century.[16] Despite the growing importance of law at Bologna—perhaps because of it—logic or natural philosophy did not grow here into as important a discipline or consume as much of the student's time as it did at Paris. The Statutes of Bologna indicate that grammar continued to be considered a separate branch of the arts course and had its own special students, even doctors. Whatever the institutional background, a more ambitious opinion of poetry's reach seems to have prevailed among Italian writers—in Dante, and later in the theories of Albertino Mussato and Boccaccio, who defends poetry precisely by linking it with philosophy.[17] The victory of logic over grammar chronicled by Henri d'Andeli in his mid-thirteenth-century *Battle of the Seven Liberal Arts* was still being disputed throughout fourteenth-century Italy.

Certainly the profound differences between the *Roman de la rose* and the *Commedia* cannot be explained away by citing such historical and institutional developments, and I will not try to do so. Yet intellectual climate determines to some extent the kind of genius that will flourish in it, and thus a climate of thought becomes responsible for the path that poetry takes in responding to intellectual developments. In the late thirteenth century, we arrive at a fork in the road for poetry: Dante strikes out in one direction, full of optimism, ready to blend the diverse strands of discourse and thought of his age into a new *summa*, a new and grand synthesis. Jean de Meun takes the lower road, a great and encyclopedic artist still, but less confident about the uses of his art; more ready to poke fun at the institutions and philosophies that make up his world, though still basically a conservator of the traditional world view.

At the same time, there is necessarily a continuity between these two poets. The directions taken by vision poets in this period were limited to those permitted by the genre. Laurent de Premierfait, whom John Fleming has called "the leading 'Romance philologist' of his day (ca. 1400)," claimed that Dante self-consciously modeled his epic vision on the *Roman de la rose* and that both poems conform to the tradition established by Virgil in the sixth book of the *Aeneid*. Fleming qualifies Laurent by suggesting that he meant that the three works were only morally, not formally, similar. Yet Laurent states specifically that Dante adhered to the "ordre" observed by Virgil in Book VI of the *Aeneid*.[18] Following the medieval critic, I will be arguing that moral and formal meaning are inseparable here. Jean de Meun's *Roman de la rose* and Dante's *Commedia* are most alike precisely in their formal shapes, in their genres, for both are philosophical visions, in which a hero—or mock-hero—is invited to ascend to truth through the Virgilian "ordre" of knowing. Both embody their age's epistemology; both protect a syncretism under serious and escalating attack.

Jean de Meun as Interpreter of Guillaume de Lorris

It has become a kind of commonplace in comparisons of Jean de Meun's and Guillaume de Lorris's sections of the *Roman de la rose* to say, as one critic does, that Jean "broadens" the perspective of Guillaume's poem; as another, that he "overload[s]" it.[19] As Charles Dahlberg puts it, "The effect of Jean de Meun's addition is to enlarge the scope and significance of the fundamental issues of Guillaume's poem."[20] In some ways, however, the contrary is also true. As well as enlarging and complicating the issues raised by the earlier poem, Jean also works to narrow and more closely focus its view, a fact that emerges most clearly from a look at how the two poems related to each other generically as philosophical visions, and not just at how their morals or messages compare. By and large, *Rose* critics have tended to ignore the fact that the work is a poem, existing in two parts, and not a unified philosophical tract. Both parts have a profoundly formal dimension, which itself cannot be grasped without an understanding of the implications that changes in generic structure have for meaning. In the history of poetic reception, Jean's text, finally, represents only a single reading of Guillaume's, a reading that I will show has as much in common structurally or generically with Dante's *Commedia* as it does with the work that served as its immediate inspiration. The choice, then, need not be one between a Robertsonian, Christian interpretation, which stresses the poem's overall irony, and a sentimental acceptance of the work's naturalistic argument about love. Nor do we need to adopt a reading that polarizes the two authors, stressing Guillaume's grace and courtliness as opposed to Jean's strenuous and far-reaching satire.[21] Instead, I wish to show how Jean develops one of the generic possibilities latent in Guillaume's more generically complex fragment and follows through its possibilities.

It was Guillaume's innovation to bring together in a single work the genres of love debate, romance, and vision; to invent, in one of those generic admixtures that characterize the progress of literary history, the love vision. He was the first to use the dream as a framework for a love problem—certainly an inversion of the more strictly moral purpose of Boethius and Alain—the first to put visionary guides, like Reason and the God of Love, into direct competition. That his synthetic intention was surely conscious is suggested equally by his opening reference to Macrobius and by the appearance to the Lover of the Boethian Reason, whom "God made . . . personally in his likeness and in his image and gave . . . such advantage that she has the power and the lordship to keep man from folly, provided that he be such that he believe her."[22] Indeed, even the images that the Lover sees soon after falling asleep, etched on the wall surrounding the Garden of Deduit, resemble in kind those encountered by Aeneas outside Apollo's temple in Book VI. Like the visible world on Natura's gown, they are imaginative presentations and, along with the nature and society he sees within the garden, they require interpretation. But of what kind? Since Guillaume tells us that his is a true dream, as readers we are prompted to interpret it as a Macrobian *somnium*, searching the allegory for a deeper, veiled meaning beneath its images; but since it is also a romantic quest, we do not know how far to make that an explicitly Augustinian or Christian one.

Lacking the poem's conclusion, we are hard pressed to determine finally how Guillaume would have resolved the generic conflict he had set up. The mirror seen in the Fountain of Love is perilous in raising two possibilities for love—one that distorts and destroys, the other that reveals and expands the Lover's vision.[23] If what we are reading is a conventional Boethian or philosophical vision, we would expect the mirror to function as it had in Alain's poem, where the vision itself was a *speculum*, reflecting an array of lush images to a heightened imagination. But in rejecting Reason, this Dreamer does not seem to follow the typical Boethian path. Alternatively, the mirror might be a means to sublimation and refinement in love, efforts more congenial to our lusty visionary.[24] Which it is we never know. Rather, the narrator only tantalizes us with the promise of the conclusion he has planned: "When I have revealed the mystery, you will never hear the truth of the matter better described" ("ja mes n'oroiz mielz descrivre / la verité de la matere, / quant j'avré apost le mistere"; p. 52, ll. 1598–1600).

In fact, the end of Guillaume's fragment only makes our task as interpreters more difficult. As it draws to a close, the different narrative voices sound together to minimize the reader's experience of irony and emotional distance from the Dreamer and thus further to confuse and frustrate him. "I would rather die thus," the Lover explains, "than that Love should have accused me of falsity or treason" ("je vosdroie morir ençois / qu'Amors m'eüst de fauseté / ne de traïson aresté"; p. 74, ll. 3074–76). Though we will find this kind of declaration called into question by Jean, Guillaume expresses such sentiments to evoke an aristocratic ideal, as they are echoed several hundred lines later in the voice of the experienced narrator: "I shall never seek elsewhere to have honors or blessings, health or joy" ("je d'aillors ne quier que j'oie / honor ne bien, santé ne joie"; p. 87, ll. 3973–74).

The Lover is only twenty years old, he tells us, when he has his dream. The dream itself, experienced to its end, and the five or more years that have elapsed since then, have given him, he implies repeatedly, a broader, more mature perspective on its events.[25] This changed outlook ought to provide a clue to the dream's allegory. Yet, as far as the fragment leads us, even the mature narrator is smitten.

Love has permanently wounded his heart with the arrow of Simplicity; "No man born, I believe, will ever dislodge it from there, for I tried, without any great joy, to pull the shaft from me, but the point remained within" ("Je n'en gerrai par home né, / car au tirer en amené / le fust a moi sanz grant contenz, / mes la saiete remaint enz"; p. 55, ll. 1743–46). The work remains, as Charles Muscatine has put it, one of "balanced pressures": "There is paradox inherent in the very terms we use in describing the poetry: earthly paradise, sensuous, even sensual idealism."[26]

However, this paradox, these tensions, were not the primary interest of the poet who took upon himself the task of finishing the work. If Guillaume's purposes were synthetic, Jean's were of a more analytic bent. Of the several genres in which Guillaume had worked, Jean selected one—the philosophical vision—and wrote as though Guillaume's work could be comprehended wholly in the tradition of Boethius and Alain de Lille. Ernest Langlois traces over 2100 lines in Jean's part of the poem directly to Boethius's *De consolatione*, which Jean later translated, and more than 5000 to the *De planctu*.[27] Direct verbal echoes from these earlier philosophical visions along with widespread borrowing of character and motif place Jean's dream poem more firmly in the tradition of the philosophical vision than Guillaume's. For Jean, the moral claims of the vision override the claims of any other genre briefly invoked by the poem.

In Pursuit of Reason

Jean's poem is, then, less a continuation of Guillaume's, as it is usually called, than a revision. It becomes, in this sense only, a kind of "anti-Guillaume."[28] It is Guillaume's poem written over as if it were a typical Boethian vision and nothing else. Like the *De consolatione* and the *De planctu*, Jean's *Rose* begins with the Dreamer's complaint. It opens with a monologue whose piteousness earns the Lover the visitation of the dream physician, Reason:

While I raved thus about the great sorrows I was suffering, not knowing where to seek a remedy for my grief and wrath, I saw fair Reason coming straight back to me; as she descended from her tower she heard my complaints. (p. 93)

> Tant com ainsinc me dementoie
> des grans douleurs que je sentoie

> ne ne savoie ou querre mire
> de ma tristece ne de m'ire
> lors vi droit a moi revenant
> Reson, la bele, l'avenant,
> qui de sa tour jus descendi
> quant mes conplaintes entendi.   (ll. 4191–98)

She takes the role of Philosophy from the *De consolatione* and of Natura from the *De planctu*, perhaps even of Reason from Augustine's *Soliloquia*, the role of instructing a visionary flawed in understanding, unable to interpret properly the world he sees and desires. Reason, therefore, becomes the one character in the poem with unquestioned authority, though this does not imply, I will demonstrate, that the whole meaning and force of this remarkable poem is detachable from her lectures.[29]

But if Reason is lifted right out of the available tradition, the Dreamer is much different from his prototypes. Unfortunately Reason's pupil has not achieved here the kind of preparatory or "medicinal" grace that in the vision form could make him ready for her teachings. When she asks him if he recognizes his master, Amors, for what he truly is, this Dreamer does not respond with the humble prostrations, the confused stupor, that such questions of identity would have elicited from the Boethian or Alainian visionary. Quite the contrary, this Dreamer answers confidently: "Yes, Lady." "You do not," replies Reason (p. 94, ll. 4223–24), who then proceeds to instruct him, employing precisely the methods, even at times echoing the language, Natura had used in Alain's poem. Like Natura, she is careful not to exceed in her teachings what he is naturally capable of understanding: "By my head," she begins, "I want to teach you, since your heart wants to hear" ("Par mon chief, je la t'en veill prendre, / puis que tes queurs i veust entendre"; p. 94, ll. 4247–48). She echoes the traditional oxymoronic description of love, borrowed from Alain to warn the Dreamer from his folly: "Love is hateful peace and loving hate. . . . It is a healthful languor and diseased health" ("Amors, ce est pez haïneuse, / Amors, c'est haïne amoureuse / . . . c'est langueur toute santeïve, / c'est santé toute maladive"; p. 94, ll. 4263–64, 4275–76).

But whereas these and other rhetorical strategies had worked ultimately to arouse Alain's Dreamer to righteous indignation and to raise him to new levels of comprehension, they do not affect Jean's

Dreamer at all: "Lady, I flatter myself that I know no more than before of how I can extricate myself from love. There are so many contraries in this lesson that I can learn nothing from it" ("Dame, fis je, de ce me vant, / je n'en sai pas plus que devant / a ce que m'en puisse retraire. / En ma leçon a tant contraire / que je n'en puis neant aprendre"; p. 95, ll. 4330–35). Similarly, Reason's descriptions of carnal love and of the divine punishment it invites do nothing for our Lover, nor does her contrast of fruitless passion with the higher love of God. "Thus Reason preached to me. But Love prevented anything from being put into practice, although I heard the whole matter word for word" ("Ainsint Reson me preescheit, / mes Amors tout enpeescheit / que riens a euvre n'en meïsse, / ja soit ce que bien entendisse / mot a mot toute la matire"; p. 99, ll. 4599–4603). Even the description of true happiness that caps Natura's argument, which Jean tells us he has taken directly from Boethius (p. 105, l. 5007), does the Dreamer no good. He responds merely that the virtues which Reason would have him seek are unattainable and therefore not worth his effort (p. 110, ll. 5348–57). What is Jean up to here?

After Reason's laudable effort, which includes almost 3000 lines of unexceptionable learning and precept, the Lover takes her to task for a seeming triviality. In narrating the story of Jupiter's assault on his father, Reason had used the word "coilles," an expression that the Lover feels is not "courteous" (p. 133, ll. 6898–6901). Having been subjected to the indignity of this word, the Lover hoards up his resentment for nearly 1500 lines until he is backed into a corner by Reason, who forces him finally to state his allegiances; then he spends his anger all at once:

"Now this is worse," I said, "than before, for I see clearly now by your bawdy speech that you are a foolish ribald; even if God made the things you have mentioned before here, at least he did not make the words, which are filled with villainy." (p. 133)

> Or vaut pis, dis je, que devant,
> car bien vois ore apercevant
> par vostre parleüre baude
> que vos estes fole ribaude,
> car, tout ait Dex les choses fetes
> que ci devant m'avez retretes,
> les moz au mains ne fist il mie,
> qu'il sunt tuit plein de vilenie.   (ll. 6949–56)

Reason has an answer to this:

> When, in addition, you object that the words are ugly and base, I say to you before God who hears me: if, when I put names to things that you dare to criticize thus and blame, I had called testicles relics and had declared relics to be testicles, then you, who here criticize me and goad me on account of them, would reply that "relics" was an ugly, base word. "Testicles" is a good name and I like it, and so, in faith, are "testes" and "penis." I have hardly ever seen any more beautiful. I made the words and I am certain that I never made anything base. (p. 135)

> > Et quant tu d'autre part obices
> > que lez et vilain sunt li mot,
> > je te di devant Dieu qui m'ot,
> > se je, quant mis les nons aus choses
> > que si reprendre et blasmer oses,
> > coilles reliques apelasse
> > et reliques coilles clamasse,
> > tu, qui si m'en morz et depiques,
> > me redeïsses de reliques
> > que ce fust lez moz et vilains.
> > Coilles est biaus nons et si l'ains,
> > si sunt par foi coillon et vit,
> > onc nus plus biaus guieres ne rit.
> > Je fis les moz, et sui certaine
> > qu'onques ne fis chose vilaine. (ll. 7076–90)

In this exchange, I think we can find the key to this Dreamer's problem—to what makes him both like and unlike the other dreamers we have been examining and to what these differences signify for our larger reading of the poem.

The Ideas in the Poem

It has been argued that Reason, in the foregoing, is taking a kind of nominalist position, that her obscenities represent an invitation to the Lover to move back along the axis of abstraction toward concrete reality.[30] Such a view would make this Lover the reverse of the traditional Dreamer. Rather than being literal minded, he would become overly prone to abstraction. The Lover with his preference for euphemism and figurative expression would become, when seen from the perspective of the nominalist Reason, something of a philosophical realist, albeit on stylistic grounds. But there is something very strange in making Reason, the abstracting principle, an advocate of her opposite. In fact, I think, almost the reverse is true. In the Lover we see not an airy-headed idealist or philosophical realist, but a caricature or cartoon nominalist. Here is a person who does not believe that any essential reality inheres in the thing itself. Sexual organs can be changed, he implies, by the words we select to describe them. As a nominalist, he seems to believe that the reality of a thing as a universal exists only as an act or object of thought and not in any actual substance.[31] In its most extreme form, the nominalist position is characterized by a feeling of arbitrariness about the physical world: it will not yield to intellect any glimpse of the ideal, so we need not look too closely at it if the ideal or universal is our aim. This is, in effect, the Lover's position. Reason, in opposition, asks the Lover to take a closer look at the thing itself, so that he can rise from that thing as *significans* to a true understanding of its *significatum*.

On one hand, then, this Dreamer, rather than overliteralizing, overabstracts. As Winthrop Wetherbee puts it, he is motivated by an "effete, languorous pseudo-idealism."[32] He believes the first crackpot who gets hold of him—in this case Amors—and he is incapable of revising his interpretation on the basis of further experience. But on the other hand, this readiness to idealize suggests, on a deeper level, that the Dreamer is not open to knowledge as a true scientist, a true seeker of truth, would be. Though he is not a literalist, then, like his predecessors in the mode, he shares with them the same kind of epistemological failure, merely put in reverse. The other visionaries we have seen are stuck in the literal level, lacking the power to abstract. This Lover is spinning his wheels among abstractions he refuses to test in the literal, real world. True knowledge comes from the confrontation of the two levels, literal and abstract. "Universal concepts," John of Salisbury writes, "derive their credibility from the fact that they are inductively inferred from particular things."[33] This Dreamer differs from others, then, in having closed himself off from this inductive process. In a more profound way, however, he is similar to them. He is finally handicapped precisely as those others were—in his reason's capacity to raise him from the images of this world to an understanding of their meaning as a reflection of God. Yet he is more seriously disabled than they, for while the Boethian narrator and the narrator in Alain's vision were, to some extent, receptive, willing to entertain new ideas, the Dreamer whom Jean inherits from Guillaume already owes his allegiance elsewhere, "not to the truth of things," as John Fleming writes, "but to various kinds of surface elegance, levels of vocabulary, rhetorical competence."[34]

Like earlier dream guides, Reason wants to enlighten the erring visionary about differing kinds of love so that he can grow out of one set of feelings and into another. She wants to teach the Lover a better kind of love, as well as the proper methods of abstraction that will help him reach that love. In this, she is much like Natura; her theories of language and literature resemble Natura's as well. Behind the Lover's objection to Reason's language lies a question roughly analogous to that of Alain's Dreamer when he asked why gods such as Jupiter, Bacchus, and Apollo are represented by poets as engaging in lewd acts. And Reason's response is not dissimilar to Natura's exhortations to *her* pupil to look through and beyond literal meaning.

> In our schools indeed they say many things in parables that are very beautiful to hear; however, one should not take whatever one hears according to the letter. In my speech there is another sense, at least when I was speaking of testicles . . . than that which you want to give to the word. (p. 136)
>
> > Si dit l'en bien en noz escoles
> > maintes choses par paraboles,
> > qui mout sunt beles a entendre;
> > si ne doit l'en mie tout prendre
> > a la letre quan que l'en ot.
> > En ma parole autre sen ot,
> > au mains quant des coillons parloie . . .
> > que celui que tu i veuz metre. (ll. 7123–29, 7131)

If anything, she is even less squeamish than Natura, in her attitude, for example, to the story of Venus and Vulcan, which had been too vulgar even for Macrobius. True poetry, as I noted in Chapter 1, discloses a philosophical referent and requires judgment for proper interpretation.

But the development of this quality also requires some sort of preparatory grace in the subject, something in the Dreamer of a readiness to learn, of that reaching upward for knowledge which the vision form is so perfectly suited to dramatize. This is what the Lover finally lacks. Alain's Dreamer had been moved to humility and understanding by Natura's lecture on the poets. Jean's Dreamer simply dismisses their significance altogether: "But as for the sentences, fables, and metaphors of the poets, I do not now hope to gloss them" ("Mes des poetes les sentances, / les fables et les methaphores / ne bé je pas a gloser ores"; p. 136, ll. 7160–62). Though he understands well enough that his problem involves a fundamental conflict of loyalties, he is incapable of reassessing the validity of his first love in order to discover a better love that would enable him to avoid the conflict:

If I promised my love to you, I would never keep my promise; and then if I did not keep my word, I would either deceive you or rob my master. (p. 137)

> et se m'amor vos prometoie,
> je voir promesse n'en tendroie;
> lors si seroie decevierres
> ver vos, ou ver mon mestre lierres
> se je vos tenoie covent. (ll. 7185–89)

And so he sends Reason away:

When you make me think elsewhere, by means of the speeches that you repeat here, until I am constantly tired of hearing them, you will see me flee away from here if you do not immediately keep quiet. (p. 137)

> et quant ailleurs penser me fetes
> par voz paroles ci retretes,
> que je sui ja touz las d'oïr,
> ja m'en verrez de ci foïr,
> se ne vos en taisiez a tant. (ll. 7193–97)

It is, of course, part of the poem's elaborate joke that, whereas Jean, like Guillaume, promises several times to reveal the significance of his work (as late, in fact, as the lines directly following the Pygmalion story), the main act of interpretation is done by the Lover. Having missed completely Reason's point about names and things, he seizes upon the equation she suggested between sexual organs and "reliques," twisting the metaphor of pilgrimage to gloss and gloss over his Herculean assault on the Rose's virginity. Jean is engaged, then, in a revision of earlier dream poems, but it is primarily a revision in the character of the Dreamer. The main part of the doctrine recommended by the Dreamer's first moral guide, Reason, is substantially identical to that provided by Natura in the *De planctu*, Jean's most important model for his poem.

A recognition of how the *Rose* both differs from its predecessors and how, even so, it is essentially like them in moral perspective can help to solve that worried problem of the role Jean plays in the intellectual drama of his age. Among other things, it ought to show that a certain kind of misreading has led to the oft-argued view that Jean is an "Averroist" and that, as such, he advocated such behavior as free love and opposed the celibate life. By "Averroism" usually seems to be meant some sort of simpleminded naturalism or nominalism such as we have seen Jean satirizing in the character of the Dreamer. "For Jean de Meun," writes Mary Katherine Tillman, "Nature is absolute, and anything beyond or above nature is unthinkable."[35] John Fleming calls this sort of misreading "perhaps the most depressing of recent critical misapprehensions about the *Roman*."[36] However, in neither his original formulation nor his recent book does Fleming really attempt to locate Jean's position on the philosophical issues current in his day, warning only that contemporary scholars "have raised enough dust to obscure the real importance of the condemnations of 1277, and of the wider context of Scholasticism generally, for the *Roman*."[37] Yet importance it does have, and we must not let this dust interfere with our vision too much. By placing a significant number of highly controversial views in the mouths of such characters as Genius and Nature, Jean clearly establishes his concern with certain trends in the thinking of his time. But we must not therefore make the error of imagining that Jean himself identifies with the views stated by either of these characters (or for that matter that he simply opposes them), as Gérard Paré and Tillman have done to determine the *Rose*'s philosophical positions. Tillman seems particularly insensitive to the dangers of reading Jean's characters as mouthpieces for the poet's real opinions. As a result, we find her, without the slightest historical evidence, arguing that the poem was "an instigation and indirect object of the decree of 1277."[38]

In fact, I do not think that Jean was truly so heterodox. He never espouses a questionable opinion in his own voice: such opinions, when they occur in the poem, tend rather to reflect on the moral character of the Lover, who is deficient in his ability to learn from experience, to use his reason to abstract truth from the flux of worldly images. One advantage of reading this poem in its generic context is that it permits us to see the Dreamer's moral development as a controlling theme in the poem. As a member of the scholastic community, this Dreamer is callow and young, a student without the wisdom to benefit from his study. The stichomythic dialogue that opens the Lover's colloquy with Reason well illustrates his learning disability (ll. 4223–31). Though Reason calls Logic "science autentique" (l. 6598), she knows it can be damaged and abused in the wrong hands. As Fleming puts it, "Simple contradiction ('Yes'–'No'—'Yes. I do') is dialectically sterile."[39] Several times in the poem, in fact, Reason accuses the Lover of being just such a sterile and sophomoric initiate: "You have not, to overcome me, examined old books; you are not a good logician" ("tu n'as pas bien por moi mater / cerchié les livres anciens; / tu n'iés pas bons logiciens"; p. 116, ll. 5724–26). In Reason alone lies this youth's chance for intellectual and moral survival. Once the Dreamer has cast off, in the character of Reason, his own reason, he is at the mercy of lesser guides, among them faculties within himself that are capable of great intuition and apprehension of truth, but only if properly disciplined by intellect.

When Reason had used the pedagogical method of exemplum, she had been accurate and sure in her glosses, in the morals she was able to derive from the materials of her art. The stories of Croesus and Manfred, for example, worked perfectly to illustrate the vanity of human dependence on fortune, which is precisely what she wished for them to illustrate. None of the Dreamer's helpmates who follows is capable of such surefooted guidance, for none is so apt at discerning the true significance of things. None possesses that ability to abstract from experience so essential to the imposition or recognition of its sentence: not the Friend, who infers from the decline of morals that one must engage in the basest forms of casuistry and deceit to make one's way in the world of love, and certainly not the Old Woman, whose speech is crammed with the inappropriate and the bathetic. Descriptions of the most hideous gluttony serve her only as warnings against the social sin of napping in the wrong places; the stories of Dido, Phyllis, Oenone, and Medea suggest that women ought to store up a backlog of lovers in case of desertion. Not even Genius is a competent moralist. Though the purveyor of some wisdom, he uses the stories of Cadmus's sowing and of Jupiter's castration of Saturn as incitements to sexual indulgence, while he condemns Orpheus for his refusal to plow.[40] Lady Nature, as many have pointed out, becomes Alain's Natura bereft of responsibility for man's understanding. Genius, likewise, becomes the Dreamer's *ingenium*—his imagination as a kind of instinct for truth—but without the training upward toward truth that reason can provide to that faculty. It cannot be said, then, that Jean advocates views stated by these characters. Instead, they provide a vehicle for making an oblique comment on the folly of one who denies to reason the proper precedence in the soul.

But neither can the poem's dialectical structure be viewed as an indictment, in the vein of Bishop Tempier, of the new naturalism. Tempier, on the one hand, had acted to quash that independence of reasonable inquiry, perceived as a threat to theology. Jean, on the other, worked to *vindicate* a mode of inquiry and to place blame instead on those who might be so precipitate as to misuse its power. The *Roman de la rose* was probably begun around 1268 and completed around 1278, the year after Tempier issued his renowned Condemnations, and after Tempier's preliminary condemnation of thirteen Averroistic propositions in 1270.[41] A number of the specific doctrines that the Bishop denounced appear in the *Rose*, espoused by such characters as Genius and Nature. But though the coincidence suggests that the *Rose* may have been a document in an ongoing philosophical debate, it does not mean that Jean bore a simplistic relation to Tempier, that he was, as critics have assumed, either "for him" or "against him."

Tempier's position itself, as I have suggested, was not simple: what he objected to was not merely a set of doctrines, many of which were neither seriously argued nor doctrinally objectionable if they had been. More profoundly, he seems to have opposed what in his view was a licentious freedom of inquiry that, by trespassing over the boundaries of Church jurisdiction, might allow heresies to flourish. Jean de Meun, for his part, offered neither direct support for, nor criticism of, Tempier's position. His was a more complex kind of response to the complexity of the situation out of which the condemnations grew—a suggestion simply for modification of the Church position. He seems, in fact, to have been asking for another chance for that spirit of reasonable inquiry to which, as a Master in the Arts Faculty at Paris, he must have felt some commitment. Tempier's warning, it may be said, went something like this: "The pursuit of reason as a discipline separate from faith can lead to a rejection of basic moral and theological principles." Jean answered, "Not quite. The *abuse* of reason can perhaps lead to heresy, but this does not call reason itself into question. Do not blame the methods of science. Blame only those of its practitioners who misuse it." "Reason," Jean answers loudly, if only we can hear him, "is no threat to revelation."

Thus, the literary vision that Jean writes does what the philosophical visions that preceded it also did, what the psychology that gave it shape did: it works to protect a world view based on a synthesis of reason and faith, though it does so in an oblique way, by using the methods of satire. To see how such an analysis of the work's intellectual matrices can help us to understand its poetic drama, let us look now at the two characters whose views are the most seditious to theology: Nature and Genius.

Lady Nature and Her Priest

Although Jean's poem cannot be read as the same sort of thoroughgoing psychological allegory I believe Alain's to be—the figures of the Friend and the Old Woman do not easily translate into psychic forces—I do not agree with Wetherbee that through most of the second half of the work, "the Lover's state of mind will henceforth be almost wholly obscured by the course of events and the interplay of forces which are, as it were, beyond him."[42] Much of the time, to be sure, the Lover reveals himself to the reader through his actions, but with the return of the character Nature, borrowed in main outline from the *De planctu*, we return to the realm of moral or psychological allegory proper for a time. Quite a number of the views expounded by Nature in Jean's poem are not quite orthodox. Certainly, she embodies what is knowable by a dreamer's human nature, just as Natura had done in Alain's philosophical vision, but she also reflects this particular Dreamer's human nature, whose reasonings are not always harmonious with the divine, because it is not a nature properly ordered to reason. She engages in the purely rationalistic study of nature, with all the defects that such study has if radically separated from its proper end in the divine.

The cause of the difficulty is that by eschewing reason, the Lover's nature has imposed an unwelcome and unnecessary limit on itself. Nature's digressive, meandering attempts to analyze and explain the universe from the top down ultimately end with man—the "new little world [who] acts worse toward me than any wolf" (p. 315, ll. 19023–24)—the subject of her confession. But it takes her 2,300 lines to get there, after being sidetracked onto several topics only tangentially related, such as the Boethian conflict between divine foreknowledge and free will, or the influence of the heavens, or the nature of true nobility. At moments Nature has genuine insight into these topics, for example, finally grasping the essence of God's foresight and vision as a mode of knowledge different from man's in her beautiful image of his eternal mirror (p. 292, ll. 17430–53). However, in her effort to connect such fleeting insight to her knowledge of the mechanics of the universe, she consistently gets off track. For instance, her culminating example of the momentous evil in the universe is the cozy one of a bad marriage match (p. 296, ll. 17733–48). Even worse, her postulation of a world where all the "dumb animals" are endowed with speech and reason—even though she offers it negatively—demonstrates a bizarre disorder in Nature's imagination, capable of envisioning a world that empowers bestiality, giving to monkeys' and marmots' hands the power to work and write like those of men (pp. 296–97, ll. 17763–829).[43] In an important sense, this inner disorder is the true "nature" of Jean's Lover.

Since she seems thus incapable of bridging the material and the abstract, the natural and the divine, Nature might even be said to echo Bishop Tempier's response to reason's encroachments on the domain of faith, as he too warns thinkers to retreat, not to investigate certain matters too closely. But by putting such a sentiment in Nature's mouth, Jean subtly calls it into question. He seems to suggest a slightly different way of defining the problem. The fault lies not in the pursuit of truth through natural study, but in the improper conduct of that pursuit. Human nature deprived of its basis in reason is not human nature at all; without reason, man becomes a beast. He cannot even solve fairly simple problems unless assisted by the goddess Reason, and this Dreamer's capacity for intellectual advancement is hindered by the fact that he has renounced all such assistance—hence Nature's final discussion of dreams and mirrors. She who ought to be herself a mirror of God—and who *was* such a mirror in the *De planctu*—gets derailed in her own discussion of mirrors and optics by diverse sorts of deceptive mirrors that can multiply and distort images. Like other characters in the poem who draw false inferences from pagan stories, she recommends as a remedy for the plight of Mars and Venus a magnifying glass in which they might have discerned Vulcan's net (pp. 300–301, ll. 18031–59).

Nature's comments on dreams reflect the same restricted insight. Her purely naturalistic discourse on dreams stands in sharp contrast to Reason's use of them in exempla and to the presuppositions of this revelatory dream poem itself, which degenerates into an *insomnium*, an unreliable dream, only because the Lover refuses the oracular wisdom originally offered him. In a tale related by Reason early in Jean's part of the *Rose*, Croesus had dreamed of two gods upon a tree, one who bathed and one who dried him. The proper interpretation of this vision, as his daughter Phanie had informed him, is that his present course of action will cause him to die on the gallows. But Croesus denies his daughter's reading and, instead, arrogantly trusts in fortune. As a result, the dream does come true (pp. 126–28, ll. 6459–6589). The king's error had been pride or presumption in rejecting the sentence provided by God under covering of a dream in favor of a literal interpretation. Nature is like Croesus in this: she is a kind of embodiment of the Lover's own tendency, as she sees in dreams only a bewildering variety of images, which she takes literally because she is incapable of abstracting from them. This attitude is reflected in her final pronouncement, that dreams indicate only the dreamer's waking preoccupations. If a man is put in prison, for example, he will dream of the gallows that occupy his daytime thoughts, or about "other unpleasant things that are not outside, but within" ("quex que choses desplesanz, / qui ne sunt mie hors, mes anz"; p. 305, ll. 18387–88). Dreams, she concludes, are merely the five senses deceiving the soul, a psychology that contrasts sharply with the explanation of revelatory dreams I outlined in Chapter 2.

Thus characterized, Nature becomes one of the naturalists condemned by Tempier when he specifically denounced those who believe "that raptures and visions are caused only by nature." Scholars have yet to locate any thinker in the age who actually argued this position.[44] As we have seen, the Arabic philosophers Avicenna and Averroes certainly did not. So Jean would have been uniquely heterodox if he had been using Nature to make known his true opinions on the subject. It is more probable that the poet, like the Bishop, defends here God's power by suggesting, through Reason's use of dreams, that He can bring about divine rapture and impart knowledge during sleep. Even so, Jean modifies the Bishop's position somewhat by granting Reason the authority to disseminate truth, for, as we have seen, Reason, like the more responsible naturalists of the day, argues acceptable doctrine on visions. Reason, the poet implies, will achieve orthodoxy if properly applied. Only because Jean's Nature remains uninformed by that abstracting capacity does she fail to realize the meaning of the phenomena that constitute her world.

Genius, too, is undermined as a spokesman to allow Jean to make a similar point. A comparison of Jean's Genius with Alain's will clarify the ways in which Jean disclaims his authority. In the economy of Alain's poem, Genius had served to demonstrate the unity of natural and divine apprehension in a spirit where the heavenly intuitions of imagination were ordered to the power of reason. Genius there had represented the faculty of the Dreamer's imagination in its redeemed state, as a power humanly capable of initiating the act of cognition whose end is God, capable both of apprehending the images that might embody transcendent truth and also of generating such images. But what happens when Genius is not ordered to reason, when the spirit does not exist in a condition of rectitude?

As I suggested earlier, precisely because of its affinities with both the worlds of sense and transcendence imagination might be the wellspring either of the most elevated kind of knowledge or the most delusive error. In our study of Alain, we witnessed a Dreamer's moral development, the reclaiming of his soul from ignorance and the purification of his imagination so that it might represent to him glimpses of the highest sort of truth. In Jean de Meun's poem, we watch something quite different: a soul trapped by its ignorance, too quick to translate desire for an image into knowledge of its value, unable to penetrate through the literal to the absolute. In Alain's poem, Genius stood for a Dreamer's imagination and demonstrated the rededication of that imagination to truth. In Jean's poem, Genius comes to represent imaginative failure—not potential grown to realized power, but potential come to nothing.

The fact that Genius—*ingenium* or imagination—in the *Rose* can still apprehend some vestige of redemptive truth as he describes the Beau Parc, just as Nature had a momentary insight into the problem of divine foreknowledge, simply deepens the tragedy for the person who, like Jean's Dreamer, does not know how to move from a glimmering to a full epiphany of truth. Nature at her forge had recalled some of her original glory. Genius, as he contrasts the eternal joy of the blessed in Paradise to the vain pleasures of the doomed in Deduit's Garden, also regains some of his dignity (pp. 332–38, ll. 20249–629). He has not lost all access to that archetypal memory which had given Alain's Genius his authority. The Triple Well provides a corrective to Guillaume's Perilous Fountain; it is a mirror of God that affords the only whole view of Paradise, the kind of view the mirror of vision ought typically to provide: "The one makes the living drunk with death, while this fountain makes the dead live again" ("cele les vis de mort anivre, / mes ceste fet les morz revivre"; p. 337, ll. 20595–96).

The foregoing is a far more Christian construction of death than Genius had earlier offered in the poem when he recommended energetic fornication to defeat the death of the species (pp. 322–23, ll. 19513–78). That attitude had anticipated the three revelers' error in "The Pardoner's Tale" when they take Death as something physical that they can overcome, even though death only has true significance when applied to the spirit. Jean's Dreamer is invited by Genius, that power within, to make the progress from image to significance that characterizes true visionaries. But the Lover's soul has not been correctly ordered to truth; the fleeting vision of redemption offered by his imagination remains only that, fading images whose significance the Dreamer cannot organize into action. Genius's lapse is thus the Lover's lapse, as it perfectly reflects the Lover's own libidinal overcharge. At the most compelling moment of his sermon to the assembled Barons of Love, Genius breaks off, "It is right for me to sheath my flute, for beautiful songs often get boring" ("Droiz est que mon fretel restuie, / car biau chanter souvant annuie"; p. 338, ll. 20631–32), and throws the burning torch into the throng.

In assessing the views of this Genius, then, we must keep firmly in mind his failure to submit the spark of his imaginative perception to the disciplines of reason—and the defect in the work's protagonist that this failure represents. In terms of the philosophical tenets of the day, Genius explicitly advocates several heresies condemned by Tempier. Indeed, in trying to understand why the celibate life is for some and not all, he veers dangerously close to the doctrine of the double truth, arguing that reasonable belief cannot prevail without special recourse to faith: "I do not know how to respond to this position," he complains, "unless faith wants to explain belief" ("Je ne sai pas a ce respondre, / se foi n'i veust creance espondre"; p. 323, ll. 19579–80). Likewise, the positions "that simple fornication . . . is not a sin," "that the pleasure in sexual acts does not impede the act or the use of the intellect," "that continence is not essentially a virtue," "that chastity is not a greater good than perfect abstinence," and "that perfect abstinence from the act of the flesh corrupts virtue and the species" are among the central beliefs in Genius's system,[45]—and, indeed, such doctrines are manifestly opposed to Christian ethics and dogma. However, we must bear in mind that it has not been possible to find plausible and accurate contemporary sources for most of these heresies. For example, when investigating the origins of No. 205, historians of philosophy are forced to attribute the advocacy of free love to none other than Andreas Capellanus and Jean de Meun himself. The argument for Jean's heterodoxy here becomes absurdly circular.[46] It is simplistic to assume either that Jean himself advocates such a puerile naturalism or that he is engaged in a systematic refutation of its claims. Genius's words are twice removed from their author; they convey only the specific moral that, as indulged in by the Lover, the untutored and undisciplined pursuit of nature for her own sake leads to base enjoyments.

By allowing Reason to retain her dignity in this as in other matters, however, Jean also implies that rational study need not end this way. Reason had earlier given a slightly different meaning to natural love; though not invoking Christian law, her definition had not violated it, either:

If you want me to tell you the definition of this love of which I speak, it is a natural inclination to wish to preserve one's likeness by a suitable intention, either by engendering or by caring for nourishment.   (p. 116)

> De l'amor don je tiegn ci conte,
> se tu veuz que je t'en raconte
> quels est li defenissemenz,
> c'est naturiex enclinemenz
> de volair garder son semblable
> par entencion convenable,
> soit par voie d'engendreüre,
> ou par cure de norreture.   (ll. 5737–44)

There is no mention here of pleasure, no establishment of a moral imperative to procreate. Indeed, Reason clearly differentiates the nobility of natural instinct from the "much more senseless enterprise" ("plus fole emprise de l'amor") embraced by the Dreamer (p. 116, ll. 5761–62). She suggests at least the possibility of a postlapsarian sexuality that would not be unreasonable or pernicious. This strategy of differentiation throws into relief the poet's criticism of rationalism as a way of being specific only to this Dreamer. Here as elsewhere, by satirizing abuse in the Schools rather than the Schools themselves, Jean moderates the point made by Tempier, and the form of his poem works to vindicate a system that allowed theological and philosophical speculation to continue side by side. No other explanation takes into account both Jean's pervasive interest in natural philosophy, his affiliation with the School of Arts,[47] and also the insistently moral and orthodox voice of Reason that qualifies every other perspective in the poem.

The Uses of Irony in Jean's 'Rose'

The *Roman de la rose* ends as a kind of anti-*Anticlaudianus* in a battle reminiscent of many medieval psychomachias, yet one in which the side of virtue rather than vice is defeated. In one of the most obscene passages in medieval literature, the Lover quickly claims his Rose:

> I scattered a little seed on the bud when I shook it, when I touched it within in order to pore over the petals. For the rosebud seemed so fair to me that I wanted to examine everything right down to the bottom. As a result, I so mixed the seeds that they could hardly be separated; and thus I made the whole tender rosebush widen and lengthen. (p. 353)

> un po de greine i espandi,
> quant j'oi le bouton elloichié.
> Ce fu quant dedanz l'oi toichié
> por les fueilletes reverchier,
> car je vouloie tout cerchier
> jusques au fonz du boutonet,
> si con moi samble que bon et.
> Si fis lors si meller les greines
> qu'el se desmellassent a peines,
> si que tout le boutonet tandre
> an fis ellargir et estandre. (ll. 21689–700)

I do not agree with Wetherbee that we are meant to see the conception of a child as a higher, providential force intervening and to some extent mitigating the corruption of the act.[48] Rather, the Lover's rejection of his reason and subsequent denial of his tutelary *genius*, his singular indulgence in the procreative and sexual *genius*, has brought Jean about as far as possible not only from the ending of the *Anticlaudianus* but also from the ending of the *De planctu*. There, an act of antigeneration had signaled the completion of a Dreamer's psychic redemption. Here, ironically, an act of generation certifies a Lover's total alienation from that redemptive promise. In his surrender to passion at the end of the poem, the Dreamer seems to have fallen into a state of complete unresponsiveness to his better instincts.

Indeed, I think we would have no trouble predicting the ending of this poem even if it, like the ending of Guillaume's, were lacking. Both the sexual act to which the Dreamer seems committed and the author's moral perspective have an irreversible momentum—the momentum of the philosophical vision, which judged human love and experience only for what they could reveal of a higher truth. If the emotional ambiguities in Guillaume's poem are lost in the transfer, the energy conveyed by Jean's careful, sustained irony as it moves toward this final *reductio amoris* are worth the sacrifice. Jean left to the age that followed a different legacy from Guillaume's, but one that must be honored as well. His gift, as Rosemond Tuve puts it, is "the large controlled structure, the way to make details 'signify' and the special decorum with which they must be controlled, the way abstractions are presented and the special understanding of 'characters,' the ironic wit, the tone not depending Romantically on associations but on other factors."[49]

Jean de Meun left something else as well: a new, more oblique approach to the literary vision. Satire had been part of the form before, in the Goliardic and "Voie de Paradis" dream poems, where the follies and abuses of the age had been held up for scrutiny and ridicule. But never had the most valued norms of the genre been manipulated to such effect. In the second part of the *Roman de la Rose*, we find the very structures that had been constitutive of meaning in earlier philosophical or Boethian visions: the ailing dreamer, literal minded and lamenting; the dream healer, figure of psychic wisdom and reason; her attempt to bring the dreamer's imagination into the proper order in the soul's hierarchy; and the natural order of knowing the poem consequently imitates. We find all of these in Jean's *Rose*, but put to very different uses. In the *Rose*'s models, the elements of vision had served to illustrate the success of poet and dreamer alike in achieving new levels of natural understanding. The success of vision was an index to the power of human rationality and an endorsement of a psychology based on that rationality. In response to the growing challenge that human experience represented to received authority, the vision could demonstrate a way to reach from the world of experience to authoritative truth. Its aesthetic appeal, we have seen, lay in this defensive power.

But in Jean's poem, there is no visionary success. No new levels of understanding are achieved. The world of the Dreamer's experience does not yield control or comprehension, only moral confusion. Like many lengthy satires that use serious coordinates, the *Roman de la rose* makes us begin to think about the validity of those coordinates themselves.[50] If this Dreamer cannot, in the natural order of things, make an imaginative truth stand for something beyond itself, then perhaps the poet means us to question the very grounds of the vision quest. Perhaps the realist or sacramentalist world view described in Chapter 1 is not operative here. Indeed, Jean has often been seen as the precursor of a new, more "naturalistic," kind of poetry that would dominate the later Middle Ages. The focus in his work, many feel, is not on otherworldly values or on controlled ascent. In his *Rose*, a critic such as Charles Muscatine has seen a general "shifting of the whole scale of values a little earthward."[51] But Muscatine and others who adopt this view fail to consider the complexities that arise as one then tries to define precisely what Jean's new "values" might be.

Although its proponents would not put the issue thus, their position depends on either disregarding literary convention or on reading as parody what was intended as satire. Only by parody and rejection of her conventional literary typology, for example, could Jean have presented the Old Woman as "emergently serious, marginally sympathetic."[52] But the *Rose* is not a parodic poem. The difference between parody and satire, as Joseph Dane has recently demonstrated, is one of object: "Parody . . . turns a sign (a text) into a referential object. Satire takes an object (e.g., society) and ultimately turns it into a sign (usually of some moral good or evil)."[53] For example, read as parody, *The Rape of the Lock* undermines epic and the values that form embodies; read as satire, it offers a criticism of a contemporary society that fails to realize those values. Since the effect of satire depends on our taking the assumptions of a text seriously, parody, which calls these assumptions into question, demolishes the possibility of satire. As we have seen, Jean's Dreamer receives the bite of his humor; therefore, the literary values of his text cannot.

Like Belinda in Pope's satire, the Dreamer in the *Roman de la rose* enacts a mental attitude that the author must deplore. It is only because a competent reader of the poem knows this, because he knows that the Dreamer's moral development conventionally depends on his submission of imaginative desire to the disciplines of reason, that he is able to understand the work by judging this Dreamer morally deficient. Our ability to respond coherently to the poem, then, rests on a capacity to take seriously the moral norms that the Dreamer violates. Value, in this poem, resides finally in the theory of vision that gave to the philosophical vision its original shape as a subgenre. Though he pokes fun at the Dreamer, in no way does Jean de Meun poke fun at that theory. Instead of endorsing, as Muscatine suggests, a "new sacramentalism,"[54] Jean defends an old one. The Dreamer's final sin becomes an index of the distance that one falls if old assumptions about the value and meaning of this world are denied.

At the same time, formal characteristics in texts carry with them profound meanings. Even though his primary focus was on the moral effect of visionary failure—hence an indirect defense of conservative values—some significance must be attached to the fact that Jean did not choose to write the history of a Dreamer's successful quest for knowledge, to the fact that he was attracted to the project of revising Guillaume's poem as well as to that of recasting Alain's. Earlier in this study, I outlined the theory of art and literature that characterized the high medieval period, an era during which men sought to comprehend literal diversity by their deep belief in the wholeness of God and nature. A poet's legitimacy depended on his almost godlike ability to create, in imitation of nature, images of truth that could take on sacramental value by their ability to represent materially a formal or spiritual reality. This was the rationale behind Alain's creative work in the *De planctu naturae*, and in turn, it was what the *De planctu* worked self-consciously to vindicate. In an increasingly unstable realist synthesis, poets and philosophers alike were forced to consider and to defend their roles as purveyors of truth. As we have seen, as a subgenre of the dream vision, the philosophical vision created special opportunities for the poet who wished to make such a defense as part of a structure of continuous change; for when the sensuous images of a dream, which Macrobius had compared to poetic images, stood for a transcendent truth, they suggested by their very existence that poetic images might also represent that truth.

But as time passed and the defensive position came to seem less tenable, the analogy between dreams and art might, we can imagine, be used to make a different point. It might serve as well to anticipate discontinuous change, when the limits of synthesis had almost been reached, with the system as a whole at its saturation point. What A. C. Spearing calls the "separability of poet from Dreamer"[55] can work either to contribute to poetic authority or to detract from it. When the images of a dream are delusive, the implications for poetry are negative as well. Even in the twelfth century, Hugh of Saint Victor had questioned the legitimacy of fictions. But poetry's status, as I noted earlier, had since fallen victim to more and more insidious attack. The classification of poetry as a technique of logic rather than as a central part of the discipline of grammar was symptomatic of the growing lack of confidence in the kind of spiritual allegory that had been popular in scholastic circles during the previous century.

For a thirteenth-century university poet, then, satire might be an appropriate mode for artistic endeavor. Its obliquity enabled the artist to reassert the validity of a world view based on the harmonies of nature and grace, while conveying at the same time a growing concern about the probability of human success in apprehending or representing the world as the mirror of truth he knew it to be. At the beginning of this book, I suggested that poetry would first begin to display the strain in the realist paradigm within its own ontology. Before poets would start to reject the world view that made the high medieval synthesis of reason and revelation possible, they would show nervousness about their own role in that synthesis; by reaching back to reflect on the grounds of their own artistic enterprise, they would begin to anticipate discontinuous change. We can see this sequence of anticipation and self-reflexiveness clearly in the poetic practice of a writer like Jean, who stands at the intersection of two metaphysical frameworks, realist in relation to the world he represents, nominalist in relation to the word.

The thirteenth-century poet does not seem really to believe any longer in the analogy between the three levels of creation—God's, nature's, and man's. When Jean comes to describe Alain's Natura, he does not proceed fully and eloquently as the twelfth-century poet had done. Instead, he explains, "It is therefore right that I make no tale either about her body or her face" ("Por ce n'est droiz que conte face / ne de son cors ne de sa face"; p. 275, ll. 16209–10). As he explains,

> However, with very attentive care, [Art] kneels before Nature and like a truant beggar, poor in knowledge and force, she begs and requests and asks

of her. She struggles to follow her so that Nature may wish to teach her how with her ability she may properly subsume all creatures in her figures. She also watches how Nature works, for she would like very much to perform such a work, and she imitates her like a monkey. But her sense is so bare and feeble that she cannot make living things, no matter how newborn they seem. (pp. 271–72)

> mes par mout antantive cure
> a genouz est devant Nature,
> si prie et requiert et demande,
> comme mandianz et truande,
> povre de sciance et de force,
> qui d'ansivre la mout s'efforce,
> que Nature li veille aprandre
> conment ele puisse conprandre
> par son angin an ses figures
> proprement toutes creatures;
> si garde conment Nature euvre,
> car mout voudroit fere autele euvre,
> et la contrefet conme singes;
> mes tant est ses sens nus et linges
> qu'el ne peut fere choses vives,
> ja si ne sembleront naïves. (ll. 15989–16004)

The inexpressibility topos is here taken quite seriously. Not Plato, Aristotle, Algus, Euclid, or Ptolemy could adequately describe Nature; nor could Pygmalion "fashion" her, Apelles paint her (p. 274, ll. 16138–52). Jean, he informs us, is not so presumptuous to imagine that his "angin" is up to this task (ll. 16135–37).

As Pygmalion's prominence at the end of the poem indicates, such confidence in one's "angin" or *ingenium*—in one's ability to know and to represent God's world accurately—is a kind of pride, a usurpation of His place and a kind of idolatry. Artist figures in this poem are often tricksters of the sort found more commonly in romances and fabliaux than in vision poetry. They are playful, deceitful masters of illusion, like the Old Woman, for whom "angin" or *ingenium* is merely a handy faculty when ladies want to connive new ways of teasing and captivating their lovers, new ways of being false in the bargain of love. Consider the following advice she gives to women (emphasis mine):

Now when she hears a lover's request, she should be reluctant to grant all her love, nor should she refuse everything, but try to keep him in a state of balance between fear and hope. When he makes his demands more pressing and she does not yield him her love, which has bound him so strongly, she must arrange things through her *strength* and her *craft*, so that hope constantly grows little by little as fear diminishes until peace and concord bring the two together. (p. 235)

> Et quant el orra la requeste
> de l'amant, gart qu'el ne se heste
> de s'amor du tout otroier;
> ne ne li doit du tout noier,
> ainz le doit tenir en balance,
> qu'il ait poor et esperance;
> et quant cil plus la requerra
> et cele ne li offerra
> s'amor, qui si forment l'enlace,
> gart soi la dame que tant face
> par son *engin* et par sa *force*
> que l'esperance adés anforce,
> et petit a petit s'an aille
> la poor tant qu'ele defaille,
> et qu'il faceint pes et concorde. (ll. 13633–47)

This sort of *engin* or *ingenium* is like that described by Robert Hanning in a study of twelfth-century romance; in this tradition, *engin* or *ingenium*, especially as here coupled with force, connotes "wit, readiness to take advantage of a situation" and conveys as well a "component of fraud." The word in slightly different contexts may also suggest an artistic striving for "illusionistic effects."[56] Such meanings for this term are far different from those we discussed in the high medieval philosophical tradition, where *ingenium* was credited with almost vatic imaginative powers.

Although Jean does not deny that the world may be made to yield truth—indeed, that it can is one of his main points—he demonstrates little sense that a correspondence between God and nature may be brought to the support of human art. Moments such as the one in which Jean de Meun dreams of a God of Love who prophesies that Jean de Meun will grow up to dream of a God of Love force us, in Spearing's words, "to realize that it is a work of fiction we are reading, and that the very existence of fiction as an imitation of reality involves fundamental paradoxes."[57] It is in his awareness of such paradoxes that Jean becomes a transitional figure to the fourteenth century. The world has begun to seem a bit confusing to the author who tries to make it an image of truth. Despite Reason's assertive defense of direct, referential language, the poet in Jean seems uneasy. Please excuse my words, the narrator apologizes self-consciously, if they seem rude, unwise, satirical, for as Sallust says, "If anyone writes something without wishing to rob you of its truth, then what he says must resemble the deed" ("quiconques la chose escrit, / se du voir ne vous velt ambler, / li diz doit le fet resambler"; p. 258, ll. 15158–60). For Jean, as for Chaucer, who borrows the phrase from the thirteenth-century poet though he attributes it to Plato, "The wordes moote be cosyn to the dede" (cp. ll. 15161–62).[58] But the resemblance, like the word "cosyn" itself, is ambiguous. Just as Jean seems drawn to consider the Lover's epistemological failure rather than his success, so also, knowing that he has made things difficult for his readers, he seems unsure that they will always get the message quite right either. A crack is appearing between the domains of experience and authority. These words—these deeds—do not always seem a clear index to truth. Instead, truth will become something to be sought, not in and through the imitation of an action, not in and through the stages of a narrative, but in that narrative's ironies, its hesitations, and its silences.

CHAPTER 5

The 'Purgatorio': Dante's Book of Dreams

Dante's Poetic Teachers

Not all of his contemporaries shared Jean de Meun's satiric bent or his consciousness of the paradoxes and limits of fictional forms, for neither literary nor intellectual history continues regularly along an unbroken line. A little more than a quarter of a century later, Dante would complete the most ambitious and confident history of a spiritual journey ever attempted. Like Jean, Dante took part in the scholastic world of ideas; he involved himself deeply in the philosophical movements of his time. Like Jean also, Dante seemed to wish to allow reason and faith each its own scope of inquiry. He advocated a freedom of philosophical pursuit that presupposed an enormous commitment to the idea that reason could not produce anything disharmonious with theology, placing, for example, Siger of Brabant—one of those most notorious as a proponent of the so-called "double truth" theory—in the fourth sphere of Paradise, along with such others as Peter Lombard, Richard of Saint Victor, and Thomas Aquinas himself.[1]

Unlike Jean, however, Dante possessed some assurance not only about his philosophical position, but also about his right to speak from that position as a poet. As a magnum opus, his *Commedia* is comparable to the *Summa theologiae*: it is a vast synthesis whose very aspiration to reveal the analogies between different levels of creation and human endeavor bespeaks its writer's confidence in a world view. Encyclopedic form becomes a defense of philosophically realist content, as the poet—like a god or like nature—creates his own kind of *speculum mundi*. Thus, the *Commedia* unites poetically an astonishing diversity of motifs and structural elements from other areas of literature and thought.

In response, to help Dante's readers appreciate fully the power and genius of this synthesis, much of the best recent criticism of the poem has sought to shed new light on its various literary and historical backgrounds. This will be my purpose, too. But in focusing on the *Purgatorio*, the canticle that most closely approaches the structure of the philosophical vision, I will necessarily bring the issue of the poem's generic intent more into the foreground than others have done. In the *Commedia*, Dante's *itinerarium mentis ad Deum*, the poet marks out three distinct phases. In the *Inferno*, though what the pilgrim sees are shades, he sees them, in Augustinian terms, corporeally. They take on a physical presence the shades in Purgatory lack for him.[2] The *Paradiso* culminates in a purely intellectual vision—which, significantly, the poet cannot remember because his memory is limited by the powers of sense and imagination. But in the *Purgatorio*, the mental traveler experiences a *visio spiritualis*, the kind of imaginative vision which we have seen is typical of dreams as analyzed in the Middle Ages and which gave the philosophical vision its unique epistemological structure. For inspiration here, Dante turned to the subgenre we have been studying—to Boethius, to Alain's poetic vision, and to the sixth book of the *Aeneid*.

Neither the *Purgatorio* nor the *Commedia* as a whole is a dream or vision per se, though *Vision* has been an alternative title for the work, which seems problematically related to the "mirabile visione" that prompted Dante's vow at the end of the *Vita nuova* to write more and "nobler" things about Beatrice. Even in contemporary reception it was often read as a dream, indeed by Dante's own son, Pietro Alighieri, who interprets the poet's opening comment that he is "full of sleep" ("pien di sonno"; *Inferno* I.11) as evidence that the poet intends the external structure to be that of a dream. This interpretation seems at least in part genre bound, as Pietro compares Dante's concluding observation that his "fantasy" has failed to the end of *Aeneid* VI and the gates of ivory and horn, which suggest a final waking. The interpretation of the poem as a dream seems to have been so widespread that Filippo Villani in the early fifteenth century felt compelled to attack it outright, arguing that the "many" ("pleri") who so read the *Commedia* are themselves the "real dreamers."[3] Most close students of the poem will agree with Villani. But perhaps the misreading occurred so frequently because the poet incorporates in a most thorough way many of the conventions of the philosophical vision, often couched as a dream, including an abstractive psychology of vision and dreams used explicitly to mark stages of spiritual progress.

There seems little doubt that, in the first two canticles of the *Commedia*, Dante is demonstrating, like earlier vision poets, the kind of psychic preparation necessary for the mind's journey to God. The *Purgatorio*, in particular, is a drama of increasing awareness and readiness for vision. This is assumed as the poet's basic intention by Charles Singleton, whose analysis of the canticle in *Journey to Beatrice* consists largely in illuminating the ways in which various motifs in the journey and in the poem's overall symbolic structure come to reflect the pilgrim's growing knowledge of and love for divinity, a love that is the human reflection of divine grace.[4] Nevertheless, in choosing to stress certain features of the allegorical journey, Singleton necessarily leaves others relatively unexplored. His emphasis is primarily on the narrator's evolving love, on his maturing will, and hence on rectification in the affective part of his soul. But, as Singleton acknowledges, an ordering of faculties to reason or intellect precedes and forms a part of this justification.[5] More can be done to illustrate the outlines of this intellectual journey.

For example, Singleton does not investigate the poetic structures Dante uses to dramatize the ordering of imagination to reason. Yet this ordering is a central event in the conventional drama of the vision poem as Dante inherited it, and Dante too insists upon its primacy. When, in Canto XXVII of the *Purgatorio*, Virgil "crown[s] and miter[s]" Dante master of himself, proclaiming "Free, upright, and whole is your will" ("libero, dritto e sano è tuo arbitrio"), he is signaling more than just the perfection of Dante's love for the good;[6] he announces the completion of an ordering process in the intellectual soul as well, the right rule of reason over imagination. As Etienne Gilson points out, in a Thomistic psychology understanding and will, though distinct, "mutually include one another."[7] In any human act, there are two parts: understanding, which apprehends an object, and will, which transmits the movement toward it. No right action can occur unless *both* these parts—intellect and will—reflect a proper order. Will must dominate sensitive appetite just as reason commands imagination, so that, though equal to intellect in dignity, a man's will can reach no higher than that rational faculty allows. Cato, Justice according to the law or reason of the ancients and unaided by love (I.85–90), precedes and makes possible the meeting with Casella, Dante's dear friend, who makes a lyric appeal to him of pure love (II.76–117). At the outset of the canticle, the two characters set the psychological poles of the journey. As Beatrice explains to Dante in the *Paradiso*, souls have delight to the extent that their sight penetrates Truth, "from which it may be seen that the state of blessedness is founded on the act of vision, not on that which loves, which follows after" ("Quinci si può veder come si fonda / l'esser beato ne l'atto che vede, / non in quel ch'ama, che poscia seconda"; XXVIII.109–11). We cannot love, in other words, what we cannot apprehend; or to know the good means to love it, but likewise loving depends on knowing. Thus, that part of the *Commedia* which traces the poet's increasing love for the divine also traces his growing understanding of it. For this rectification in the intellectual soul, Dante finds a convenient paradigm in the literature of visionary ascent we have been studying.

The first significant literary precedent for Dante's journey was Aeneas's descent to the underworld, a voyage that Dante invokes immediately at the beginning of the second canto of the *Inferno* when he likens himself to the father of Silvius (II.13–15). Notes and motifs from that previous epic journey resound throughout Dante's epic; their specific character may suggest some of the special strengths the poet saw in the literary archetype. The reading of the *Aeneid* that informs the *Commedia*, it has been noted, is strongly influenced by the twelfth-century commentary on the poem I have already discussed in some detail.[8] It was from this commentary, no doubt, that Dante appropriated his dark wood of error, for his "selva oscura" bears marked resemblance to the wood of temporal goods ("bona temporalia") there portrayed as "obscura" because uninterpreted by reason: "Just as groves are dark because of the lack of sun, so too temporal goods are dark because of the lack of reason." The suggestion, of course, is that the pilgrim Dante, like Aeneas, is misguided because he has placed his affection in the world and is incapable of seeing past it to God. As the commentary goes on, "And just as woods are impassable places because of the multitude and variety of paths, so too are temporal goods impassable because of the various paths which seem to lead to the highest good but which do not."[9] In particular, Dante's error has been reflected in the imperfect and temporal way that he has loved Beatrice. Significantly, just at this moment, Virgil appears as his leader, his master, and his teacher to show him the passage up and away from the maze of error.

That Virgil is Dante's maestro in two senses—spiritually and poetically—seems obvious. As a figure of the reason that was granted to Christians and pagans alike, he becomes the sinner's moral guide, able to achieve high levels of natural vision, though levels that fall short of beatitude. As a poet, he provides Dante with the structural model for a genre designed to trace that moral and natural journey toward truth. The first two canticles of the *Commedia*, during most of which Virgil is Dante's guide, recapitulate Aeneas's underworld journey to the point at which he faces the wall of the Cyclops, symbol of the firmament.[10] "Before flying aloft to see God face to face, Dante undergoes a *descensus*, a *conversio* and an *ascensio*," writes David Thompson. "He travels the same spiritual path along which the Sybil had led Aeneas. Both journeys have the same pattern and the same basic epistemology."[11]

Thompson provides an important insight into the structure of Dante's poem, but one whose implications have yet to be fully examined, for Thompson and others who have written on the relation of the *Aeneid* commentary to the *Commedia* fail to define precisely the way that the epistemological assumptions operative in Virgil's narrative determine its pattern. As we saw in Chapter 2, the twelfth-century reading of the *Aeneid* projected onto that epic the "natural order of knowing," the progress through imagination, reason, and memory toward truth, which we have seen to exert such ordering force on the philosophical vision poem. In recalling immediately to his readers' minds that earlier journey, Dante raises an expectation as well that his poem will also play out this epistemological drama. Like Aeneas, Dante should come to represent a misguided, but properly humbled, imagination; Virgil, something like the Sybil in his own epic poem, should become that reason which can help imagination realize its true purpose in the human soul. The twelfth-century commentary tradition implied such psychological identifications, and Dante's poem also repeatedly suggests them. First of all, the misguided love that precipitated Virgil's appearance is an appetitive error in the imagination. It arises from the Lover's failure, which Dante had explored in the *Vita nuova*, to submit imaginative desire to a higher truth. Virgil, as reason or natural justice, leads the mental traveler to that truth in stages.

But these equations become much more central in the *Purgatorio* than in the *Inferno*, which is not strictly a philosophical vision, as I have defined it; it has a different set of conventions and rhetorical functions. One of these, Dante tells us in the *Letter to Can Grande*, is "to remove those living in this life from a state of misery, and to bring them to a state of happiness," a purpose Beatrice affirms even at the end of the *Purgatorio*, when she tells the pilgrim to write the poem "for profit of the world that lives ill" ("in pro del mondo che mal vive"; XXXII.103).[12] The *Inferno*, however, is the section of the poem most devoted to this sort of didacticism. In this canticle, though he tells us "io non Paulo sono," Dante gives us a work partly modeled on *The Vision of Saint Paul*, a panoply of vividly imagined tortures and personalities. Here the pilgrim is established in a set of proper emotional attitudes that relate primarily to the way he deals with the corporeal world, rather than the visionary world of spiritual images. His fear of the power of sin, his sympathy with the damned, his excessively human curiosity about their quarrels and complaints —these are the sorts of mental postures in which he has been squandering his spiritual energy. These are the attitudes that Virgil starts out to correct, more nearly in the style of the early Christian otherworldly vision than in the twelfth-century philosophical tradition.

Up to a point, then, the visionary's ontogeny recapitulates the phylogeny of the vision form itself, for the pilgrim's real psychological reordering does not properly begin until the *Purgatorio*, when he is first named as a pilgrim, or even until *Purgatorio* IX, when he actually reaches the gates to that region. Then, from his arrival in Purgatory through his emergence into the Earthly Paradise, Dante can more usefully be seen as the conventional dreamer, figure of divinely inspired imagination, yet desperately in need of reason's tutelage so that he can learn to pass through an earthly image to a heavenly truth. Here the poet wishes us as readers to focus not on the images of torture, which may convert us from evil, but on the path of ascent, which will confirm the good: "Heed not the form of the pain: think what follows, think that at the worst beyond the great Judgment it cannot go" ("Non attender la forma del martìre: / pensa la succession; pensa ch'al peggio / oltre la gran sentenza non può ire"; X.109–11).

This model breaks down, though, in the *Paradiso*, when the pilgrim has passed beyond humanity (I.64–72). There the focus is not on struggle, growth, and ascent, but on the more static and lyrical descent of God, disseminating Himself throughout the universe and revealing Himself gradually to man. The appropriate visionary form for this sort of movement is the pure *oraculum*, represented in the *Paradiso* by the Cacciaguida episode, which itself makes manifest and charges Dante also to reveal "tutta tua visïon" (XVII.128). Cicero's *Somnium Scipionis* is Dante's model here, where under the pressure of political prophecy the distinction between personal and universal vision collapses altogether and leaves the poet gasping like Scipio at the insignificance of earthly life: "With my sight I returned through all and each of the seven spheres, and saw this globe such that I smiled at its paltry semblance; and that counsel I approve as best which holds it for least" ("Col viso ritornai per tutte quante / le sette spere, e vidi questo globo / tal, ch'io sorrisi del suo vil sembiante; / e quel consiglio per migliore approbo / che l'ha per meno"; XXII.133–37).

The Order of Knowing

Dante has marked out, then, a distinct region in the second canticle, neither of unregenerate sin and corporeality nor of beatitude, but of the human desire and imperfection that make a bridge between the two. Within this scheme, the sins that Dante encounters on the ascending terraces of Purgatory are appropriately earthly or human sins of the imagination. They are explicitly portrayed by Virgil as errors of misplaced imaginative desire, like those exhibited by Aeneas in the first book of his epic as he fed his eyes on "empty pictures."[13] To achieve recognition of this fact, the Dante of the *Purgatorio* is educated in spiritual sight and insight. "I go up hence," the pilgrim tells us later in the canticle, "in order to be blind no longer" ("Quinci sù vo per non esser più cieco"; XXVI.58).

This process begins in Canto IX, typically enough, with the poet's dream of an eagle, in which his mind is "more a pilgrim from the flesh and less captive to thoughts" ("peregrina / più da la carne e men da' pensier presa"; IX.16–17). The dream motif is used here as it had been in earlier vision literature: to announce that a certain kind of education of the imaginative faculty had begun. In this dream, the eagle, who had strong—even medicinal—associations with sight, sweeps Dante up with him into the sky, "as far as the fire: there it seemed that it and I burned" ("suso infino al foco. / Ivi parea che ella e io ardesse"; IX.30–31).[14] At this point, vision is interrupted, and we discover from Virgil that Lucy, herself patron saint of the blind, has brought the sleeping Dante to the gates of Purgatory. The dream marks an advance in the pilgrim's journey—he has earned his vision—but it also signifies the spiritual problem that will plague him through the next phase of his climb to Beatrice. The imagined fire which scorches the Dreamer so searingly that he awakens is analogous to the scorching process which will constitute his purgation. It suggests as well, as at least one critic has pointed out, the literalizing tendency of the kind of imagination that would interpret a metaphorical fire as physical fact.[15]

The fire, of course, also brings to mind the fire he must pass through at the end of his purgatorial ascent just past the circle of lechery, at least in part the fire of lust; this fire Dante must learn to transform in this canticle to a purer—though still physical—desire, to the Edenic love he feels ultimately for Matelda.[16] Indeed, in this dream, Dante is quite self-conscious in stressing that vision comes to him *in* the body; the soul sleeps within him, not without ("l'anima tua dentro dormia"; IX.53), and his sleep comes to him as a response to bodily need, to the "Adam" in him (IX.10). Likewise, the mythological references in this canto—to Tithonus's "concubina," rather than wife, and to Ganymede, desired by the gods for his physical beauty—suggest the poet's emphasis on his pilgrim's physicality at this point and on the physicality of a desire that he must learn to understand and accept before he can move on. Like the fire, which is both cause and instrument of his purgation, the dream provides a fine vehicle for conveying an experience that both uses and moves the pilgrim past his body, and Dante draws effectively on that liminal quality of dreams we examined in an earlier chapter.

With the literal-minded Dreamer's admittance into Purgatory proper, then, we have entered the world of the conventional philosophical vision poem. The three steps that lead up to the gate of Purgatory, representing confession, contrition, and absolution, recall another motif from the vision form. The first of these steps is a mirror, polished so brightly that the visionary can see in it his true likeness. Purgation, the poet implies, involves proper sight and insight before anything else. Dante needs experiences to provide him with this clarity in the reflecting power of his imagination. He is confronted, then, with the *speculum* of the conventional vision poem, simply put into a more explicitly penitential framework. That the pilgrim does advance in contemplative power as a result of traveling through the landscape of purgation is made clear in his third dream, when he views the *speculum* again, this time perfected, as it is held by Rachel. The active life—the practice of virtue and purgation of vice—leads to perfection of the intellectual or contemplative virtue.

Once inside the realm of Purgatory, the traveler encounters yet another generic marker of the philosophical vision—the visual images carved on the encircling banks. Here to his side and later on this terrace underfoot, Dante can read images of great humilities, the first group illustrating antidotes to the sin of pride, the second the effects of that sin. These are controlling images for the entire canticle—they cast their influence forward—for just as pride itself is a root evil, a proper imaginative comprehension of its causes and effects is a key to the total redemptive vision. Once the poet enters the second terrace, the region of the envious, he will be leaving such visual images behind for a time. Here spiritual blindness is experienced as a physical fact; on the third terrace, the place of the wrathful, it has become a thick and blinding smoke.

Emerging at that time from the world of the literally blind prompts from Dante an apostrophe to imagination (XVII.13–18). In the absence of sensation, he tells us, it is this faculty that has presented to him and others in Purgatory the images that they need to ascend to God; it is this faculty inspired by divine light. The examples that the pilgrim had seen in a kind of ecstasy on the terrace of the wrathful, images of the meekness which opposes vice, had been freely given to his inner sense from above. There he had seen Mary's mildness in the temple, Pisistratus calming his wife, and the stoning of Saint Stephen. Here he provides a psychology to account for that sort of vision, which becomes retrospectively a *visio spiritualis*, the kind of vision that informs man of God through the mediation of images. The poet's method is like that of other vision poets, except that just as Dante's pilgrim has access ultimately to three guides, and takes place in three distinct regions, within the *Purgatorio* itself the narrator's progress upward is expressed by a series of three spiritual visions rather than by a single one. Virgil, representing the light of natural reason, explicates the visions in the intervals in a way that is perfectly consistent with contemporary dream psychology. The wayfarer's movement to God is still a collaboration of nature striving ever upward and the divine love that is grace diffusing itself downward.

In the following canto, XVIII, an exchange between Dante and Virgil clarifies beyond doubt the roles that these two figures play here in relation to each other as they articulate together Dante's progress upward through nature. Dante's experiences, like those of the Dreamer in the *De planctu*, have fired him with a desire to know more, and specifically to know more about love. "Wherefore . . . I pray that you," he says to Virgil, "expound love to me, to which you reduce every good action and its opposite" ("Però ti prego . . . / che mi dimostri amore, a cui reduci / ogne buono operare e 'l suo contraro"; XVIII.13–15). Virgil responds with the conventional psychology: "Your faculty of apprehension draws an image from a real existence and displays it within you, so that it makes the mind turn to it" ("Vostra apprensiva da esser verace / tragge intenzione, e dentro a voi la spiega, / sì che l'animo ad essa volger face"; XVIII.22–24). This inclination, Virgil explains, is love. But love is founded on accurate perception of the "intenzione"—the *intentio*, as Aquinas defines it, the principle of benefit or harm in an object as apprehended by an individual's reasoning powers. Thus, if the reasoning is not sound, the love, as Virgil cautions, will not be either: "Not every imprint is good, although the wax be good" ("non ciascun segno / è buono, ancor che buona sia la cera"; XVIII.38–39).

Dante has followed this discourse, he tells Virgil, with "ingegno" (XVIII.40). But, as imagination must be, he is still confused: Why isn't every love good? Virgil answers, "As far as reason sees here I can tell you" ("Quanto ragion qui vede, / dir ti poss' io; XVIII.46–47). Like Lady Philosophy, he then proceeds to explicate, as well as he is able, the notion of free will, a power that man possesses because he has as his substantial form the intellectual soul. Though Virgil's emphasis here is on the will—on the affective part of the human response to choice—his definition of will conveys, in addition, a sense of the intellectual act that must precede any act of volition. Will, in his discussion, is dependent on an innate faculty in man that "counsels" ("consiglia") and "garners and winnows good and evil love" ("buoni e rei amori accoglie e viglia"; XVIII.62, 66).[17] As we have seen repeatedly, this winnowing faculty, this reason, is what the typical visionary stands in need of. It is what Virgil, as reason, is able to provide to Dante's imagination. Dante, at the conclusion of this dialogue, tells us that he has "garnered clear and plain reasons" to his questions (XVIII.85–86). Though he still remains as one drowsy or slumbering, his dream in the canto that follows will indicate the kind of intellectual progress, the kind of awakening, also going on in his soul.

Just as the first dream marked a stage in the visionary's development and indicated the next phase of his spiritual preparation, the second dream, which follows at the beginning of Canto XIX, reveals the nature of the dual affective and imaginative problem the pilgrim is now experiencing. Before, he had been too literal minded; now, something like the Dreamer in the *Roman de la rose*, he is overly prone to idealize. He has learned to look past the literal for truth, but still the faculty of reason that discriminates among images is weak. The woman seen in this dream is not innately attractive. In fact, she is hideous in ways that indicate her identification with false art and perception; she is "a woman, stammering, with eyes asquint and crooked on her feet, with maimed hands, and of sallow hue" ("una femmina balba, / ne li occhi guercia, e sovra i piè distorta, / con le man monche, e di colore scialba"; XIX.7–9). Her sallow hue reminds us of Dante before the sun of Purgatory disclosed the natural color of his complexion; her crooked feet and squinting gaze indicate that she is spiritually directionless, incapable of divine perception; her maimed hands, lastly, call to mind the more positive, artful hands of the creators in Geoffrey of Vinsauf, Bernardus Silvestris, and the Aristotelian tradition, revealing her incapacity to inspire in the poet who turns to her any wholesome images.

With imagination, however, the Dreamer is able to color her pallid face "even as love requires" ("com' amor vuol"; XIX.15), and she sings, riveting the poet's attention on her. Imagination, Aquinas tells us, is the faculty responsible for such errors rising from a "dissimilarity between the sense and its object."[18] A holy lady, a "donna" fortunately, appears to put the other, the "femmina," to confusion. "O Virgil, Virgil, who is this?" she demands of the Dreamer's mentor, who then disrobes the offensive Siren, "rending her garments and showing me her belly" ("fendendo i drappi, e mostravami 'l ventre"; XIX.28–32). This sundering of the veil that conceals truth abruptly wakes Dante, who within the dream has clearly failed at the task of piercing the veil of the Siren's allegory.

The holy lady, in fact, stands for the grace necessary to every habit of divine goodness in man; Virgil, as is customary in the poem, represents intellect's right response to that grace, a response that the dream shows us the narrator is only part way to achieving.[19] The dream confirms in him the beginnings of a real understanding of that psychological truth which Virgil had explained in the previous canto. Forced to confront the demon's real nature, her true psychological meaning to him, the pilgrim forms the appropriate *intentio* in her regard, illustrating his reordered affections and redirected love. Or, one might say, here at the center of Purgatory, near souls immobilized by sloth, the pilgrim awakens through a dream to a new insight that is destined to help him in the next stage of his journey. The sins of avarice, gluttony, and lechery, which he will next encounter, are faults only of imaginative excess, of weakness in discriminating, like the fault represented in his vision of the witch. They are not, like pride, envy, and wrath, signs of a more serious inversion of psychic hierarchies. By the end of the canticle, we will see the process of psychic regeneration reach its conclusion as reason gains even firmer control over imagination, which then is put more securely in service to the good.

The narrator's psychological advance, his growing recovery of control, is represented by a third dream, described in Canto XXVII. We can understand this dream only by noting the events that precede it. In this canto, Virgil attempts to persuade Dante to enter into the purifying flames. With his reason, it may be said, the pilgrim knows that the fire signifies something beyond itself and knows that he must pass through it. But when he gazes into the flames, his imagination takes hold, and he vividly pictures to himself charred human bodies. A trace remains of that literalizing imagination which felt itself scorched by the empyrean fire in the first dream—and, we must note, of the lust which fire had represented then and signals again in the terrace of the lecherous. Some remnant of this desire had drawn him as well to the Siren of his second dream. Virgil responds to his passion not by asking the poet to transcend it, but by giving him the opportunity for transformation. He presents to his charge now another image, a very different one, of Beatrice waiting for him on the other side of the wall of fire. Dante's demeanor alters immediately at the thought of his lady, and Virgil smiles "as one does to a child that is won with an apple" ("come al fanciul si fa ch'è vinto al pome"; XXVII.45). The maestro condescends affectionately to his pupil's humanity, since the taking of this apple reverses man's enslavement to his lower, imaginative nature, and hence the effect of the original apple in an earlier Eden. As mortals, we are like children, limited, only to be won over, by our imaginations. In recognition of this fact, Virgil continues to encourage Dante through the searing fire with the image of Beatrice.

Love, and the imagination that realizes it, are here turned toward the ultimate good, enabling the pilgrim to move through and past the literal-mindedness that, early on, had interfered with vision and to combat the pseudoidealism that later had cut it off. The dream that follows the fire is brief, lasting only long enough for Dante to envision Leah and Rachel, but it will be the only dream in the poem that is not interrupted. Its completion suggests the perfection of imaginative vision, the realization of the promise the poet had made to us in the *Vita nuova* that he would convey his dream of a pure and noble love for his lady. The harmony of Rachel and Leah here—active and contemplative modes of being—suggests a harmony in the pilgrim's own soul between its affective and intellective parts, between its inclination to action and its knowledge of the good, which I have glossed here primarily by reference to increasing knowledge. But both parts, as I said before, are necessary—Leah's "fair hands" ("belle mani") and Rachel's "fair eyes" ("belli occhi") to balance fully the image of the maimed and squinting Siren.

The lover has imposed intellect on the natural passions; he has given acceptable shape to imaginative desire. "No longer expect word or sign from me" ("Non aspettar mio dir più né mio cenno"; XXVII.139), says Virgil, whose guidance as reason is not required any more, though his presence will continue as long as natural reason is the sufficient cause for the pilgrim's growth. The conclusion of this dream prepares the way for Virgil's pronouncement of right order in both the intellectual and affective parts of his disciple's soul: "Free, upright, and whole is your will, and it would be wrong not to act according to its pleasure; wherefore I crown and miter you over yourself" ("libero, dritto e sano è tuo arbitrio, / e fallo fora non fare a suo senno: / per ch'io te sovra te corono e mitrio"; XXVII.140–42).

Return to the Earthly Paradise indicates return to the condition of rectitude in the soul which existed in man before the Fall. The pageant witnessed by the narrator there, as Joseph Mazzeo has noted, is seen in "that mode of prophecy effected through imaginative similitudes, a mode . . . that Saint Thomas places below a purely intellectual kind of prophetic vision."[20] It corresponds, then, to the pageant at the end of the *De planctu*, which had culminated in the imaginative insight represented by Genius's anathema. The change in quality of insight is indicated by the kind of sleep the pilgrim experiences in Canto XXXII, which makes no concessions to the Adam within him and which, unlike any other sleep in this canticle, culminates in no dream.[21] Indeed, in a strange *occupatio* the poet seems almost to avoid image making about this sleep at all. If I could describe the eyes of Argus, he writes, lulled to sleep by Mercury's song of the Syrinx, I would; but no, instead "I pass on . . . to when I awoke" ("trascorro a quando mi svegliai"; XXXII.70). We are leaving the book of "spiritual vision," the book of dreams. Dante seems to be anticipating what will come next, as he must travel even further, into Paradise, where he will experience a more completely intellectual sort of vision. For this, he must purify the one faculty that has not yet been involved in the drama of the poem—memory. The journey through the faculties will not be complete, the pilgrim's spiritual state not perfected, until he does so.

The narrator's crossing of the two rivers of memory, rivers whose presence in the poem has never been adequately explained in criticism,[22] signals the completion of this phase of his psychic journey, the end of that education conventionally treated in the philosophical vision. The mirror of vision, the first step up to the gate of Purgatory, now reflects nature clearly to the poet, both his own nature and that outside him, thus suggesting the cure of imagination. After insight comes contrition, the second step, stimulated in the pilgrim by Beatrice's sternness when she calls Dante by name in Canto XXX, signaling the reformulation of his identity according to her reason and justice. Matelda's portage of Dante through the river of Lethe marks the third and final step, absolution. Rivers of oblivion abound in visionary writers, from Virgil to the author of *The Voyage of Saint Brendan*. Dante deftly exploits this tradition with his River of Forgetfulness, which forms an ideal psychological parallel to this third step through purgation, an ideal third term to complete the sequence of imagination and reason; forgetfulness paradoxically becomes the perfect embodiment of memory. As Aquinas writes, in a state of transcendence or absolution such as we may expect after death, we will remember nothing of what in this life was purely sensual; "activities, such as loving or understanding, decay likewise, and the soul itself neither remembers nor loves any more."[23] Thus, after Lethe, Beatrice stands unveiled in her true essence, which though still conceived imagistically, exerts none of that old, sinful attraction. As wax, Dante's imagination is perfectly imprinted with her figure (XXXIII.79–81).

"From fear and from shame I wish that you henceforth divest yourself, so that you may no more speak like one who is dreaming" ("Da tema e da vergogna / voglio che tu omai ti disviluppe, / sì che non parli più com' om che sogna"; XXXIII.31–33). No longer is Dante the typical flawed dreamer; no longer can he even recall that part of his love that was sin. Aeneas, too, had been like this in the Elysian Fields, according to Lorenzo de' Medici, remembering earthly things no more.[24] But a River of Memory is unique to Dante, and here he draws directly on scholastic philosophy, fusing it with his own synthetic invention. There is a kind of memory other than the bodily one described by Aquinas, one that will enable the pilgrim to remember his origin in God, to recall the images through which God manifests Himself, and to apprehend that supreme truth which lies beyond images. This memory, claims Bonaventure, is thus an image of eternity, "capable of being informed not only from the outside by phantasms but also from above, by receiving and having in itself simple forms that cannot enter through the doors of the senses, nor through sensible phantasms."[25] This is the sort of memory intended by the River of Eünoè, good memory. The passage through the second river of memory, which concludes the *Purgatorio*, strengthens Dante in the power of this second sort of remembering, which he will need for the altogether different vision of the *Paradiso*, a vision beyond dream.

The Place of Vision

Purgatory, Dante's realm of dreams, is indeed the appropriate locus for the sort of highly differentiated rectification we have seen

Dante's pilgrim undergoing. The two poles of Heaven and Hell had always been part of the Other World, even in classical times; in early Christian visions like *The Vision of Saint Paul*, the visionary was simply transported from one to another place without any sense of intervening space. Sometimes, as in Bede's vision of Drycthelm, one might find waiting areas outside Paradise and Inferno, but still clearly attached to one or the other. It was not until the end of the twelfth century, the height of the High Middle Ages, that Purgatory took its central place in Catholic theology, under the influence of figures like Peter the Chanter, and in literature, the *Purgatorium Sancti Patricii*. Along with the new focus on penance, on close analysis of sin and intention, and with the attempt to balance the human demand of living in the world with the absolute demand for perfection, a need evolved for a "liminal" space in the afterlife, participating in both earth and heaven and, in the form of prayers, allowing for some communication between the two. Purgatory, as Jacques Le Goff argues, is that region, "a place . . . for subtlety, justice, accuracy, and measure."[26] And Dante is its poetic master, partly because he discovered a way to make his *visio spiritualis*—neither wholly physical nor wholly beatific—tap into that region's liminality, demonstrating not only that the earthly kingdom should be a reflection of the divine, but also that by following the "natural order of knowing," man could ascend from one to the other. Man ends in heaven only by beginning on earth. The new life is achieved by risking one fixed state to reach another, and the *Purgatorio* is the domain of that risk, the region of growth, change, and initiation into higher truth.

Because it thus mediates between figure and fulfillment, Purgatory is also the region most comfortable for traditional poetic allegory. In the *Purgatorio*, image is joined to its gloss or interpretation: we learn Virgil's role, we meet Beatrice, we become acquainted with the epistemological and metaphysical universe in which they exist. T. S. Eliot claims that "from the *Purgatorio* one learns that a straightforward philosophical statement can be great poetry." I do not think, however, that it thus becomes the most "difficult" of the canticles.[27] In the *Inferno*, Dante has the arduous task of speaking systematically about moral chaos, which he represents as punishments turning inward on sinners trapped by their own corporeality. In the *Paradiso*, he comes up against the limits of his own imagination, the bark of his *ingegno*, always smaller than the reach of his intellectual vision, as both memory and words fail him.[28] As John Freccero indicates, "For both of these realms, a different rhetorical strategy is required."[29] But among the shades of Purgatory, Dante can make a kind of allegory that is simple and direct. Once Jean de Meun's "truant beggar" (p. 271, l.15992), Dante's Art shakes hands with Nature. Like Boethius and Alain, Dante lets the validity of the images in this canticle—Beatrice, the griffin, the tree of life—serve as an index of the pilgrim's grasp of truth. He even tells us directly that the wellspring of his poetry is divine in Canto XXIV of the *Purgatorio*, when Bonagiunta da Lucca announces that the inspiration of Dante's *dolce stil novo* differs from other poets' in being heavenly, and in Canto XXVIII, when his guides ("miei poeti"; 146) smile at finding their dreams of Paradise confirmed.

Both Dante and Jean, then, use the spiritual vision's marginality—its liminality—to formulate anew the terms upon which nature and grace could meet. And both make that liminality as well a way of commenting on the role of poetry in effecting and representing this meeting. But Jean's approach, significantly, is negative and satiric, whereas Dante's is clear and sure. At a time when other poets were modestly indirect in their approach to God—something less than sure of their ability to express the ineffable—Dante's poetry was always aimed confidently upward, like a steadily drawn bow; his expectation was always firm that the arrow would reach its goal. The images vouchsafed to the pilgrim in the dreams of the *Purgatorio* are analogous to the poetic images with which God had inspired him in the larger vision of the *Commedia*, bearing clear proportion to truth. As it had for Alain, the spiritual itinerary of the philosophical vision served Dante well as he demonstrated in the *Commedia* the vast reaches of human apprehension and expression, as he defended, simply by practicing it, a poetry that, in the most humanistic tradition of his age, could honor not only the stars but also the demands of mere imagination.

CHAPTER 6

John Gower's Fourteenth-Century Philosophical Vision

Elements of Vision in the 'Confessio Amantis'

John Gower's *Confessio Amantis* is neither explicitly framed as a vision, nor was it written during the time period on which this book has mainly focused. Why, then, continue our study of the high medieval philosophical vision past Dante? The hesitance of the narrator in the *Confessio Amantis* as he learns to renounce the world makes him in some ways a closer spiritual brother to *late* medieval visionaries—the stubbornly uncomprehending Jeweler in *Pearl* or Chaucer's vision narrators with their apparent unlikeliness for love. But such similarities also break down at crucial moments. I will show here that for the most part Gower's shaping of his poem provides a conservative response to previous works in the subgenre, as he capitalizes on the psychology of visionary ascent to make a point not theoretically or poetically dissimilar to that of earlier writers. In temperament and orientation, the moral Gower is a transitional figure belonging partly to a previous generation, which perhaps explains why his work may seem, in comparison to Chaucer's or Langland's, static, decorative, or old-fashioned.

Like other fourteenth-century poets, however, John Gower is extraordinarily self-conscious in his role as poet and in his use of literary forms, matched among medieval English writers in his dedication as a reviser only by Langland. This care and attention to form makes him a useful subject in the study of what elements were received by the fourteenth century as most essential to the high medieval vision genre. Of course, the *Confessio* draws from other genres as well. The roles played by the penitential tradition, medieval complaint and satire, sermon exempla, belletristic poetry, and erotic love verse have been well examined in modern criticism.[1] But none of these supplies the external structure of the poem that determines its true, overriding genre. Here the poet turned to a tradition of literary visions. Indeed, along with the Lover's confession to the priest of Venus, the other scene in the poem chosen most frequently as a subject for manuscript illumination was Nebuchadnezzar asleep, dreaming of the figure of gold, silver, earth, steel, and brass.[2] Although Gower's poem is not, then, explicitly presented as a dream or vision, it is introduced by a dream whose interpretation provides a key to many of the poem's concerns and is closed by another dream, this time the Lover's.

Even more important, much of the opening setting in Book I—the spring landscape, the wood that opens into a *locus amoenus*, and especially the complaining narrator whose malady is that he has a lapse in the memory of his true identity—also frequently appears in high medieval visionary literature. In Book I, Gower even hints that all we are witnessing may, in fact, be a literal dream; here the Lover falls to the ground in what seems to be a swoon, structurally parallel to the one that will come at the end of the poem. He "awakens" from this to call upon Venus, who in turn summons her priest, Genius, a character whose appearance and confessional role are borrowed directly from Jean de Meun's philosophical vision.[3] But except in somewhat distorted form, Genius, descendant of the classical demons who appeared to men in dreams, is found nowhere outside the vision tradition until well into the sixteenth century, unless we count Gower's poem itself.[4] That audiences naturally read this poem with the vision genre in mind is suggested by the reactions of modern critics from Russell Peck, who places the work confidently in the genre of Boethius's *De consolatione*, to Donald Schueler, who calls the action "a waking dream," to Jane Chance Nitzsche, who dubs it a "pseudo-dream vision."[5]

Gower himself was clearly aware of the kinds of poetic effects that visions might have, of the various ways that visions might serve as structuring devices in literature—and not only in the *Confessio*

Amantis. As he says in the *Vox Clamantis*, echoing statements of earlier dream theorists,

> What dreams may mean is clear from Daniel, and Joseph's vision in his sleep was not meaningless. Indeed, the good angel who is the guardian of the inner man always protects him with vigilant love. And granted that sleep may envelope the outer body, the angel visits the interior of the mind and sustains its strength.[6]

We have here a clear description of the sorts of oracular, healing dreams that had dominated the philosophical vision, and indeed that would inform Gower's own *Confessio*. Following this passage from its Prologue, the first book of the *Vox Clamantis* forms a kind of literary vision in miniature, in which the narrator falls asleep to witness the Peasants' Revolt figured in the changing of the different social estates into various beasts.

But although Gower relies on some of the typical features of the vision poem in constructing this book—for example, the enigmatic shapes of the *somnium* interpreted to the Dreamer by an oracular celestial voice (I.xx.2020–50)—he uses the dream here mainly as an authenticating device, to secure for himself the authority of prophecy. His primary concern is with how this Dreamer, on the model of that John "whose name I bear" ("cuius ego nomen gesto"), author of the biblical *Apocalypse*, can help his reader "better understand the conditions of the time" ("magis in causis tempora noscat"; I.Prol.58, 14), and not with elucidating a single Dreamer's psychological development. A similar apocalyptic purpose also informs Nebuchadnezzar's vision, which, as we have noted, dominates the middle of the Prologue to the *Confessio Amantis*. Nevertheless, the vision seen by Amans—a vision that in a sense begins as he falls to the ground and prays to Venus in Book I but that culminates in Book VIII, when he faints into a true swoon and dreams the pageant of lovers—is different, for it is used more self-consciously as a poetic instrument and is structured more in accordance with the subgenre of the philosophical vision. This vision borrows, as I will show, from previous poets just those elements of the form that the author felt were significant, and thus provides unique evidence about fourteenth-century reception of the subgenre.

The *Confessio Amantis* also borrows courtly motifs from the French love vision, another visionary subgenre, which as I noted in

Chapter 4 found its starting point in Guillaume de Lorris's *Roman de la rose* and which continued, throughout the late thirteenth and fourteenth centuries, to use the form to express refinements of *fin amor*, to develop a more purely secular idealism. But as John Fisher has pointed out, despite superficial similarities, the debt in Gower's poetry to this tradition was not as profound as, say, Chaucer's.[7] The influence of a fourteenth-century court poet like Guillaume de Machaut comes largely in tone and scale, matters that may have been more or less unconscious for Gower, compared to the poet's clearly intentional and rather conspicuous return to the thirteenth-century *Rose* for his literary personae. Contrast Gower's choice with, for example, Chaucer's method in *The Book of the Duchess*, where the lamenting knight, his lady, and to some degree the voyeuristic narrator all have precedents in Machaut's *Fonteinne amoureuse* and *Jugement dou Roy de Behaingne*, which also supply, respectively, an embedded version of Ovid's Ceyx and Alcyone, along with the *Dit dou lyon*, an analogue to Chaucer's puppy or animal guide, not to mention some of the exact language the later poet uses. In opposition, the *Confessio Amantis* borrows its specific content most fundamentally from the tradition of philosophical visions whose growth as a genre I have traced from Boethius through Jean de Meun and Dante. This narrator is not just a lover, Amans, but a man, the word play suggesting that his spiritual journey stands in some sense for our own.

In thus locating Gower generically, I may appear to be claiming too much for the poet who has seemed to many modern readers —as I suggested earlier—lifeless and oppressive. According to one nineteenth-century critic, reading Gower's work is a penance, his style a coffin, he an undertaker, and dullness his legacy.[8] But, interestingly, this was not always the verdict rendered. For the two-and-a-half centuries following Gower's death, he was revered almost as highly as Chaucer, sometimes more so. The decay in his reputation may indicate, among other things, increased misunderstanding over the centuries of just what purposes the poet's scope and conservatism might serve. In recent work, however, several critics and a new John Gower Society have sought to rescue the *Confessio Amantis* from critical iniquity.[9] Still, in this endeavor, emphasis has frequently been placed on the richness—the "unity and coherence," in John Fisher's words—of the poet's moral philosophy, to the detriment of those architectonics that Gower struggled for as a poet and that C. S. Lewis had the sensitivity as a reader to admire so frankly in his epoch-making reappraisal of the poem.[10]

It must be admitted that one quickly encounters the limits of Gower's poetic talent, and this even beyond the necessary dullness and bathos that is inevitable in any writer of Gower's earnest ambition and prolixity. But his faults are mainly local infelicities. Even Gower's non-English works have now been shown to exhibit unusual strengths of originality and coherence in combining traditional sources.[11] And as Fisher himself points out, by uncommon efforts of revision in the direction of rigor and structural consistency, Gower managed to make his three major poems, in three different languages, "in a very real sense . . . one continuous work."[12] Still, relatively little has been done since Lewis to examine the basis of Gower's aesthetic in the *Confessio Amantis*, to discover the "unity and coherence" of his poetic plan there,[13] or to try to determine as a kind of adjunct to this what kind of "speculative" philosophy or epistemology might inform deep poetic structure. Indeed, the majority of readers still feel that an imperfect synthesis between the poem's courtly frame (the love confession by Genius, priest of Venus) and the didactic lore in the Prologue and in Books V and VII mars its overall achievement.[14]

The Lover's Confessor

The classic criticism of poetic structure in the *Confessio Amantis* is offered by G. C. Macaulay, the poem's editor:

The scheme itself, with its conception of a Confessor who as priest has to expound a system of morality, while as a devotee of Venus he is concerned only with the affairs of love (I.237–80), can hardly be called altogether a consistent or happy one. The application of morality to matters of love and of love to questions of morality is often very forced, though it may sometimes be amusing in its gravity. The Confessor is continually forgetting one or the other of his two characters, and the moralist is found justifying unlawful love or the servant of Venus singing the praises of virginity.[15]

But Macaulay was by no means the first to suggest this line of attack. He got the idea, I imagine, from Gower himself, whose Genius at length apologizes for the limitations of his own priesthood. Gower did not have to make Genius the priest of Venus; in his sources, Genius was the priest of Nature. But as a result of this change the poet was able to investigate the dichotomy between competing views of his subject matter, between *honeste love* and *love seculer*, more subtly and thoroughly. Part of his method includes exploiting the disjunction involved in the yoking of two codes of love through the character of Genius and ultimately in showing the way to their unification. As I have noted, Genius himself calls attention to the disjunction both at the transition from Book VI to VII and at his first introduction in Book I:

> For I with love am al withholde,
> So that the lasse I am to wyte,
> Thogh I ne conne bot a lyte
> Of othre thinges that ben wise:
> I am noght tawht in such a wise;
> For it is noght my comun us
> To speke of vices and vertus,
> Bot al of love and of his lore,
> For Venus bokes of nomore
> Me techen nowther text ne glose.   (I.262–71)

He alludes to his double office again in Book VIII, when he suggests that an effectual resolution of its contradictions has been reached (VIII.2075–86).

Such self-awareness suggests to me a sense on the author's part that the seeming impropriety of the poetic frame may be made to serve the poet's overall intention, as stated in his colophon, of founding a work "on love and the promises of lovers," and of making history, fiction, and philosophy exemplify the resulting insight into his subject.[16] An analysis of the external structure of the poem and of Genius's role in that structure, as Gower works toward this insight, should help to clarify how this thematic coherence is achieved. Like the Ladies Philosophy, Nature, and Reason, Genius attempts to lead Amans from *visibilia* to truth, from the confusions and frustrations represented in his individual experience to a deep, personal acceptance of authority as a means of transcendence. By explicating different aspects of earthly love, through his tales he leads Amans and the reader ultimately to a deeper understanding of that heavenly love which is finally for Gower their *significatum*.

The fact is, though, that Genius guides Amans obliquely. He does not speak directly for Gower, but rather for a point of view that is ultimately exposed in the work as limited, even seriously misdirected. There is something to Macaulay's criticism after all, something problematic in reading Genius in his mythographic character as the proponent of *caritas* or even of reasonable, generative love. How do we explain this confessor who presents some rather equivocal love tales as the matter of *honeste love*? In recent criticism, the quest for Genius's prototypes has worked primarily to sharpen Macaulay's definition of the poem's main structural difficulty: the poet seems to have drawn upon both Genius's generative, sexual, and scribal role, and at the same time upon his tutelary or priestly one, yet—many feel—without finding a way to resolve unambiguously the moral problems raised by the combination of reason and sexuality that the character thus embodies.

Alain's Genius, the argument goes, had clearly been in service to the Chartrian Nature; his tutelary role was properly fulfilled in the directing of sexual energies to procreation in the marriage bed. Jean de Meun's Genius was, on the other hand, like his Nature in the *Roman de la rose*, divorced from Reason for purposes of irony and hence alienated from this proper tutelary role: natural love becomes *cupiditas*. By making Genius a major actor in his own poem, Gower means, as Denise Baker puts it, "to restore to this figure the moral authority exercised by Alain's true priest."[17] Yet unlike Baker, many readers still feel that Gower's reconciliation of Love and Reason, for all its literary authority, ultimately has its limits; the poet's most avid detractors have dubbed it unconvincing, arbitrary, even evasive. "Genius," writes Michael D. Cherniss, "is the most problematical figure in the poem. Gower defines this character's functions more clearly than his conceptual identity, perhaps because the device of the lover's confession took precedence in the poet's mind over philosophical clarity."[18] I mean to show, to the contrary, that within the generic contexts invoked by this poem, Genius has a very clear and carefully defined conceptual identity.

If Genius is primarily meant to serve as Venus's priest in a static confessional encounter, then his role *is* ambiguous, for his tales frequently instruct in Christian virtue, and he is even forced at one point in the poem to deny Venus explicitly. If he is intended as Reason, as Baker has argued, then his character is still more disturbing, for surely Reason would never relate some of the tales Genius tells or attach to them his interpretations. Even Chaucer balks at the "wikke ensample of Canacee," a story which may indeed warn against wrath but in which Genius also seems "curiously sympathetic" to the "kindly," yet incestuous, longing of brother and sister for each other.[19] Yet the "device of the confession," as Cherniss calls it, did not take precedence for Gower; the philosophical vision did, and the expectations of both content and form it raised can go a long way toward explaining what seems troubling in this work when it is read chiefly as a confession.[20]

The narrative order or sequence of the philosophical vision is controlled by the profoundly dynamic sequence of the visionary's moral or psychic growth. Moreover, in contrast to a confession, a vision articulates the stages of a dreamer's growth through allegorical characters who embody a trait or faculty he possesses. Natura's confusion at the Dreamer's question about the behavior of the pagan gods in the *De planctu naturae* we understood there as a confusion within the mind of the poem's narrator and not as the poet's consistently held view of Nature. Similarly, the changes and inconsistencies in the character of Genius in Gower's *Confessio* can be comprehended as changes and inconsistencies in Amans, as Genius tries to instruct him in a manner typical of dream guides by accommodating his lore to the natural limits of the Lover's knowing. The problems Genius encounters as Amans's teacher become even more revealing if we consider him as embodying the faculty that is traditionally his province in the poems we have been studying—as he becomes the spiritual pilgrim's imagination or his *ingenium*.[21]

C. S. Lewis was not far off when he called Genius "the lover's deepest 'heart.'"[22] Genius initially warns Amans not only to guard his five outer wits, but also "thin hertes wit, which is withinne, / Whereof that now thi love excedeth / Mesure" (I.540–42). This inner wit, suggestively like *ingenium*, is what Genius seems to embody. It is what he consistently works hardest to temper, for the establishment of a proper relation between wit, as a "kindly" quality, and reason is a constant theme in his tales. Further, in establishing this relationship, the priest is, according to a marginal note, Genius *secundum poetas*, and the Genius that Gower inherited from the poets had an association we have studied in detail with imagination or *ingenium*.[23] I would not want to limit the meaning of wit in Gower to *ingenium* nor of Genius to either.[24] He is, in a sense, the governor of the entire natural man—perceptive, productive, reproductive. Indeed, the first sins about which he instructs Amans are sins of the outer wits, the eye and ear. And, of course, his ostensible role is as Venus's priest. But as guardian of his inner wits too, he is not only that goddess's emissary but also the Lover's imagination as it functions in the larger epistemological structure of the work.

As well as helping to explain changes in Genius's character throughout the poem, which occur uniformly in the direction of spiritual growth, seeing the sort of wit that Genius represents as, at the same time, the aspiring *ingenium* and the more debased and acquisitive form of this faculty, *engin*, can also account for what seem to be inconsistencies in his overall function within the allegorical framework. As *ingenium*, Gower's Genius might command an almost unlimited vista of things spiritual, but as *engin*, he would demand a complex, ambivalent response, using as he does his priestly craft for purposes that do not always seem in Amans's best interests. The priest and confessor is Amans's guide, just as *ingenium* or imagination might be, in the Lover's journey toward fuller understanding; yet because he is only imagination, he can be a limited guide. The devotee of Venus and preacher of the ideals of earthly love is a creative, generative power—imagination as it experiences the attractions of the physical world. The figure of imagination in the poetic sense crafts tales that provide the Lover with artistic images of nature and social life. However significant his role, though, Genius remains mere imagination, or rather an embodiment of this faculty in the Lover, whose lusts are undisciplined, untutored by that power which ought to reign in the soul—reason. This human failure is what makes Gower's frame, and the narrative strategy within it, seem at times faulty or inconsistent. To see Gower's greater method in exploiting the limitations of Genius as a guide, we must now look closely at the way the priest and storyteller handles a few of the more problematic aspects of the shrift.

Genius's Narrative Art

Although in many ways Genius is a remarkable storyteller—and his narrative art has many times been praised[25]—there are problems in his tale telling that reflect problems in his overall tutelage. He often simply misses the point of his own stories, at times quite comically. There is a kind of fixity to this character who seems bent upon instructing and shriving Amans on every sin, regardless of whether or not the poor fellow has ever even had the desire, let alone the power or opportunity, to commit it. It has been noted that Gower's poem echoes penitential handbooks, which were a response to new requirements for penance laid down by the Fourth Lateran Council. Among other things, these handbooks popularized the notion that penance should be a "cure" for sin. By this metaphor, they indicated that the confessor should suit the medicine to the illness, that he should individualize his shrift.[26] By this standard, Genius seems a rather poor confessor.

Hypocrisy, Genius tells Amans, is the first category of the first sin, Pride. The Lover certainly requires instruction on this sin, for when Genius asks him if he has been guilty of it, he answers quite simply, "I wot noght, fader, what ye mene" (I.588). But after Amans has been enlightened by a lengthy definition of the sin, he quickly protests that he has not been fortunate enough to have had occasion for this form of pride. If he has dissimulated, it has been in the opposite direction from hypocrisy. Instead of beguiling his lady by sighs and pretended lovesickness, Amans has had to bear up as cheerfully as possible under the real discomforts of love:

> As forto feigne such sieknesse
> It nedeth noght, for this witnesse
> I take of god, that my corage
> Hath ben mor siek than my visage.   (I.713–16)

Nevertheless, Genius insists on telling the character John Gower a tale for this sin, as he will insist on telling them, like it or not, for each division of each sin throughout. By the end, we feel that Amans must be as bored as we are at times by this compulsive explication of faults, without regard to the Lover's real condition. Henri Bergson has defined the comic as "mechanical inelasticity" where one would expect to find "life" or "adaptability."[27] Though Gower has many times been criticized for lacking humor, by this definition Genius approaches the essence of the comic when he repeatedly substitutes a pre-arranged sequence for the kind of shrift that would be truly responsive to Amans's developing needs.

Such comic inaptitude, such replacement of a mechanical propriety or decorum for a true one, is a characteristic of Genius's narrative and exegetical methods as well. Nearly every critic of the poem, no matter how sympathetic, finds himself remarking at one point or another on how curiously some of the tales seem to fit their stated morals. Genius himself seems puzzled by their relation at times, commenting, for instance, thus on the exemplary force of the tale "The Patience of Socrates": "I not if thilke ensample yit / Acordeth with a mannes wit, / To soffre as Socrates tho dede" (III.699–701). Even Derek Pearsall, whose work has been highly influential in the reevaluation of the tales as exempla, admits that "sometimes . . . Gower's overt moral betrays his own best understanding."[28] Or as John Fisher puts it, "The fit between the . . . stories and either the Seven Sins or courtly love varies from mediocre to poor."[29] Not even readers who grant Gower some method in the matter tend to feel that he has full control over the view of Genius's character that the poor fit of his tales causes.[30] However, a dissertation by James Foster on the influence of the mythographic tradition on the poem indicates considerable skill on Gower's part in manipulating the accepted significance of each tale for his own artistic purposes. As Foster points out, Gower does more than simply alter conventional morals: "The degree of distance between Genius's interpretations of a fable and the mythographic ones will show how far the Lover yet has to progress toward enlightenment."[31] Moreover, as I will argue, this distance is measured by the distance between a tale's explicit moral and the real effect it seems designed to have on the reader.

Basically, there are two kinds of pointing in medieval literature—visual and verbal. As a technique of guiding reader interpretation, the second is obvious: it consists simply of the stated significance that literary material is given by its author. Visual pointing operates more subtly, for it is made up of those images that the author presents in the most detailed way and that the reader thus retains most vividly in his memory. As J. A. Burrow notes, "to point" was a technical term in the poet's vocabulary and indicated the medieval writer's overt consciousness of the type and scale of his description and the effect it might have on an audience in a variety of narrative contexts.[32] V. A. Kolve describes this effect, even as it works upon a modern reader:

If, in respect to a medieval narrative poem, we put to ourselves the question 'What is remembered?', and limit our answer to what comes to mind immediately and intact, requiring no linear reconstruction of the narrative itself, the answer most often concerns something seen with the eye of the mind, something which the narrative caused us to image with particular force as we attended to the verbal process, and which is instantly accessible as image to the memory.[33]

Despite the fact that the tales in the *Confessio* have frequently been characterized as relatively barren of visual effect—C. S. Lewis, for example, complains that "the pictorial imagination finds little to feed on in the *Confessio Amantis*"[34]—the memorable image is an important part of each tale's effect. Pointing, indeed, is done on a smaller scale by Gower than by many of his contemporaries. But although Gower's "plain style" would seem to militate against the sort of vivid picturing we are talking about, it actually provides a contrast against which images stand out in relief and, in areas where Genius lacks competence, often stand in clear tension to the purported moral significance of the tale as an illustration of a particular sin.

An example of this narrative method and the tension it creates can be found in the tale "Iphis and Araxarathen," offered by Genius as an example of the wanhope that is a kind of sloth in love. In the rapidity of its narrative and the economy of its descriptive pointing, this story is typical of those told by Genius in the *Confessio*. The tale is only about two hundred lines long, and most of the action occurs in the first 150 lines, during which there are only three moments that might be called "pointed." The first is Iphis's approach to the house of his beloved; the second, her complaint. The third moment, Iphis's suicide, provides an instant of potentially intense visual drama, which Gower chooses deliberately *not* to point. In Ovid's *Metamorphoses*, Gower's source for this tale, Iphis attaches his noose to the lady's doorpost and his feet convulsively pound against her door as he dies (*Metamorphoses*, XIV.739–42). But since it would distract him from the real end of his telling, Gower omits such gory detail, concluding simply and indeed bathetically, "He hyng himself, that was pite" (IV.3594).

In contrast, the last fifty lines of the tale etch a startlingly clear image in our minds of the funeral procession bearing the transformed Araxarathen and her faithful lover:

> And forto kepe in remembrance,
> This faire ymage mayden liche
> With compaignie noble and riche
> With torche and gret sollempnite
> To Salamyne the Cite
> Thei lede. . . .

> This ilke ymage as for miracle
> Was set upon an hyh pinacle,
> That alle men it mihte knowe,
> And under that thei maden lowe
> A tumbe riche for the nones
> Of marbre and ek of jaspre stones.
>
> (IV.3648–53, 61–66)

Set against the plainness of the rest of the story, the portrait of the funeral party stands out sharply. As Burrow notes, the effect of such spare pointing may be like that of the sudden close-up in films.[35] But the effect is not simply a manner; it has its meaning for the tale, too. When the reader who keeps this tale "in remembrance" pictures later in his mind's eye the funeral procession, he will also see the marble tombstone, "the lettres graven in a table / Of marbre" (IV.3672–73): "He was to neysshe and sche to hard" (IV.3681). Here Gower goes beyond the story's literal warning against despair as a branch of sloth and guides us toward the more general value of "mesure" or moderation in love, a value that Amans finally requires far more than he does the kind of encouragement to pursue his lady that the tale seems overtly to provide.

Even beyond this moral recommendation, however, the hardness of Araxarathen (or Anaxarete, as she is called in Ovid) had received a spiritualized interpretation at the hands of medieval mythographers, which also stands in opposition to the tale's moral in its present context and which has implications for the grace and love to which Amans must finally give himself over. In the interpretations made by the *Ovide moralisé* and Pierre Bersuire's *Ovidius moralizatus*, Anaxarete becomes a type of the soul who rejects Christ's love, her punishment the hardness of heart which is its lot.[36] Of the three possible readings of the tale—the courtly, the moral, and the spiritual—Genius's is clearly the most limited and the least appropriate to Amans's serious psychic and spiritual needs.

Similarly, we remember, because it is highly pointed, the speech of Thisbe over Pyramus's body, added by Gower to Ovid's rendition of this tale (*Metamorphoses*, IV.55–166), a speech that makes us contemplate the recklessness of those who singlemindedly pursue worldly pleasure and the fate they must suffer in the jaws of the lion (glossed as the devil by the *Ovide moralisé*).[37] "Helas," complains Thisbe to Venus, "why do ye with ous so? / Ye sette oure herte bothe afyre, / And maden ous such thing desire / Wherof that we no skile cowthe" (III.1472–75). What is made poetically significant in this tale, then, is not its admonition against foolhaste in love, Genius's moral—or even the more general warning against "impetuosity" offered by the Latin marginalia—but rather its foreshadowing, as Foster points out, of "the renunciation of love which even Genius finally advises."[38]

The tale "Canace and Machaire," likewise, is mentioned rather frequently in Gower criticism not only because Chaucer inveighs against it in the Prologue to "The Man of Law's Tale," but also because it seems so strange an exemplum against wrath. Indeed, Ovid's main purpose in telling this tale, through Canace's epistle in *Heroides* XI, had been to memorialize King Eolus's horrible wrath, and Gower rightly picks up on details in the Latin poet's telling that emphasize this aspect of the story. But he adds some of his own too, and the additions work primarily to elucidate, though not explicitly to condemn, the emotions and motives of the young, incestuous lovers:

> And so it fell hem ate laste,
> That this Machaire with Canace
> Whan thei were in a prive place,
> Cupide bade hem ferst to kesse. . . .
> And as the blinde an other ledeth
> And til thei falle nothing dredeth,
> Riht so thei hadde non insihte. . . .
> So that thei felle upon the chance
> Where witt hath lore his remembrance.
> (III.166–69, 179–81, 187–88)

We never feel that these innocent lovers have deserved their punishment—indeed, Gower uniformly enhances our sympathy for them[39] —but we do come to suspect that one of the poet's purposes in the tale has been to make *us* prudent as Canace and Machaire were not, to effect in us a union of "witt" and "remembrance." Finally the reader comes upon that terrible scene—perhaps the most intensely realized and horrifying touch added by Gower to any story in the entire *Confessio*—dominated by the image of Canace's baby tumbling from her lap after she has committed suicide, "And for the blod was hot and warm, / He basketh him aboute thrinne" (III.314–15). This image will cause the attentive reader to think not only of the unfortunate effects of ire; he will also see here a picture of fertile, productive sexuality gone wrong, a picture of desire unbridled by reason—as the wording of the Latin marginal gloss betrays, "intolerabilis concupiscentia,"[40] like Amans's desire itself.

In essence, the level of pointed detail in these stories is consistent with the high medieval theory of poetic imagery examined in Chapter 1. This theory held that the sensuous image had specific moral value as it was able to raise the soul through its contemplation to an understanding of disembodied truth. The images in Gower's tales, thus, are not neutral, but are placed there to accommodate the weakness of man's sensual nature and are intended for meditation, intended for the soul that wishes to rise through the natural order of cognition to God. Works of art, including those "olde bokes" that Gower cherishes so much as examples for his own writing, contribute to the poet's cultural as well as his personal memory—an important word for this work—providing images that can be used for his countrymen's edification. By giving these new application, the *Confessio Amantis* thus becomes a kind of *ars memorandi*, an arrangement of visual images not simply for the delight of the age, but also for its instruction.[41] As they will ultimately be remembered, these images become part of a nexus of themes and images that transcend their limited applications and acquire more profoundly moral and spiritual meanings. The reader at last will understand them not primarily as they exemplify the seven sins of courtly love, but as they are embedded within the larger pattern of Christian values.[42]

Gower's attention to this larger pattern can be demonstrated by a discussion of certain images of central importance to the poet in his exposition of love, which he repeats in a variety of contexts until they acquire their fullness of meaning. In a given instance, these images may or may not work to reinforce a tale's stated moral, but the gloss on any tale will never provide the whole context for their understanding. As the *Confessio* works to expound a social and political philosophy and to present a model of kingship for young Richard II, for example, Gower keeps before our eyes the image of a king who experiences a profound fellowship with his subjects and who, through his humility, is thus better able to rule. Such kings appear everywhere in the poem, providing corrective counterparts to wicked kings like Eolus. Nebuchadnezzar himself is one, as are Constantin and Appollinus. So is the king in the tale "The Three Questions," at least for that memorable moment when he looks in the face of the humble maiden, his future wife, who has answered his curious "demandes" and at last understands "reson" (I.3322). In a parallel "demande tale" in Book VII, the answer itself becomes the mnemonic when Zorobabel responds to the question asked in the tale "King, Wine, Woman and Truth" (VII.1783–1984). Here Gower departs from his primary biblical source in drawing the hierarchy of these four goods to point a new lesson in right rule: kings—not wine, as in the source—are weakest in power, exceeded in strength by both wine and women, but above all else, surpassed by truth.[43]

Like the king's humility, Cupid's arrow lodged in a lover's heart also becomes an object for our repeated meditation. It consistently works to call to mind ill-timed or unregulated passion, but neither Genius nor the Lover sees this clearly until Cupid removes his dart from Amans's heart in Book VIII.[44] In the rather plainly told "Phebus and Daphne" (III.1685–1720), for example, the most strikingly pointed passage is the one which describes the fiery gold dart that lodges in Phebus's heart as it contrasts with the arrow of cold lead in Daphne's and which points the difference in the arrows' effects:

> And thus Phebus in love brenneth,
> And in his haste aboute renneth,
> To loke if that he mihte winne;
> Bot he was evere to beginne,
> For evere awei fro him sche fledde,
> So that he nevere his love spedde.   (III.1707–12)

The reader cannot fail to note the parallel between Phebus, who is going to "failen of his wille" (I.1720), and Amans, who fares likewise. But though the story is intended by Genius only as a warning against the sin of foolhaste as it hinders success in romantic love (III.1721–28), Phebus's failure must finally be seen by reader and Lover in its largest moral context. This re-visioning will occur as the moral frame that takes precedence over the frame of the courtly sins comes increasingly to govern our response to such images as the dart of love. Recognizing that this is the case can help make sense of the somewhat puzzling tale "Eneas and Dido" (IV.77–146), used by Genius to caution against the kind of sloth practiced by Eneas when he deserted Dido.

Two traditions in interpreting this story existed in the Middle Ages, one emphasizing Aeneas's falseheartedness in leaving Dido, the other his virtue in traveling onward toward his destiny. The first—in medieval texts often laced with irony—may be called the

Ovidian, the second the Virgilian approach. Adopting the tone of Ovid's *Heroides* rather than of the *Aeneid*, Jean de Meun follows the first tradition by relating the story in order to condemn Aeneas's treachery,[45] even though he relates it in the voice of the Old Woman, who may be misappropriating the story as a measure of her own limitations. Chaucer also seems more intrigued by the value of love than of imperialism. Indeed, the degree of irony in Chaucer's tone is more difficult to locate as he follows Jean's Ovidian approach, first in *The House of Fame*, as L. B. Hall has shown, with some ambivalence about the character of Aeneas, then in *The Legend of Good Women*, where he ultimately resolves his ambivalence in Dido's favor, unequivocally stressing Aeneas's falseness.[46]

On the other hand, for the twelfth-century *Aeneid* commentator, Dido, not Aeneas, had been the vicious one. In that commentary, she had come to represent the soul's natural concupiscence. Aeneas's renunciation of her was a part of his spirit's laudable journey upward to God.[47] Given the ending of the *Confessio*, Gower would seem to be more sympathetic to this spiritualized approach. In the *Vox Clamantis*, Gower had warned knights against "battles" of love, in which women with their "silly love" entrap men and keep them from higher duties.[48] Indeed, if the actual telling of the tale in the *Confessio* works to reinforce either interpretive tradition, it must be this second, Christian one, rather than the first, more courtly and sentimental, approach. For example, Gower's presentation of the tale confuses the Ovidian narrative with the Virgilian moralization, thus shifting the tale's moral focus by renaming Aeneas's treachery "lachesce." Any competent reader would have known that when moralists called Aeneas slothful, it was for hesitating to pursue his true destiny, not for neglecting passion or courtesy to Dido.

But Gower provides an even more important sign to his reader of the irony in this tale: the dominant image, a totally original touch found to my knowledge in no other redaction of the episode, recalls that significant arrow of disruptive passion. This moment of detailed pointing occurs just where Gower borrows most from the epistolary form of the *Heroides*, in the letter Dido sends to her lover threatening that if he tarries she will become like the swan who lost her mate:

> For sorwe a fethere into hire brain
> She schof and hath hireselve slain;
> As king Menander in a lay

> The sothe hath founde, wher sche lay
> Sprantlende with hire wynges tweie,
> As sche which scholde thanne deie
> For love of him which was hire make.   (IV.107–13)

The fact that it pierces the brain, not the heart, and is aimed by Dido herself simply makes the sign more explicit. Like other images of its kind, this feathery dart is a symptom of "loves lawe out of rule" and casts its influence over the rest of the tale, seriously complicating our judgment of Dido, not to mention Genius and Amans.

Similarly, significant images of old age and death recur throughout the work—a recurring *memento mori* with clear implications for the aging Amans, whether or not the reader at this point has picked up on the clues that he is old.[49] The tale "The Trump of Death" is dominated by such images; the trump itself is one, as are the two pilgrims

> of so gret age,
> That lich unto a dreie ymage
> Thei weren pale and fade hewed,
> And as a bussh which is besnewed,
> Here berdes weren hore and whyte;
> Ther was of kinde bot a lite,
> That thei ne semen fulli dede.   (I.2041–47)

An illumination in a late-fifteenth-century manuscript indicates the power of this scene by juxtaposing a picture of the king, tenderly kissing an aged pilgrim on the mouth, with his courtiers, who laugh and converse to the side, ignorant of the significance of his act.[50]

This passage forms part of a new context for understanding the highly pointed description of the loathly lady in "The Tale of Florent" less than four hundred lines earlier (I.1678–91)—far more realistic and loathlier than anything in Chaucer's version of this story told by the Wife of Bath. Both "The Trump of Death" and "Florent" are constructed so as specifically to contrast an anxiety about reputation with an inner conformity to truth, alternatives here embodied in the images of pilgrim and courtiers: the king's brother shows such anxiety by criticizing his sovereign for dishonoring his "oghne name" (I.2096), and Florent is torn between his promise to marry the loathly lady and his desire to avoid public disgrace, perhaps even by concealing her on an island "wher that noman hire scholde knowe, / Til sche with deth were overthrowe" (I.1579–80). By putting this choice into relief, "The Trump of Death" helps us retrospectively to understand the final victory in Florent's obedience to an inner bond (I.1798), when he turned over in bed to embrace his new wife and the relationship of this fidelity to acquiescence in the face of age; likewise we appreciate more deeply the intervening figure of Capaneus, hit by lightning in the fullness of his pride (I.1980–2006). In the manuscript mentioned earlier, a picture of Capaneus struck down appears on the same leaf as the honest king humbling himself to the pilgrim, as though the two somehow formed a pair. They both exemplify the pride that grows from not fully comprehending one's human limits, indeed of not coming to terms with mortality, a sin that is not just a subject of this book, but of the entire *Confessio*.

An odd twist on the theme of age and deterioration is provided, this time by the Lover himself, in Book IV when he likens his condition to that of a green tree. No use counseling restraint in love, he tells Genius; that would be like cutting off my root. He will not realize the inapplicability of the image until Book VIII: "The Wynter wol no Somer knowe, / The grene lef is overthrowe" (VIII.2853–54). One might say the Lover begins by being remarkably out of touch with reality. The lesson suggested by the haunting pictures of old age scattered throughout the work will attain full significance only as Amans contemplates the image of his own age in Venus's mirror in Book VIII, in a passage that reminds us of the portrait of the pilgrims quoted from Book I:

> Wherinne anon myn hertes yhe
> I caste, and sih my colour fade,
> Myn yhen dymme and al unglade,
> Mi chiekes thinne, and al my face
> With Elde I myhte se deface,
> So riveled and so wo besein,
> That ther was nothing full ne plein,
> I syh also myn heres hore.
> Mi will was tho to se nomore.   (VIII.2824–32)

But despite his revulsion at this point, Amans is able to progress in Book VIII beyond the stark recognition of his age to a deeper understanding of it. He does this, in fact, by drawing on another pattern of imagery, embedded in the scientific lore provided by Genius in Book VII. The passing of the different months associated with astrological signs becomes for Amans an image of time, and he thus feels himself into the seasonal rhythms of generation and decay.

In a sense, then, Genius as he represents *ingenium*—or that capacity of imagination to invent appropriate images—functions perfectly, and perfectly in character. As we saw earlier, *ingenium* in the medieval rhetorical tradition was the capacity for inventing images that could be an accurate representation of ineffable ideas. By "pointing" with memorable images just those moments in each tale that have the potential to become spiritually meaningful for the Lover, Genius is what he should be: he is Amans's inspired imagination, his instinct for the good if only he will attend properly to it. Genius in Jean de Meun's *Rose* had played this role to the Dreamer in that poem also when he described the Beau Parc. But as we saw there, it is not enough to have a talented, informed imagination. If one is going to use the world of sensuous nature or the world of delightful fictions correctly, one needs as well a faculty to determine the abstract truth of those worlds. And that determination cannot be made by imagination or *ingenium*, but only by reason.

Genius's superficial interpretations of many stories in the *Confessio* suggest that we may expect too much of him. He is an embodiment of the Lover's imagination, not his reason, and since abstraction occurs only in the reference of what the soul apprehends to reason's analysis, the guidance of Genius, however prolonged, will not serve to raise the Lover from the literal and practical ethics of courtship to a consideration of the sublime and transcendent love offered to man by God. The "expert confessor" in the penitential handbooks was supposed to be sympathetic and of course learned, but above all "spiritually minded—free from the cares and desires of the flesh."[51] Given his traditional procreative and tutelary roles, Genius is a markedly poor choice for spiritual mentor; the limits of his guidance point to the problems any man experiences when he orders his soul to the self-indulgent fantasies of imagination. Genius's incompetence as moralizer thus forms part of Gower's larger poetic intention. Although that intention may not redeem the sheer magnitude of the poem for us, Gower's supreme skill and control over artistic form is indicated by Genius's subtle growth as a character. As the poem progresses, Genius begins to come up against the limits of his own exempla, an experience that serves to make him increasingly aware of the boundaries of his capacity as teacher, healer, and priest, and that prepares the way for real growth in the narrator's soul.

Amans's growth as it is reflected in his relationship to his mentor is modeled in important ways on that of other dreamers from the vision tradition. In both the *De planctu* and the *Roman de la rose*, we have seen that a significant moment of impasse occurs when the Dreamer questions his allegorical guide on the nature of the pagan gods and pagan mythology. Such a moment occurred in Alain's poem when the Dreamer chastised Natura for bemoaning mankind's sins when the gods, as they were treated by the poets, were guilty of even worse moral transgressions. Natura, in answer to his complaint, had pointed the way toward an acceptably philosophical reading of pagan literature, toward a reading that looks beyond literal to symbolic meaning. The Dreamer comes to internalize this lesson and advances because of it. A similar objection underlies the protest made by the Dreamer in Jean de Meun's version of the *Rose* when he finds distasteful the language Reason had employed in discussing Jupiter's castration of Saturn, though Reason's rejoinder to his objection, which essentially resembles Natura's, fails in this case to make a significant impression on the *Rose* Lover. Amans in the *Confessio* fits into the pattern: he seems troubled by a doubt parallel to that experienced by these earlier dreamers and, as we will see, is ultimately striving after an attitude like one the dreamers' guides in previous visions were trying to instill in *their* charges.

After the tale "Vulcan and Venus" in Book V—surely that pagan story which shows the gods in the most compromising of positions—the Lover questions the credibility of a polytheistic mythology; "for there is bot o god of alle, / Which is the lord of hevene and helle" (V.732–33). Genius responds with a lengthy disquisition on the history of religions that has frequently been criticized for its digressiveness but that serves a very precise function in the poem. It ultimately brings Genius and the Lover he guides up against the tacit contradiction between Christian moral truth and the "religion" of courtly love. It asks them to look beyond the literal meaning of pagan *integumenta* to a higher meaning. The crucial moment occurs when the Lover asks Genius why, in his discussion of Greek and Roman gods, he has not mentioned that god and goddess whose emissary he is supposed to be. "For schame," he answers, "Be cause I am here oghne Prest" (V.1382–83).

As Russell Peck points out, Genius is never the same after this moment: "The earthy priest . . . becomes more reflective."[52] James Foster has indicated the way that this change is mirrored in the kinds of tales that Genius tells from this time on and in the kinds of glosses he provides on them:

> Before Genius has recognized that the service of the illegitimate Venus and love *paramours* is idolatry, he does not perceive the warnings against their moral and spiritual dangers which the mythographers saw in the tales. His exegesis omits those warnings and focuses upon those portions of the conventional interpretations which, taken out of context, constitute secular and practical advice about maintaining an amorous intrigue. After Genius' conversion, the character of the exegesis changes. Genius usually perceives the full moral significance conventionally given the tales.[53]

Although, as Foster goes on, the full spiritual significance of the tales continues to escape the priest, he does become capable from this point on "of leading the Lover to rightful earthly love," which as natural inclination is Genius's proper function. "The Tale of Tereus" becomes, as it was for the mythographers, an example of "ravine."[54] The tale "Ulysses and Telegonus" in Book VI of the *Confessio* represents what it also did in conventional moralizations: the connection of libido with the black arts and the inability of human wrongdoing to subvert the providential plan.[55]

But many of these later stories, for all their newfound sentence, continue to stress as well images and themes that go beyond the standard moralizations. The sorcery that both Ulysses and Nectanabus practice is condemned only partly in and of itself—and not really for its connection with the sin of gluttony warned against in Book VI— but mostly because it is a false art. This meaning is developed slightly by Genius in Book VII when he makes sorcery a false use of the word (VII.1558–71). Indeed, the scenes and images we remember most vividly from these two tales—Nectanabus, for example, changing from dragon to ram to seductive lover—are of men manipulating images not to convey the truth but to pervert it for lustful gain. These are images that accumulate their full meaning only in Book VIII of the poem, in the tale "Apollonius of Tyre," for example. Here the physician Cerymon, Appollinus's daughter Thaise, and Appollinus himself realize the possibility first embodied in Arion, whose forgotten art had been described in the Prologue. His was an art that healed rather than destroyed, an art based on "mesure" and "acord" that could bring "the Hinde in pes with the Leoun" (Prol. 1059), the soul in peace with itself. The unity that may exist between the words and cadences of a song or poem and the Word of God is finally affirmed last and most powerfully in the kind of prayerful art recommended by the poem's conclusion.

Visionary Success

Beyond their recognition of the limits of Venus's service, a recognition substantially achieved in Book V, Genius and Amans require a deeper understanding of the way that the world is organized to reflect God's plan. It is not enough to be acquainted with doctrine. The real ascent to God, we have seen, must begin in the world, must be the soul's reaching between the realms of heaven and earth, though as the headnote to Book VII indicates, such knowledge is "doctrine" in that it must be taught. The philosophical vision poem had always sought to dramatize this reaching and teaching. And this is what Book VII, no more digressive structurally than Book V, attempts to do: to reorient Amans in the divisions and hierarchies of the created world, to make the world a *speculum* that can ultimately reflect for Amans something like divine love. True, policy is an important part of this book, which sets forth Aristotle's guidance of the young King Alexander, but it is policy firmly rooted in an understanding of the way that earthly governance functions as part of the system that is God's plan for the world. It is policy as a response to the soul's demand for accord between earth and heaven.

Amans's inquiry precipitates this discussion. At the end of Book VI, he really is much like the typical protagonist in the philosophical vision, beginning to ask for the first time the right questions, exhibiting his increasing rational strength by his request for a different kind of healing or lore. I heard you say something about Aristotle's teachings of Alexander, he remarks, "wherof min herte sore longeth / To wite what it wolde mene" (VI.2414–15). Genius provides Amans in Book VII sufficient knowledge of the organization of natural systems and their ordained hierarchies for Amans to cast off the service of illegitimate love, though his efforts do not immediately have their effect—for as the Lover says, "The tales sounen in myn Ere, / Bot yit myn herte is elleswhere" (VII.5411–12). Even this late in the poem, he repeats what he has affirmed many times throughout the work:

> Suche lore couthe I nevere gete,
> Which myhte make me foryete

> O point, bot if so were I slepte,
> That I my tydes ay ne kepte
> To thenke of love and of his lawe. (VII. 5415–19)

His *genius* is making progress, though, and by the end of the poem, Amans advances in just the way he had claimed would be impossible for him; it is even, as he has humorously predicted, a change that comes while he sleeps. When Venus asks him near the end of Book VIII what love is, he does not know, "so ferr it was out of mi thoght, / Riht as it hadde nevere be" (VIII.2876–77). What brings about this major change in the Lover's psyche? Significantly, it is a vision—in fact, a kind of philosophical vision in miniature, an epitome of the kind of poetry we have been studying. As a framing device, simply because it involves falling asleep and waking, the dream contains the literal conditions for its own closure and hence may be useful for creating in the reader a feeling of ending. But this dream does much more. Its placement at the poem's end to signal the conversion of a sentiment that was narrow, unproductive, and literal minded in its origins to one that is charitable, expansive, and spiritually fruitful indicates clearly the way that the form works for Gower, as it had for the other writers we have studied, to raise the earthly to the divine.

Up until this point in the poem, it seemed that we had wandered into a kind of philosophical vision poem gone haywire. All the traditional elements of the subgenre had raised our expectations that some sort of transformation in the Lover was about to occur. But his guides were all wrong. Where was the figure of Reason? Venus and Cupid certainly could not qualify, and Genius as imagination was also limited in his outlook. No matter how completely his powers were prepared to convey revelation, alone they could not discover it. Moreover, where was the device of the vision, within which the narrator might be led to truth? The answer and the proper guidance comes—and the literal vision too—but not until the Lover's imagination, his *genius*, has been completely prepared for it, not until near the end of Book VIII, when his complaint indicates new readiness for cure. At long last he will accept either salve for the arrow through his heart or its removal. The second, more rigorous, alternative is, in fact, stated first (VIII.2289–90). His original complaint had indicated no such poetic or psychic organization. Indeed, the delay heightens our desire for this conclusion, which satisfies us completely by its enormous self-consciousness and by the thoroughness with which it meets the conventional demands of the subgenre.

Around VIII.2183—with wonderful generic playfulness—the poem seems to make a new beginning. The Lover's rhyme royal complaint marks the start of a new movement, a revision of the previous complaint in Book I and, we might add, of the complaints in earlier poems. In a remarkable inversion of Alain's and Jean's visions, it is Amans—rather than Nature or Venus—who complains about disorder in creation. Only *he*—only this man—is denied full participation in nature, denied the upward swing on Fortune's wheel:

> Ferst to Nature if that I me compleigne,
> Ther finde I hou that every creature
> Som time ayer hath love in his demeine,
> So that the litel wrenne in his mesure
> Hath yit of kinde a love under his cure;
> And I bot on desire, of which I misse:
> And thus, bot I, hath every kinde his blisse.
> (VIII.2224–30)

Continuing this ludic inversion, the Lover sends his message via Genius to Venus. She descends in the same playful mode, "as it were halvinge a game" (VIII.2319), asks the Lover his name, and proceeds to give him remembrance, gently but realistically, of his age and state in life:

> Mi Sone, if thou be well bethoght,
> This toucheth thee; foryet it noght:
> The thing is torned into was;
> That which was whilom grene gras,
> Is welked hey at time now.
> Forthi mi conseil is that thou
> Remembre wel hou thou art old. (VIII.2433–39)

This realization causes the Lover to fall upon the ground in a swoon, during which he dreams that he sees a spectacle of lovers, all of whom are drawn from Genius's stories in the previous seven books; a whole "lusty route" of lovers parade before him, some virtuous, some sinful, some young, some old. They look at him lying on the ground and understand his plight as little as he understands theirs. This part of the swoon is a kind of recapitulation of all that has gone before in the poem. It represents the first movement of the conventional philosophical vision: the presentation of images to the imagination.

In the last part of the swoon, from VIII.2792 through Amans's waking at VIII.2857, the dream moves successfully to its conventional conclusion as the first seven books of the poem had not done. Here the Lover is finally provided with the reason and psychological maturity to give to those images that had made up the *materia* of the work their rightful interpretation. Here they reach finally their fullness of meaning. Cupid removes the lancegay from the Dreamer's heart. Venus seems to have developed too, along with Genius. As Amans's capacity to love, she is now the goddess of honest love, not love *paramours*, *Venus caelestis* rather than *Venus scelesta*. In her new role, she is a healer of the Dreamer's body and soul. With a cold ointment, she anoints his wounded heart, his temples, and his loins. Her action signals that his "Reins" (or loins), seat of lust and fleshly desire, no longer have improper precedence in the Lover's moral or physical make-up.[56] His heart, no longer wounded by love, becomes properly the seat of magnanimity and the ruler of the other bodily organs, a function for this organ that Gower himself had suggested earlier (VII.463–74). And his temple, the locus of imagination or *ingenium*, also healed, is submissive finally in the right way to reason.

In the mirror then given to him by Venus—the traditional *speculum* of the vision—the Lover sees at long last truly. In this penitential inner mirror, he confronts an accurate image of himself for the first time. His imagination has received the proper preparation, and it takes heed of what it finds there (VIII.2820–33). The Lover is old, his "colour fade," his "heres hore," his passion as unnatural and infertile as Canace and Machaire's was perverse and fertile. In the lines that follow, Amans names the other faculties he has recovered: his remembrance and his reason. He knows his position in nature and awakens from his swoon (VIII.2834–59). In VIII.2860, he begins to call home his wits, both inner and outer:

> And whan Resoun it herde sein
> That loves rage was aweie,
> He cam to me the rihte weie,
> And hath remued the sotie

> Of thilke unwise fantasie,
> Wherof that I was wont to pleigne,
> So that of thilke fyri peine
> I was mad sobre and hol ynowh. (VIII.2862–69)

The Lover's "hertes wit," his inner genius, is ordered now to reason; no longer necessary, Genius and Venus take their leave. Memory too is cured, for at last Amans cannot even remember what earthly love or lust is; he is like Dante, having crossed the River Lethe, who is no longer cognizant of the part of love that is sin. In VIII.2904–2908, when she gives him the black beads of penance and calls him for the second time by name, Venus also brings to a close his experience of visionary or liminal passage. She gives him an identity—or perhaps more accurately, redefines the one he had. Amans has learned the deepest meaning of the question, "Who are you?"—a question that has preoccupied seekers after self-knowledge from Boethius to Dante, who also, as we have seen, had been addressed by name only at the end of his natural ascent in the *Purgatorio*. In the return to spiritual health, the Lover's journey through the faculties has reached its expected conclusion in a dream. He will think hereafter only of that heavenly love: "thilke love which that is / Withinne a mannes herte affermed, / And stant of charite confermed" (VIII.3162–65).

Just as absolution—such as Genius administers in Book VIII to Amans—was considered the form that perfected the matter of penitence, just as this Book's number, Eight, raises a series to eternity, so finally the conclusion of the *Confessio Amantis* transcends all confusions. The poem begins as an ambitious experiment—as a shuffling together of some of the most popular genres of the age—some old, some new, some self-consciously fictional and literary, some not. Part of the poem's encyclopedic intention becomes to comprehend the great variety of experience by rendering the variety of current literary forms in all their complexity and confusion. But finally it gives to the multiplicity of tales and their contradictory interpretations a new meaning by subordinating them to the traditional framework of the philosophical vision, a framework that took as its basic purpose the ordering of experience to significance, of image to abstraction. As C. S. Lewis says so aptly of the vision passage in Book VIII, "The handling of this quiet close is so beautiful, and the thing itself so wisely and beautifully imagined that it constitutes Gower's highest claim as a poet; and that not only for its content, but for its artistry."[57]

Gower and Dante

I have made a comparison of Gower and Dante several times in the foregoing discussion. That likeness may seem at first strained. Though Gower's borrowings from Boethius, Alain de Lille, and Jean de Meun are relatively obvious, it is not usually suggested that Gower and Dante had anything significant in common or that Gower may have had the *Commedia* in mind when writing the *Confessio Amantis*.[58] Just this, however, is what I wish to argue now. Though Gower's characteristic tone as a writer differs sharply from Dante's, there are a number of things that the two poets share, both superficial and profound: for one, the desire to compose in the subgenre of philosophical vision; that is, to write a poem about human growth, a first-person account of an individual's liminal encounter with a guide who teaches him to replace a static, confined definition of the self with a liberated, expansive one. Both wished also to write poems that move beyond the particular, the microcosmic, to engage an entire society in the challenge that individual growth presents. Attention to this social challenge lies very near the surface for both Gower and Dante; neither could ignore for any length of time the poet's role as prophet. Nor could either keep submerged for long a powerful concern with the poet's role in general. Gower, like Dante, had a deep interest in language and poetic forms. Like Dante, he was revered in the years that followed his death as a refiner of his native tongue. And like Dante, he composed in more than one language while at the same time striving self-consciously to make of his works a single, comprehensible corpus.

In addition, Gower has a number of specific structural devices in common with Dante. Both poets trace the corruption of the individual and the different levels of his society explicitly to a misguided love. Both Dante's pilgrim and Amans have as their basic tasks the redefinition and redirection of a love that was earthly and romantic in its inception. More specifically, though, the idea of curing this failure within a framework that combined the penitential and visionary traditions was Dante's first. The pilgrim in the *Purgatorio*, like

Amans, must be absolved of each of the seven deadly sins. Indeed, the notion of using exempla, initially to show the kind of behavior to avoid, but finally to embody positive ideals, may have been taken from this canticle. (See, for example, the tales "The Three Questions" and "Constantine and Sylvester," which close the first two books of the *Confessio*, or the tale "Apollonius of Tyre," last in the entire work.) So might Gower have taken from Dante the idea of using dreams to mark stages of spiritual growth in a poem that is not technically a dream vision itself—though he might have gotten such an idea from a source like the *Anticlaudianus*. I think, though, that the number of important similarities, taken along with Gower's own reference to Dante as example of honest poet and social critic (VII.2329–39; 1st rec.), argue for a direct and conscious imitation of Dante on Gower's part, or at the very least, suggests some awareness of a relationship between what he was doing and what the Italian poet had done. But whether or not such influence can finally be proved, the comparison of Dante and Gower is instructive for another reason as well, for what it can show us about the moral and speculative philosophies that inform the works of these two authors.

C. S. Lewis writes, "Gower is not enough of a philosopher to achieve, like Dante, or even to attempt, like Alanus, any reconciliation between the claims of his two worlds."[59] This is a common criticism of the poet, echoed more recently by Michael Cherniss. Cherniss complains that although, by the end of the poem, "Venus, Nature, Genius and Reason are in harmony in *honeste*, married love, and in the rejection of earthly love . . . this is no final reconciliation of the forces and concepts these figures represent."[60] I think just the opposite: the conclusion does represent a reconciliation of exactly these forces—of celestial and earthly love, of reason and imagination—however oblique and tentative it may seem when compared with other syntheses. Cherniss protests that the reconciliation cannot be made for every conceivable instance of earthly love, but this objection could be raised about any work—the *Commedia*, for example—that understands the allure of life in this world by showing how it can be transformed within one individual's experience to something higher. It is unfair to condemn Gower for not accomplishing a broader task than the one he set for himself.

Of course, there is a residue of doubt about this reconciliation that has taken so long to reach; its final achievement is quiet, playful, ambiguous, more an eschewal of the value of the world than an embrace of it. In this poem, the dream is truly framed by—and hence qualified by—a worldly, social perspective. The narrator's experience does not end with the dream, but continues past it, just as the Lover's quest is introduced by the voice of the Prologue. As it had for Jean de Meun, the distance provided by such narrative layering and by a comic perspective on the Lover and his Genius suggests that Gower's affirmation of the traditional world view is somewhat more problematic than Dante's. It must be allowed that such modulations of tone do assert themselves as part of the poem's "meaning." But also like Jean, Gower does finally suggest that the world is at least the bottom rung on the ladder to truth. He joins these other poets in working within a framework of continuous change, finding in normal experience as interpreted by human reason the sufficient condition of knowledge and uprightness. As Lewis puts it, in this poem, "life itself manages the necessary palinode."[61] It is through real experience that we grow, as living men and women that we are transformed.

Twenty-five years ago R. H. Green recognized a need for the kind of study in which I have been engaged, a study of the "convention by which the mediaeval poet makes of himself the dreamer or narrator of a fictional vision, and the variety and subtlety of poetic effects which this practice made possible." He suggested that, among other things, it would show "that Dante's fictional method, his serious moral purpose, his graceful exploitation of Scriptural and classical traditions, are not unusual as allegorical method, however unusual the quality of his performance is found to be."[62] So far, this study of philosophical vision poets from Boethius to Alain, even to the time of Gower, has, in fact, borne out Green's projections. But there is a limit to how far generalizations made chiefly about twelfth- and thirteenth-century poems can be extended into the fourteenth century.

With Gower, we have completed a full circle in our investigation of the philosophical vision poem. Though writers of vision poetry did not exactly falter in their moral or philosophical purpose, with the arrival of discontinuous change in the medieval world view a new hesitation about the form's teleology did develop. Among English vision poets, Gower is the last to use the form as a way toward the essentially realist position that had informed the blending of traditions in the *Commedia*. He is the last, that is, to use it to make the kind of "mythic" statement that Alain had made in defense of the continuity of God and nature, the last to find in nature an accurate reflection of divinity. I say this despite the fact that, compared to Dante's pilgrim, Amans is a kind of low comic hero. As a visionary, the character John Gower, like Chaucer's Geffrey in *The House of Fame* and—even earlier—certain dreamers in the French tradition, falls considerably short of the heroic. The visionary's heroism had always been hedged against the greater authority of his guide—confrontations with higher powers always thwart heroism—so it is not just for this reason that Amans and other fourteenth-century dreamers lack grandeur.[63] The stages of their visionary growth are simply not articulated with the kind of confidence in final solutions necessary for high seriousness. Gower, then, does show the signs of the times.

Indeed, for Gower, romantic, erotic love can never mature to the point that, as in Dante or Alain, it can stand for a nobler, spiritual love. The courtly perspective can only be criticized, not made over into something else. Even so, the fact that the Lover is able to use the acceptance of his sexual impotence to progress from a partial understanding of love to a more complete one suggests Gower's deepest similarity to Dante, his fundamentally conservative epistemological position in the poem. Gower's Amans, for all his diminished stature, all his essential irony, finally accomplishes the conventional, gradualistic journey toward truth, moving from the world of creatures to their Creator, through experience to a new understanding of authority. Of course, other fourteenth-century dreamers—the Jeweler in *Pearl*, Will in *Piers Plowman*, for example—are ultimately educated in some way too by their visionary experiences. But their visions are meaningful and important to us not for the way their narrators abstract the truth from images, but rather for the thoroughgoing self-consciousness with which they extend the genre to new ways of viewing experience, making it work to represent new formulations of man's relationship to God and of the relationship between ordained and absolute truth. The means by which these mental wanderers proceed, not to mention the problems that remain for them even after vision, are much different from Amans's methods and hesitations, as I hope to show more fully in another book.

For our present purposes, three brief comparisons must suffice. To start, Guillaume de Deguileville's substitution of Grâce-Dieu for Reason as dream guide can stand as an emblem of the sort of change that would be typical of the later Middle Ages as a whole, for modes of knowing based on intuition, illumination, and grace were coming to dominate the high medieval theory of abstraction I described in Chapter 1. New theories of knowing, effectually nominalistic in their approach to reality, attacked the old models precisely in their assertion of reason's capacity to disengage universals from sense-mediated images.[64] And in this poem, while Reason and Nature are summoned to provide important lore, they also come to be chastised soundly by Grace, the real queen of the poem.[65] Consider as well how a similar change dominates Petrarch's *Secret*, where memorializing the truth is a "secret," individual matter; where dreaming is eschewed, sleep being instead a metaphor for the body's execrable weakness; where Augustine stands in for Truth; and where the narrator is continually admonished to distrust every earthly impulse, including his purest love for Laura. Finally, note the effect of the age on the structure of *Piers Plowman*: a kind of vision-in-little appears in Passus XI and XII remarkably like the central archetype of vision we have traced here. But though the Dreamer in this inner vision looks into the mirror of Middle Earth, sees the various kinds of creatures, and is instructed by Reason—all the essential elements of the philosophical vision—he lacks the proper sufferance for spiritual growth and so is rebuked by the appropriately named Imaginatif, whose lessons themselves remain opaque. Langland thus illustrates the crucial difference between using the classic vision as a framing or closural device, as Gower does, and as one of a number of models of ascent that work, as they do in *Piers Plowman*, to qualify and supplement each other. In short, God and nature were not wedded as peaceably in the fourteenth century as they had been in the twelfth.

And evaluated against such new developments, Gower displays at least qualified agreement with the kind of realist epistemology that had traditionally informed the philosophical vision poem, that the subgenre had in part evolved to protect. In fact, there are times when his philosophy as it can be inferred from the poem might even be characterized as extreme in its assessment of the material world as mirror of God and thus assumes quite strikingly the defensive position I have noted in the genre. The harmony between the concepts of Fortune and Providence, for example, is remarkable in the *Confessio*. Happy endings, or at least just ones, abound in Genius's tales. Boethius would never have argued, as Gower does in the Prologue, that virtue usually triumphs, that the good man commonly will first "winne worldes welthe / And afterward his soule helthe" (Prol. 1051–52). As a social reformer, Gower brings his speculative philosophy to bear on his moral one: he wants to take the world as it is, with all its faults and divisions, and where it fails, to make it over into a true mirror of God. This effort grows out of a basic optimism and faith in the possibilities of this life.[66] However often Gower mentions the blind goddess, Fortune is not really sightless in the *Confessio*. Each individual makes his own destiny, not just in the hereafter but *here* in the literal present:

> Of that the regnes be muable
> The man himself hath be coupable,
> Which of his propre governance
> Fortuneth al the worldes chance.   (Prol. 581–85)

In the view of art that the *Confessio Amantis* recommends, too, there is a share of Alain and Dante. Although as a moralist Genius leaves something to be desired, and so reminds us of Jean de Meun's doubts about the power and authority of the human artist, Genius seems to grow past his limits. Where he leaves a need, he also satisfies. Ultimately, as in the *De planctu* and the *Commedia*, the images provided as part of imagination's vision become sacramental; they are truly mediating images. As subjects for Amans's meditation— and indirectly our own—they are finally the means by which advance is made on the spiritual pilgrimage. Patrick Gallacher is absolutely right in *Love, the Word, and Mercury* when he argues for Gower's artistry in making the Word—creating, sacramental, self-defining— a poetic theme. Gower's concern extends past the Word in its scriptural, prayerful context, to all rhetoric, all words, biblical, poetic, conversational—although this should not make us think that the Word is thus the privileged subject of this poem. Such artistic self-awareness had been a characteristic of the vision poem for two centuries, and had worked, we have seen, to make a larger philosophical point too. The success of vision had also typically served, as it does here, to validate a certain divinely ordained poetic, for the images of vision from Macrobius onward had been analogous to poetic images.

Such analogies are here simply made explicit. Genius's teachings are not only like poetic images; they take the form of poetic images. His words are not only like pagan rhetoric; they imitate such rhetoric directly. Enlarging on these self-conscious identifications, at one point in his discussion of rhetoric in Book VII Genius overtly defines for us the ideal toward which the poet in his teachings and in his art has been reaching all along. Rhetoric or eloquence, he tells us, has a marvelous persuasive power. Therefore, it must be yoked to some sort of ethical vision to prevent the great deceit that may come otherwise:

> For whan the word to the conceipte
> Descordeth in so double a wise,
> Such Rethorique is to despise
> In every place, and forto drede.
> (VII.1554–57; see also Prol.113)

Indeed, this is just the sort of error toward which, benignly, Genius has been tending up to this point, just the sort of tension between verbal effect and conscious intention that has marred Genius's narrative method. But his error has been double: through Genius's practice throughout the *Confessio*, Gower has been offering a tacit criticism of courtly modes of poetry that enchant the hearers but that do not incline to moral virtue. At the same time, paradoxically, the effect of the pointing in Genius's tales has also frequently exceeded in morality the tale's conceit or intended significance. In a variety of ways, then, practice, effect, and intent have been out of balance; Gower's has been a poetry of self-division rather than moral and thematic unity.

But ultimately "word" and "conceipte" will come into accord, an accord that is God's greatest gift to man. In the following passage, Gower echoes a conventional sentiment, expressed also by Dante in the *De vulgari eloquentia*. As we have seen, it formed the philosophical basis of the poetics that dominated the twelfth and thirteenth centuries:

> Above alle erthli creatures
> The hihe makere of natures

> The word to man hath yove alone,
> So that the speche of his persone,
> Or forto lese or forto winne,
> The hertes thoght which is withinne
> Mai schewe, what it wolde mene. (VII.1507–12)

This accord comes most perfectly in prayer,[67] a fact that helps explain why Gower continued past the "heartfelt peace" of the Lover's "softe pas" homeward, where Lewis and others have wished that he had ended.[68] Instead, he concludes with a simple prayer to his God and to his age for a renewed harmony between fate and providence, between the rule of heaven and earth. Prayer is the purest though most artless art, thought in perfect consonance with deed and with divine intention, beyond indirection, beyond even rhetoric, as Gower himself indicates (VIII.3106–37).

I do not wish, however, to suggest that the tension between earthly and heavenly love makes no claim on the poet as he works toward a final resolution. It is this conflict, as we have seen, that gives that resolution its unique force and poignancy. If the last movement of the poem presents any difficulty, it is not, as in other works, the lack of an ending but of one or two endings too many, as though the final symphonic chord had to be sounded again and again. Twice Amans has to confront his "final ende" from Venus (VIII.2394, 2939). And after his prayer for the nation, in his farewell to reader and book, the poet bows again to the difficulty of his subject matter, twice determining to make no more of love (VIII.3143, 3154–55).[69] But in this gesture itself, there is a kind of simple, human directness which transcends the moral stridency of the *Vox Clamantis* or of the *Confessio*'s own Prologue, where Gower had discussed similar political issues; a directness which transcends even the artificiality of the tales offered by Genius throughout. There is nothing wrong with the art of Genius, at least as it had served to bring the Lover to terms with the human condition. But we have passed even beyond that art and the love it sought to treat; the poet now asks God simply, no longer as an earlier marginal note had indicated "quasi in persona aliorum,"[70] but in his own voice directly, for

> thilke love which that is
> Withinne a mannes herte affermed,
> And stant of charite confermed,
> Such love is goodly forto have,

> Such love mai the bodi save,
> Such love mai the soule amende,
> The hyhe god such love ous sende
> Forthwith the remenant of grace. (VIII.3162–69)

This is the kind of prayerful art with which the moral Gower ends, with which inevitably he had to end. The subtle transformation of one kind of love into another, of one kind of art into another too, constitutes Gower's most profound achievement as a poet and his own tentative fourteenth-century reconciliation of the claims of this world with those of the next.

For his own time, Gower drew upon the wisdom of an earlier age, when nature was a more trustworthy index of truth, when the world could be a real mirror of the Word. During years when Chaucer was turning away from the dream vision to combinations of genres that allowed him to focus more directly on the diversity of human experience, Gower was finding a new way to make the genre work to transform experience. Gower's statement of poetic purpose at the beginning of Book I was somewhat more modest than this aim:

> I may noght strecche up to the hevene
> Min hand, ne setten al in evene
> This world, which evere is in balance:
> It stant noght in my sufficance
> So grete thinges to compasse. (I.1–5)

In this deceptively simple formulation, the poet's hand rests suggestively between the rhyming word "hevene," which brings one line to a close, and "world," which begins another. The verses' syntax betrays their meaning. We saw in earlier chapters that the reach of a man's creative hand can have no more meaningful extension than this between heaven and earth. What looks at first, then, like a primarily moral treatise, engaged in providing practical advice for living well in the world, becomes finally something much more. Gower finally gives his reader a new awareness of the true spiritual *significatum* of this life, the true end of the spirit's journey for men who, as Rosemond Tuve puts it, "not only have moral responsibilities but belong to . . . a Kind beloved and sought and espoused and owing fidelity to, a loving Creator."[71] In his own way, by gently and humorously setting one soul "in evene," the vision poet in Gower points the way to transcendence on a grander scale.

REFERENCE MATTER

NOTES

Complete authors' names, titles, and publication data for the works cited in short form are given in the Works Cited, pp. 237–51. The following abbreviations appear in the Notes and the Works Cited.

CSEL *Corpus scriptorum ecclesiasticorum latinorum* (Vienna, 1866–)
PG   J.-P. Migne, *Patrologiae cursus completus, series graeca* (Paris, 1857–66)
PL   J.-P. Migne, *Patrologiae cursus completus, series latina* (Paris, 1844–64)

INTRODUCTION

1. Computed from charts in Dinzelbacher, *Vision und Visionsliteratur*, pp. 13–28.
2. Nolan, *Gothic Visionary Perspective*; Spearing, *Medieval Dream-Poetry*; Piehler, *Visionary Landscape*; Hieatt, *Realism of Dream Visions*; and Newman, "*Somnium*." Related studies include Payne, *Chaucer and Menippean Satire*; Means, *Consolatio Genre*; Owen, *Vision of Hell*; and Patch's classic *Other World*.
3. Spearing, *Medieval Dream-Poetry*, p. 4.
4. Piehler, *Visionary Landscape*, p. 38.
5. Ibid., p. 19.
6. Hieatt, *Realism of Dream Visions*, p. 57.
7. Ibid., p. 52.
8. Nolan, *Gothic Visionary Perspective*, p. 155.
9. Piehler, *Visionary Landscape*, p. 20.
10. See Reichert, "More than Kin."
11. Hirsch, *Validity in Interpretation*, p. 71.
12. Frye, *Anatomy of Criticism*; Hernadi, *Beyond Genre*.

13. Jauss, "Theory of Genres," p. 78; originally published in *Grundriss der Romanischen Literaturen des Mittelalters*, 6 (1972).
14. Fowler, *Kinds of Literature*, p. 24.
15. Jauss, "Theory of Genres," p. 80; Fowler, *Kinds of Literature*, p. 22.
16. Fowler, *Kinds of Literature*, p. 112.
17. Ibid., pp. 115–17.
18. Ibid., p. 127.
19. Ibid., p. 277.
20. Holub, *Reception Theory*. See also Holub, "Trends in Literary Theory."
21. See also Fowler, *Kinds of Literature*, pp. 48–52.
22. Jauss, "Theory of Genres," p. 105.
23. Ibid., p. 108.
24. Jauss, "Literary History," pp. 28–32; previously published in *Literaturgeschichte als Provokation* (Frankfurt, 1970).
25. Jauss, "Theory of Genres," p. 89. Jauss himself has retreated from this position in some of his recent work on aesthetic pleasure; see, for example, his *Aesthetic Experience*, originally published as *Ästhetische Erfahrung und literarische Hermeneutik* (Munich, 1977). See also Holub, *Reception Theory*, pp. 69–76.
26. Holub, *Reception Theory*, p. 63.
27. Fleming, *Reason and the Lover*, p. 75 and passim.
28. Fowler, *Kinds of Literature*, p. 114.
29. Leff, *Medieval Outlook*, pp. 5–6. In his turn, Leff clearly relies on the theoretical model of scientific paradigms and displacement offered by Kuhn in *Scientific Revolutions*.
30. For an introduction to the idea that the year 1277 marks the great turning point in medieval philosophy, see Leff, *Medieval Outlook*, pp. 1–21. See also Gilson, *History of Christian Philosophy*, pp. 387–410; also Steenberghen's *Aristotle in the West*, pp. 320–28. Even for historians like Oberman who deemphasize the influence of Thomistic thought, the condemnation marks the outset of what Oberman calls the "Franciscan alternative," in "Fourteenth-Century Religious Thought," p. 84. See also Copleston, *History of Medieval Philosophy*, pp. 209–12. Taken as a whole, modern study suggests certain patterns for late medieval—as differentiated from high medieval—thought. Franciscan Augustinianism called for a new emphasis on faith, on the study of God apart from nature. This movement, in its turn, provided a counterpoint to the quickening pursuit of scholastic dialectic independent of theology. For further elaboration of this point, see Leff's "Seeds of Reformation," p. 1232. See also my Ch. 4.
31. Leff, *Medieval Outlook*, p. 5.
32. Kiser, *Telling Classical Tales*. For Chaucer's relationship to the philosophical movements of the day, see also Peck, "Chaucer and the Nominalist Questions."
33. Delany, *Chaucer's House of Fame*.
34. Fowler, *Kinds of Literature*, p. 162.
35. Geoffrey of Vinsauf, *Poetria nova*, trans. Nims, pp. 16–17. For the

Latin, see Geoffrey of Vinsauf, *Poetria nova*, ed. Faral, p. 198:
>Si quis habet fundare domum, non currit ad actum
>Impetuosa manus: intrinseca linea cordis
>Praemetitur opus, seriemque sub ordine certo
>Interior praescribit homo, totamque figurat
>Ante manus cordis quam corporis; et status ejus
>Est prius archetypus quam sensilis.

36. Aquinas, *Summa theologiae*, Blackfriars, vol. 4, Ia.15.2: "Forma . . . domus in mente aedificatoris est aliquid ab eo intellectum, ad cujus similitudinem domum in materia format."

37. William of Ockham, *Ordinatio*, D.II.Q.viii, *prima redactio*; translated by Boehner in William of Ockham, *Philosophical Writings*, pp. 44–45. Though Ockham slightly modified this in a second opinion about whether universals are an object of thought or act of intellect, the variations do not alter the basic point I make here; cp. pp. 46–48. For the Latin of the passage translated here, see William of Ockham, *Ordinatio*, ed. Brown and Gál, pp. 272–74: "Sicut enim artifex videns domum vel aedificium aliquod extra, fingit in anima sua consimilem domum et postea consimilem producit extra, et est solo numero distincta a priori, ita in propositio, illud fictum in mente ex visione alicuius rei extra esset unum exemplar. . . . Artificialia in mente artificis non videntur habere esse subiectivum sicut nec creaturae in mente divina ante creationem."

38. William of Ockham, *Ordinatio*, D.II.Q.viii, *prima redactio*; translated by Boehner in William of Ockham, *Philosophical Writings*, p. 44; cp. Geoffrey of Vinsauf, *Poetria nova*, ed. Faral, p. 199. My emphasis on the high medieval period necessitates some simplification of the highly complex epistemological changes in late medieval philosophy, which specialists in the past few decades have been in the process of reevaluating. For further discussion, see Courtenay, "Nominalism"; see also Peck, "Chaucer and the Nominalist Questions."

39. Wetherbee, introduction, in Bernardus Silvestris, *Cosmographia*, p. 55.

40. Silverstein, "Fabulous Cosmogony," p. 116.

CHAPTER 1

1. *Commentary on the Aeneid*, ed. Jones and Jones, p. 44. The editors make persuasive arguments against assuming the author of this commentary to be Bernardus; see their introduction, pp. ix–xi. I am following their lead in ignoring the traditional attribution. I have also consulted Schreiber and Maresca's valuable translation of this work, *Commentary on the Aeneid*, and, although I do not use it here, I will be following it whenever possible. Schreiber and Maresca retain the traditional attribution to Bernardus.

2. Bloch, *Feudal Society*; Little, *Religious Poverty*.

3. Little, *Religious Poverty*, p. 41.

4. Ibid., p. 190.

5. Southern's initial discussion of this humanism, which denies Chartres its uniqueness, appears in two essays, "Medieval Humanism" and "Human-

ism and the School of Chartres," in *Medieval Humanism*, pp. 29–85. His basic point was refuted by Dronke, "School of Chartres"; Häring, "Chartres and Paris Revisited"; and Giacone, "Library at Chartres." Southern has reaffirmed and extended his earlier position in *School of Chartres*; the observations noted here on institutional characteristics are taken from Southern, "Schools of Paris." For our purposes, it is not necessary to suppress all institutional differences, merely to note their underlying unity.

6. For the appeal of literary texts primarily to the *affectus*, see Minnis, "Literary Theory." The willingness to admit the more affective modes into the study of sacred texts during the later Middle Ages may correspond to the more affective and intuitive epistemologies of that age. The grounds for poetry's defense thus also change.

7. John of Salisbury, *Metalogicon*, trans. McGarry, I.i, pp. 11–12. *PL*, 199, 827B–C: "Mercurio philologiam invidet, et ab amplexu *Philologiae* Mercurium avellit, qui eloquentiae praeceptionem a studiis philosophiae eliminat; et, quamvis solam videatur eloquentiam persequi, omnia liberalia studia convellit, omnem totius philosophiae impugnat operam.... Non ergo unam, non paucos, sed omnes simul urbes et politicam vitam totam aggreditur Cornificius noster, studiorum eloquentiae imperitus et improbus impugnator."

8. See Wetherbee, *Platonism and Poetry*; and Dronke, *Fabula*.

9. Henri d'Andeli, *Battle of the Seven Liberal Arts*, ed. and trans. Paetow, l. 450, p. 60: "Seignor, li siecles vait par vaines."

10. Averroes's commentary was translated into Latin in the thirteenth century by Hermannus Alemannus. See Averroes, "Averrois Cordubensis Commentarium," ed. Boggess; and "Middle Commentary of Averroes," trans. Hardison. Though poetry is assigned the ethical task of praising and blaming, for limits on its speculative range see, for example, "Averrois Cordubensis Commentarium," pp. 6–7, 22; and "Middle Commentary of Averroes," pp. 350–51, 356. The decorum I speak of comes through mainly in the commentary's technical discussions, for example, in its treatment of narrative unity and metaphor. See "Averrois Cordubensis Commentarium," pp. 23–87; and "Middle Commentary of Averroes," pp. 357–82. For changes in the character of late medieval literary theory and attitudes, see my Ch. 4; for changes in poetic practice, Ch. 6. See also Allen, *Ethical Poetic*, esp. pp. 3–66.

11. Wetherbee, "Theme of Imagination," p. 45.

12. Gilson, *Saint Thomas Aquinas*, p. 280.

13. Chenu, *Théologie*, esp. pp. 159–90, and *Nature, Man and Society*, pp. 99–145.

14. Chenu, *Nature, Man and Society*, p. 36 (and *Théologie*, p. 43).

15. Leff, *Medieval Outlook*, p. 8.

16. See, however, the Franciscan tradition of the thirteenth century, where the two approaches to knowing—abstraction and illumination—intersect; e.g., in St. Bonaventure's *Itinerarium mentis in Deum*, trans. Boehner.

17. For the integrity of each power, see Aquinas, *Summa theologiae*,

trans. Dominican Fathers, quoted by Bundy, *Theory of Imagination*, p. 217. See also John of Salisbury, *Metalogicon*, IV.9, trans. McGarry, p. 218.

18. I am following here Aquinas's useful, broadly conceived, and straightforward definition of the verb *abstrahere* as provided in Aquinas, *Summa theologiae*, Blackfriars, vol. 12, Ia. 85.1: "Now to know something which in fact exists in individuated matter, but not as existing in such or such matter, is to abstract a form from individual matter, represented by sense images" ("Cognoscere vero id quod est in materia individuali, non prout est in tali materia, est abstrahere formam a materia individuali, quam repraesentant phantasmata").

19. The best comprehensive treatment of medieval faculty psychology, and of much use to me in making final revisions of this summary, occurs in the first chapter of a manuscript in preparation by my colleague Katharine Park, the working title of which is *The Imagination in Renaissance Thought*. I am very grateful to her for having allowed me to use a draft of this chapter in preparing my own manuscript. See also Clarke and Dewhurst, *Illustrated History of Brain Function*; Harvey, *Inward Wits*, esp. ch. 1, pp. 4–30; Wolfson, "Internal Senses"; and Michaud-Quantin, "Classification des puissances."

20. Luca, *De differentiis animae et spiritus*, pp. 129–30 (cited by Park). Also Guillaume de Conches, *De philosophia mundi*, PL, 172, 98D.

21. See Abbas, quoted by Harvey, *Inward Wits*, p. 14. Aquinas, *Summa theologiae*, Blackfriars, vol. 12, Ia.84.7. See also McKeon, "Medicine and Philosophy"; Olson, *Literature as Recreation*, esp. pp. 39–89.

22. Bonaventure, *Itinerarium mentis in Deum*, trans. Boehner, II.6, pp. 54, 55: "Abstrahit igitur a loco, tempore et motu, ac per hoc est incommutabilis, incircumscriptibilis, interminabilis et omnino spiritualis."

23. Aquinas, *Summa theologiae*, Blackfriars, vol. 12, Ia.78.4: "cui medici assignant determinatum organum, scilicet mediam partem capitis."

24. Park is especially good at tracing these two traditions; see above, n. 19.

25. John of Salisbury, *Metalogicon*, trans. McGarry, IV.17, p. 229. PL, 199, 926B–C: "velut quemdam senatum in Capitolio animae, rationem quasi dominam in arce capitis statuit, mediam quidem sedem tribuens inter cellam phantasticam et memoriam, ut velut e specula sensuum, et imaginationum, possit examinare judicia. Proinde quidem, quia haec ipsa vis, etsi divina sit, quasi quodam sensuum et imaginationum ventilabro excitatur."

26. Gilson, *Saint Thomas Aquinas*, p. 9.

27. Aquinas, *De anima*, trans. Foster and Humphries, III.iv.692, p. 409. The Latin can be found in Aquinas, *Sancti Thomae Aquinatis*, ed. Pirotta, p. 230: "non est autem intelligibilis actu, nisi secundum quod est a phantasmatibus abstracta et remota." See also III.iv.686, pp. 406–7, and III.iv.716, p. 418 (*De anima*). Mine is, of course, a simplification of a much more complex process; see Lonergan, *Verbum*, pp. 141–81. For example, in Lonergan's "intellectualist" analysis of abstraction, the soul's ultimate act of "formative abstraction" requires a return or reflexive movement after the act of apprehension, in order to apply universal knowledge to the particular.

28. Aquinas, *De anima*, trans. Foster and Humphries, III.vii.774, p. 448. Aquinas, *Sancti Thomae Aquinatis*, ed. Pirotta, p. 253: "quia est aliquid unum respectu omnium sensibilium, sicut intellectus est terminus omnium phantasmatum."

29. This description of abstraction is based largely on Aquinas's discussions in *Summa theologiae*, Blackfriars, vol. 11, Ia.78.4, and vol. 12, Ia.84. On the importance of abstraction to proper self-realization, see also Gilson, *Saint Thomas Aquinas*, p. 210. For the mechanics of this transition from potency to act, see Aquinas, *De anima*, trans. Foster and Humphries, III.iv, pp. 411–19, text and commentary. See also Lonergan, *Verbum*, pp. 178–79.

30. Aquinas, *De anima*, trans. Foster and Humphries, III.iii.664, p. 398. Aquinas, *Sancti Thomae Aquinatis*, ed. Pirotta, p. 222: "Et propter hoc etiam quia effectus est debilior causa, et quanto magis aliquid elongatur a primo agente, tanto minus recipit de virtute et similitudine ejus; ideo in phantasia facilius adhuc quam in sensu potest incidere falsitas, quae consistit in dissimilitudine sensus ad sensibile."

31. Hugh of St. Victor, *Didascalicon*, trans. Taylor, II.v, pp. 66–67. Hugh of St. Victor, *Didascalicon*, ed. Buttimer, p. 29: "Intelligentia vero est de solis rerum principiis, id est, Deo, ideis, et hyle, et de incorporeis substantiis, pura certaque cognitio. Imaginatio est memoria sensuum ex corporum reliquiis inhaerentibus animo, principium cognitionis per se nihil certum habens."

32. Bundy, *Theory of Imagination*, p. 178. See also Chenu, "*Imaginatio*."

33. Hugh of St. Victor, *Didascalicon*, trans. Taylor, I.iii, pp. 49–50. Hugh of St. Victor, *Didascalicon*, ed. Buttimer, p. 9: "Haec tantum humano generi praesto est, quae non solum sensus imaginationesque perfectas et non inconditas capit, sed etiam pleno actu intelligentiae, quod imaginatio suggessit, explicat atque confirmat." See also Hugh of St. Victor, *De unione* (*PL*, 177, 287B–C):"Postea eadem imaginatio ab anteriore parte capitis ad mediam transiens, ipsam animae rationalis substantiam contingit, et excitat discretionem, in tantum jam purificata et subtilis effecta, ut ipsi spiritui immediate conjungatur."

34. Dante, *Convivio*, trans. Jackson, III.iv, p. 138. See also III.ii, pp. 131–32.

35. Dante, *Purgatorio*, in *Divine Comedy*, ed. and trans. Singleton, XVII.13–18. Further references to the *Commedia* are from this edition.

36. Averroes, "Averrois Cordubensis Commentarium," ed. Boggess, p. 12; and "Middle Commentary of Averroes," trans. Hardison, p. 353.

37. Bundy, *Theory of Imagination*, pp. 257–80. See also Robertson, *Preface to Chaucer*, p. 69.

38. Bundy, *Theory of Imagination*, pp. 105–16.

39. Bloomfield, *Piers Plowman*, p. 171.

40. John of Salisbury, *Metalogicon*, trans. McGarry, I.xi, pp. 34–35. *PL*, 199, 838B: "Excitat enim primo ingenium ad res aliquas percipiendas: et cum eas perceperit, deponit quasi in custodia et thesauro memoriae; ratio vero quae praecepta et commendanda vel commendata sunt, studio diligenti

examinat. . . . Haec tria quidem, quasi omnium artium fundamenta, et instrumenta, natura praemittit." For the essential unity of *ingenium* and imagination, see also the many references provided by Silverstein in "Fabulous Cosmogony," p. 98, n. 34.

41. Guillaume de Conches, London, B. M. Egerton 628, f.167v, quoted by Wetherbee, *Platonism and Poetry*, p. 95, n. 56: "uis intelligendi que uocatur phantastica."

42. Adelard of Bath, *Questiones naturales*, p. 22: "In cerebro enim utitur phantastico motu, id est ingeniali, rationali etiam, id est iudicio, sed et memoriali, id est recordatione." See also Meerson, "Bernard Silvester's Commentary on the *Aeneid*," p. 42.

43. Macrobius, *Saturnalia*, ed. Willis, V.i, p. 44.

44. John of Salisbury, *Metalogicon*, trans. McGarry, I.11, p. 35. *PL*, 199, 838D: "Horum autem tria sunt genera, sicut Carnotensis senex Bernardus, frequenti colloquio, suis auditoribus tradere consuevit. Aliud enim advolans, aliud infimum, aliud mediocre est. Advolans quidem eadem facilitate, qua percipit, recedit a perceptis, nec in aliqua sede invenit requiem. Infimum autem sublimari non potest, ideoque perfectum nescit; at mediocre, et quia habet in quo sedeat, et quia sublimari potest, nec de profectu desperat, et philosophantis exercitio accommodissimum est."

45. Alain de Lille, prologue, in *Anticlaudianus*, ed. Bossuat, p. 55.

46. Wetherbee, "Theme of Imagination," p. 47. Wetherbee traces the involvement of *ingenium* with sensual matter to two commentaries on Martianus, one by John the Scot and one by Bernardus Silvestris; see p. 47.

47. Trans. of Dante, *De vulgari eloquentia*, ed. Marigo, II.iv.10, p. 194.

48. Alcher de Clairvaux, *De spiritu et anima*, included among the works of Augustine in *PL*, 40, 787B–C; see also 808D–809A: "Ingenium est vis ea animae, sive intentio, qua anima se extendit et exercet ad incognitorum cognitionem."

49. Guillaume de Conches, "Les Gloses sur le Timée," ed. Parent, pp. 145–46: "Et est ingenium naturalis vis ad aliquid cito intelligendum, et dictum ingenium quasi intus genitum." Cp. Guillaume de Conches, *Glosae super Platonem*, ed. Jeauneau, p. 102.

50. Camb. Univ. Lib., Mm.I.18, f.10r, quoted in Stock, *Myth and Science*, p. 42n: "Nam ingenium habet mensuram ad capienda quedam futura."

51. Petrarch, *Secretum*, ed. Carrara, p. 70.

52. Isidore of Seville, *Etymologiae*, ed. Lindsay, vol. 2, X.122: "Ingeniosus, quod intus vim habeat gignendi quamlibet artem."

53. "Qui vince la memoria mia lo 'ngegno; / che quella croce lampeggiava Cristo, / si ch'io non so trovare essempro degno." See, for example, *Paradiso* IV.40 and X.43.

54. *Commentary on the Aeneid*, ed. Jones and Jones, pp. 47, 115.

55. Silverstein, "Fabulous Cosmogony," p. 98, n. 34.

56. See Quintilian, *Institutio oratoria*, trans. Butler, vol. 4, X.i.88, X.ii.12. In this second reference, the rhetorician makes the connection be-

tween invention and *ingenium* clear: "Adde quod ea, quae in oratore maxima sunt, imitabilia non sunt, ingenium, inventio, vis, facilitas et quidquid arte non traditur." See Curtius's discussion of the use of the term in Quintilian and Martianus Capella, in *European Literature*, p. 296. For Horace's notion of *ingenium*, see *Ars poetica* in Brink, 'Ars Poetica,' where Horace seems to mean by *ingenium* natural wit or talent (see ll. 295, 323, 410), which plays a role complementary to *ars* (ll. 295–98) and *studium* (ll. 408–11); for further discussion, see Brink, *Prolegomena*, pp. 255–61, and 'Ars Poetica,' pp. 328–30, 394–400, and passim. As Brink points out, within the context of his didactic purpose, "Horace sometimes satirizes *ingenium*, at other times . . . makes it a condition of *ars*" ('Ars Poetica,' p. 329). In both Quintilian and Horace, then, *ingenium* was a crucial faculty but not one defined with much rigor. The faculty does not play any significant role at all in either Cicero's *De inventione* or in the pseudo-Ciceronian *Rhetorica ad Herennium*, the other two rhetorical tracts that, in addition to Quintilian and Horace, would have been reasonably well known in the Middle Ages.

57. Trans. of Geoffrey of Vinsauf, *Poetria nova*, ed. Faral, p. 203:
    Formula materiae, quasi quaedam formula cerae,
    Primitus est tactus duri: si sedula cura
    Igniat ingenium, subito mollescit ad ignem
    Ingenii sequiturque manum quocumque vocarit,
    Ductilis ad quicquid. Hominis manus interioris
    Ducit ut amplificet vel curtet.

58. Ibid., p. 205.

59. Kelly, *Medieval Imagination*, p. 34.

60. Bernardus Silvestris, *Cosmographia*, ed. Dronke, pp. 100, 102, 121, 124, 144–45; and *Cosmographia*, trans. Wetherbee, pp. 71, 73, 91, 94, 117. Interestingly, the *Cosmographia* is found in several manuscripts along with the *Poetria nova*; see Gallo, "*Poetria nova*," p. 69.

61. Alain de Lille, *Anticlaudianus*, trans. Sheridan, p. 89; compare Grammar's actions to those of Logic on p. 95 and Rhetoric on p. 102. The corresponding Latin passages can be found in Bossuat's edition on p. 86, ll. 488–89; p. 92, ll. 100–105; and p. 96.

62. Aquinas, *De anima*, trans. Foster and Humphries, III.viii.789–90, p. 453; and *Sancti Thomae Aquinatis*, ed. Pirotta, p. 256. See also Aristotle, *De partibus animalium*, IV.x.687a5–b24, cited by Schupbach in an excellent survey of the hand's significance in classical and Renaissance scientific treatises, *Paradox of Rembrandt's 'Anatomy of Dr. Tulp,'* pp. 57–65. The medieval tradition of the hand may also draw from Galen's *Parts of the Body*, trans. May, known in the twelfth and thirteenth centuries through an abridgment and corrupt translation made by Burgundio of Pisa (see May's introduction, p. 6); see esp. Books I and II, pp. 67–153.

63. Aquinas, *De anima*, trans. Foster and Humphries, III.viii.790, p. 456.

64. Aquinas, *Summa theologiae*, Blackfriars, vol. 11, Ia.76.5: "quia per eas homo potest sibi praeparare instrumenta infinitorum modorum, et ad infinitos effectus."

65. "*Chess of Love*," trans. Jones, pp. 39–40.
66. Alain de Lille, *Anticlaudianus*, ed. Bossuat, III.3–5, p. 89: "Mentem manus excitat, urget / Ingenium, sensus proprios inuitat, ut axis / Effigiet speciem." Alain de Lille, *Anticlaudianus*, trans. Sheridan, p. 91.
67. Bernardus Silvestris, *Cosmographia*, ed. Dronke, pp. 121, 122; and *Cosmographia*, trans. Wetherbee, pp. 91, 93.
68. Bernardus Silvestris, *Cosmographia*, ed. Dronke, p. 97; Wetherbee, p. 67.
69. See particularly Wetherbee's introduction to the *Cosmographia*, p. 56. A perception of dualism is in part responsible for the modern critic's sense that one must define this poem either as rigorously Christian or pagan. See Economou, *Goddess Natura*, pp. 60–62. For other useful critical histories of the *Cosmographia*, see Stock, *Myth and Science*, p. 278n, or Wetherbee's introduction to his translation, pp. 4–5. Stock's account of Bernardus's "existential naturalism" works to counter the dialectic of pagan vs. Christian interpretations.
70. Bernardus Silvestris, *Cosmographia*, ed. Dronke, p. 127; and *Cosmographia*, trans. Wetherbee, p. 98.
71. Bernardus Silvestris, *Cosmographia*, ed. Dronke, p. 155; and *Cosmographia*, trans. Wetherbee, p. 127.
72. Wetherbee, introduction, *Cosmographia*, p. 56; see also Bernardus Silvestris, *Cosmographia*, ed. Dronke, p. 49.
73. Trans. of Dante, *De vulgari eloquentia*, ed. Marigo, I.v.1, p. 26: "sentiri quam sentire." See also Averroes's comment that the imaginative urge to express likenesses through artistic images is unique to man and a characteristic from his infancy, in Averroes, "Averrois Cordubensis Commentarium," ed. Boggess, p. 11; and "Middle Commentary of Averroes," trans. Hardison, p. 352.
74. See the discussion of man's miraculous ability to create statues of the gods in the *Asclepius*, ed. Nock, trans. Festugière, pp. 324–26; see also Dronke, *Fabula*, p. 17, and the material he includes from the *Asclepius*, pp. 72–73; Stock, *Myth and Science*, pp. 187–226. Other Hermetic texts also suggest the power of intellect and word to help man realize his godhood; see Yates, *Bruno and the Hermetic Tradition*, esp. p. 33.
75. Fletcher, *Allegory*, p. 22.
76. Alain de Lille, *De planctu*, ed. Häring, p. 825: "archetipa uerba idealiter preconcepta, uocaliter produxit in actum."
77. Tuve, *Allegorical Imagery*, p. 26.
78. Wetherbee, *Platonism and Poetry*, p. 8.
79. Wetherbee, "Theme of Imagination," p. 45.
80. Allen, in *Ethical Poetic*, lays important groundwork for this study; see esp. pp. 67–178.
81. Alain de Lille, *De planctu*, ed. Häring, X.19–20, p. 845, and XVIII.90, p. 876: "seriale prefinite narrationis propositum."
82. Peter Damian, *Sermones*, PL, 144, quoted by Alford, "Grammatical Metaphor," p. 742: "ipsa descriptionis series, et ordo verborum magnum contineat sacramentum." Stock, in *Implications of Literacy*, provides an ex-

cellent discussion of the centrality of oaths, words, and the Word in determining the very evolution of the word and concept sacrament (see especially his discussion of Tertullian and Augustine, pp. 254–59). Peter Damian seems to be drawing here on this background that makes the mystery itself a function of words, signs, and their ordering.

83. Boethius, *Consolation of Philosophy*, trans. Green, Book IV, Prose 6. See also Boethius, *Philosophiae consolatio*, ed. Biehler, Book IV, Prose 6.12: "Sicut enim artifex faciendae rei formam mente praecipiens mouet operis effectum et quod simpliciter praesentarieque prospexerat per temporales ordines ducit, ita deus prouidentia quidem singulariter stabiliterque facienda disponit, fato uero haec ipsa quae disposuit multipliciter ac temporaliter amministrat."

84. Dante, *Convivio*, trans. Jackson, II.ix, p. 94.

85. Geoffrey of Vinsauf, *Poetria nova*, ed. Faral, pp. 200–203. In *Poetria nova and Its Sources*, pp. 137–39, Gallo tries to find the roots of this distinction. Although he claims the division between natural and artificial order "rests on a tradition of long standing in classical and early medieval rhetoric" (p. 137), his examples show that, in the classical tradition, the distinction was not so named or formulated; indeed, order—whether normal or inverted—was based then on rhetorical convention rather than on temporal sequence. For elaboration of this distinction in medieval interpretation of Lucan, see Quadlbauer, "Lukan."

86. Guillaume de Conches, *Commentaires inédits*, ed. Jourdain, p. 74.

87. *Commentary on the Aeneid*, trans. Schreiber and Maresca, p. 5. See also *Commentary on the Aeneid*, ed. Jones and Jones, p. 3: "Modus agendi talis est: in integumento describit quid agat vel quid paciatur humanus spiritus in humano corpore temporaliter positus. Atque in hoc describendo naturali utitur ordine atque ita utrumque ordinem narrationis observat, artificialem poeta, naturalem philosophus."

88. Peter Abelard, *Expositio in Hexaemeron*, PL, 178, 733A. According to Abelard, Moses in speaking to an uneducated people began with a discussion of physical creation, thus "naturalem quidem ordinem in hoc prosecutus." Following up on an analysis of the twelfth-century *Aeneid* commentary, Gallo shows how the natural order of knowing could inform a secular poem, Guido Cavalcanti's *Canzone d'Amore*, in "*Poetria nova*," pp. 76–80.

89. Newman, "*Somnium*," p. 145.

CHAPTER 2

1. Owen, *Vision of Hell*. See also Patch, *Other World*, pp. 80–133; Dinzelbacher, *Vision und Visionsliteratur*. For an example of one of these visions and a fine introductory discussion of the characteristics of the tradition, see *Walahfrid Strabo's Visio Wettini*, ed. and trans. Traill.

2. "Apocalypse of Paul," trans. James.

3. Bede, *History*, trans. Sherley-Price, pp. 289–94.

4. Turner and Turner, *Image and Pilgrimage*, p. 2.

5. Ibid. The difference in terminology between "liminal" and "liminoid" need not concern us here, as being largely a quantitative rather than a qualitative distinction (see pp. 1–39, 253).
6. Ibid., p. 3.
7. Ibid., pp. 7–8.
8. Gennep, *Rites of Passage*, p. 101.
9. Macrobius, *Commentary*, trans. Stahl, pp. 86–87.
10. Turner and Turner, *Image and Pilgrimage*, p. 2.
11. Bede, *History*, trans. Sherley-Price, p. 289.
12. Jean de Meun, *Le Roman de la rose*, ed. Lecoy, ll. 18441–46; and *Romance of the Rose*, trans. Dahlberg, p. 306.
13. Alcher de Clairvaux, *De spiritu et anima*, PL, 40, 795D: "Jacebit enim corpus tuum, ambulabit illa. Tacebit lingua corporis tui, loquetur illa. Clausi erunt oculi tui, videbit illa. Et ita in ea tota et integra cernetur similitudo carnis tuae."
14. I am following the translation in *The Jerusalem Bible*, 2 Corinthians 12:2.
15. Augustine, *De Genesi*, CSEL, 27 (1), xii, pp. 379–435. See also Newman's discussion of the Augustinian distinction between the three levels of vision, in "Somnium," pp. 110–15. Useful commentary on these categories is also provided by Bundy in *Theory of Imagination*, pp. 165–72, and by Mazzeo, *Paradiso*, pp. 87–90. Augustine's divisions can be harmonized with later epistemologies of vision without too much difficulty. For example, both what Aquinas calls "natural" knowledge and knowledge "by grace" (e.g., in *Summa theologiae*, Q.12. Art.13) are aspects of the *visio spiritualis*; even though the second, which derives from "divinely formed" images rather than from those received "naturally from sensible things," is more perfect than the first, still both require the operation of imagination and the use of images for their effect. See Aquinas, *Introduction to Aquinas*, ed. Pegis, pp. 94–96.
16. Alain de Lille, *Summa de arte praedicatoria*, PL, 210, 196A.
17. Alain de Lille, *Distinctiones dictionum theologicalium*, PL, 210, 950D: "videre per speculum et in aenigmate est per visibilia quasi per quasdam imagines comprehendere Deum." Cp. 1 Corinthians 13:12.
18. That dreams and visions may be treated as one category is also clear from Avicenna's psychological analysis of prophecy in *Liber de anima*, ed. van Riet, vol. 2, pp. 18–19; see also Newman on dreams and prophecy, "Somnium," pp. 196–212.
19. Though strictly speaking the *De consolatione* alternates prose and verse sections, I will refer to it here as a poem, for convenience's sake. Four recent books provide excellent background material and a cross section of critical approaches to Boethius: the *Atti* of the Congresso Internazionale di Studi Boeziani; Gibson, ed., *Boethius*; Chadwick, *Boethius*; and Reiss, *Boethius*.
20. I have used the text of Augustine's *Soliloquia* reproduced in the PL, 32, 869–904. For further discussion of Boethius's debt to this work, see Silk, "Boethius's *Consolatio*." The argument that Boethius was indebted to Au-

gustine's dialogues is undermined by Courcelle, in "Personnage de Philosophie," then reaffirmed by Fleming in *Reason and the Lover*, p. 48 and passim. Augustine's relation to Boethius is also discussed by Seth Lerer as part of a broader treatment of Boethius's literary and cultural contexts in *Boethius and Dialogue*, a work that reached me too late to be incorporated into my discussion here. A useful text of Cicero's *Somnium Scipionis* can be found in Book VI of his *De re publica*, trans. Keyes. For the English of this work, however, I use Stahl's translations both of Cicero's dream and also of Macrobius's commentary on it, in Macrobius, *Commentary*.

21. Cicero, *Somnium*, in Macrobius, *Commentary*, trans. Stahl, pp. 72–73; Cicero, *De re publica*, ed. Keyes, p. 268: "Stellarum autem globi terrae magnitudinem facile vincebant. Iam ipsa terra ita mihi parva visa est, ut me imperii nostri, quo quasi punctum eius attingimus, paeniteret. Quam cum magis intuerer, Quaeso, inquit Africanus, quousque humi defixa tua mens erit? Nonne aspicis, quae in templa veneris?" (I have omitted chapter headings.)

22. For the metaphor of captivity, see Augustine, *Soliloquia*, PL, 32, 882B–C, where Reason says, "Unum est quod tibi possum praecipere nihil plus novi. Penitus esse ista sensibilia fugienda, cavendumque magnopere, dum hoc corpus agimus, ne quo eorum visco pennae nostrae impediantur, quibus integris perfectisque opus est, ut ad illam lucem ab his tenebris evolemus: quae se ne ostendere quidem dignatur in hac cavea inclusis, nisi tales fuerint ut ista vel effracta vel dissoluta possint in auras suas evadere."

23. This "order" is described at the end of Book I, Chapter 13 of the *Soliloquia*, PL, 32, 881D–882B.

24. I am following the English translation of this work in Synesius of Cyrene, *Essays and Hymns*, trans. Fitzgerald, pp. 326–59. The Greek may be found in *PG*, 66, 1281–1320.

25. See, for example, Synesius of Cyrene, *Essays and Hymns*, trans. Fitzgerald, pp. 332–41.

26. Ibid., p. 357.

27. I do not mean, of course, to base my argument on the certainty that Boethius was directly acquainted with Synesius's work. He might well have been, however, since Synesius wrote about a hundred years before Boethius and since Courcelle has shown that Boethius probably was trained in Greek philosophy in Alexandria. See Courcelle's *Lettres grecques*, pp. 257–300. Even Vogel's more recent investigation suggesting that he may also have studied in Athens upholds Courcelle on this point; see her "Boethiana I." Additionally, Courcelle (see p. 286) twice notes verbal parallels between Boethius's *De consolatione* and Synesius's works, one of them from the *De insomniis*, and Schmidt-Kohl notes several parallels between the *De consolatione* and Synesius's hymns in *Neuplatonische Seelenlehre*, pp. 5–6, 25, 28–29. But my argument rests only on the presumption that chronology and geography indicate that the ideas about dreaming, and even about poetry, held by Synesius would have been possible in some form also for Boethius. Unfortunately, though his *Encomium on Baldness* was recovered as early as

the ninth century, little evidence has been unearthed to show that Synesius's theories would have had wide currency again in the West until the fourteenth century; see Synesius of Cyrene, *Essays and Hymns*, trans. Fitzgerald, p. 437.

28. See the plates at the back of Courcelle's *Consolation de philosophie*, esp. 29, 30, 40, 50–62.

29. A comparison of the plates referenced above with photographs printed in Kerenyi's *Asklepios*, esp. pl. 18, p. 35, suggests a similarity between the incubation situation or healing dream and the situation in Boethius's poem. See also Schouten, *God and Serpent of Asklepios*, pp. 49–64; Flacelière, *Greek Oracles*, pp. 22–23; Majno, *Healing Hand*, pp. 201–5; Walton, *Cult of Asklepios*; and Edelstein and Edelstein, *Asclepius*. For the persistence of healing ritual into the Middle Ages under the names of certain saints, see Hamilton, *Incubation*, pp. 109–73.

30. See Patch, *Tradition of Boethius*, pp. 87–113.

31. Means, *Consolatio Genre*, p. 19n.

32. Jauss, "Literary History," p. 22; previously published in *Literaturgeschichte als Provokation* (Frankfurt, 1970).

33. Guillaume de Conches, "Commentaires inédits," ed. Jourdain, vol. 20, pt. 2, p. 74: "A practica adscendendum est ad theoricam."

34. Piehler, *Visionary Landscape*, p. 39.

35. Boethius, *Consolation of Philosophy*, trans. Green, Book V, Meter III. The Latin may be found in Boethius, *Philosophiae consolatio*, ed. Biehler, Book V, Meter 3, ll. 26–31. The characterization of the seeker of truth there is as follows: "nam neque nouit / nec penitus tamen omnia nescit, / sed quam retinens meminit summam / consulit alte uisa retractans, / ut seruatis queat oblitas / addere partes." I will be using this edition and Green's translation throughout.

36. Boethius, *De interpretatione*, PL, 64, 433.

37. Courcelle, *Lettres grecques*, p. 301.

38. See Jourdain, in Guillaume de Conches, "Commentaires inédits," p. 44. See also Courcelle, *Consolation de philosophie*, pp. 301–15.

39. *Commentary on the Aeneid*, ed. Jones and Jones, p. 61. Analysis of the literary use of this order can also be found in Gallo, "*Poetria nova*."

40. Servius Grammaticus, *In Vergilii carmina commentarii*, ed. Thilo and Hagen; Fulgentius, "Exposition," trans. Whitbread. Whitbread's translation is based on Helm's edition, *Fabii Planciadis Fulgentii opera*, pp. 83–107. Also see Mythographus Tertius, "De diis gentium et illorum allegoriis," ed. Bode.

41. Thompson, *Dante's Epic Journeys*, p. 26. See also his article on this subject, "Dante and Bernard Silvestris."

42. Thompson, *Dante's Epic Journeys*, p. 23.

43. Meerson, "Bernard Silvester's Commentary on the *Aeneid*," pp. 36–38.

44. *Commentary on the Aeneid*, trans. Schreiber and Maresca, p. 12; *Commentary on the Aeneid*, ed. Jones and Jones, p. 11.

45. *Commentary on the Aeneid*, trans. Schreiber and Maresca, p. 55. *Commentary on the Aeneid*, ed. Jones and Jones, p. 56: "Sed animus corporis mortalitatem ad tempus patitur ut deinde corpus immortalitatem sortiatur."

46. Meerson, "Bernard Silvester's Commentary on the *Aeneid*," p. 38.

47. Jones and Jones, in the *Commentary on the Aeneid*, p. xiv. As the commentator says, "profundius philosophicam veritatem in hoc volumine declarat Virgilius"; see ed. Jones and Jones, p. 28; *Commentary on the Aeneid*, trans. Schreiber and Maresca, p. 31.

48. Fulgentius, "Exposition," trans. Whitbread, p. 132.

49. Schreiber and Maresca, in *Commentary on the Aeneid*, p. xvii.

50. *Commentary on the Aeneid*, ed. Jones and Jones, p. 30; *Commentary on the Aeneid*, trans. Schreiber and Maresca, p. 32. Although here the *Aeneid* commentator is clearly talking about rising above and rejecting worldly concerns, he indicates that the way this is done is by moving through the created world to its Creator. Therefore, he does not, as Schreiber and Maresca's translation would have it, turn away from frail things to "acknowledge more clearly in thought the Creator of creatures"; rather, "by a cognition of creatures he knows the Creator more plainly" ("per creaturarum cognitionem creatorem evidentius cognoscat"). This seems a minor difference, but it is a significant one.

51. See *Commentary on the Aeneid*, ed. Jones and Jones, p. 12; *Commentary on the Aeneid*, trans. Schreiber and Maresca, p. 13. In this description of Aeneas's psychological state in Book I, the commentator writes, "Aeneas 'feasts his eyes on empty pictures.' Because the world is then new to him and he is wrapped in a cloud (that is, in ignorance), he does not understand the nature of the world; therefore these please him, and he admires them. We understand his eyes as the senses, some of which are true and some false; just as there is a right eye and a left one, so too we know certain senses are true and others false. We understand the pictures to be temporal goods, which are called pictures because they are not good but seem so, and therefore Boethius calls them 'images of true good.' And thus he fills his eyes (his senses) with pictures (that is, with worldly goods)." The Latin of this passage is quoted in my Ch. 5, n. 13.

52. *Commentary on the Aeneid*, ed. Jones and Jones, pp. 43–44; *Commentary on the Aeneid*, trans. Schreiber and Maresca, pp. 44–45.

53. For the identification of the bough of philosophy, see *Commentary on the Aeneid*, ed. Jones and Jones, p. 60; *Commentary on the Aeneid*, trans. Schreiber and Maresca, p. 59. That this entrance to Elysium might be connected to the perfection of memory is also suggested by Fulgentius, "Exposition," trans. Whitbread, p. 132. Fulgentius, however, in no way celebrates the strengthening of the other faculties, nor does he concentrate elsewhere on a psychology of ascent to God or Truth as the twelfth-century commentator does.

54. *Commentary on the Aeneid*, trans. Schreiber and Maresca, p. 106; *Commentary on the Aeneid*, ed. Jones and Jones, p. 114. Aeneas's initiations

into truth frequently begin with the imaginative contemplation of pictures (see above, n. 51), pictorial history (as depicted on the outside of the temple of Apollo; trans. Schreiber and Maresca, p. 38), or other representations of *visibilia* (as on the Cyclops' wall; trans. Schreiber and Maresca, p. 106).

55. See esp. the following: *Commentary on the Aeneid*, trans. Schreiber and Maresca, p. 44, and *Commentary on the Aeneid*, ed. Jones and Jones, pp. 43–44 (where the Sybil is compared to Lady Philosophy); trans. Schreiber and Maresca, p. 60, and ed. Jones and Jones, p. 61 (where the commentator describes the sequence of knowing observed by Boethius); trans. Schreiber and Maresca, p. 74, and ed. Jones and Jones, p. 77 (where the emotional states of Boethius and Aeneas are compared).

56. Wetherbee, *Platonism and Poetry*, p. 110. Even the first three Hesperides were interpreted by Guillaume de Conches in his Boethius commentary as the three internal senses *ingenium, ratio,* and *memoria*; see Silverstein, "Fabulous Cosmogony," p. 98, n. 34.

57. Nitzsche, *Genius Figure*, pp. 57–58.

58. For example, Piehler, *Visionary Landscape*, p. 13; Spearing, *Medieval Dream-Poetry*, p. 54; Hieatt, *Realism of Dream Visions*.

59. *Commentary on the Aeneid*, trans. Schreiber and Maresca, p. 67. *Commentary on the Aeneid*, ed. Jones and Jones, pp. 69–70: "Sompnus est quies animalium virtutum, id est otium quinque sensuum. Domus est huius humanum corpus quod merito figuratur per ulmum. Sicut enim ulmus quamvis sterilis vitem tamen fructuosam sustinet, ita caro quamvis sterilis anime, tamen virtutibus et scientie fecunda sedes est."

60. The entire passage in question can be found in John of Salisbury, *Policraticus*, ed. Webb, vol. 1, pp. 87–94.

61. Avicenna, *Liber de anima*, ed. van Riet, p. 18: "Tunc id quod apparet in ea intus est tale quale est quod apparet foris." For the full description of this psychology, see pp. 12–34. Scholars are now beginning to recognize the importance of Avicenna to the history of ideas in the West. It was through this Neoplatonist, first translated in Toledo as early as 1130, that the twelfth and thirteenth centuries first became acquainted with a synthesis of established Aristotelian doctrine. See Goichon, *Philosophy of Avicenna*, pp. 73–105. His epistemology, though, was widespread. Averroes's psychology of dreaming, for example, was very near to Avicenna's; see his "Libri Aristoteles," ed. Shields and Blumberg, pp. 75–125. A useful English translation of the Arabic text of this same work can be found in Averroes, *Epitome of Parva naturalia*, trans. Blumberg, pp. 31–53.

62. Both have their origins in Aristotelian and Galenic categories, but Aquinas places more emphasis on the delusive power of imagination when reason or intellect doze, and Avicenna more on its visionary power. See, for example, Aquinas, *De anima*, trans. Foster and Humphries, esp. secs. 669–70, pp. 375–400.

63. Avicenna, *Liber de anima*, ed. van Riet, p. 18: "Contingit autem aliquibus hominibus quod haec virtus imaginativa sit creata in illis fortissima et praevalens, ita ut non dominentur ei sensus nec formalis resistat ei, et

quod anima eorum sit fortissima, ita quod propter hoc quod contemplatur intellectum et id quod est supra intellectum, non destruatur eius condescensio ad sensus. Isti habent in vigiliis quod alii in somnis, sicut postea dicemus." On this power of imagination, see also Hugh of Saint Victor, *De unione* (*PL*, 177, 287A); Wetherbee's discussion of Hugh in "Theme of Imagination," pp. 48–49; and Bloomfield, *Piers Plowman*, pp. 172–74.
64. Macrobius, *Commentary*, trans. Stahl, p. 88.
65. Newman, "*Somnium*," p. 300.
66. See, for example, Avicenna, *Liber de anima*, ed. van Riet, pp. 32–33. Alcuin had made a similar point in his *Liber de animae ratione* when he argued that Nebuchadnezzar could not interpret his own oracular dream because he was not "divino illuminatus spiritu" as was the prophet who *could* explicate it; Alcuin, *De animae ratione*, *PL*, 101, 644D.
67. John of Salisbury, *Frivolities of Courtiers*, trans. Pike, p. 83. John of Salisbury, *Policraticus*, ed. Webb, p. 96: "Personis quoque quibusdam ueritas frequentius illucescit, utpote compositum habentibus animum, alias frequentior error inuoluit."
68. Alain de Lille, *Anticlaudianus*, ed. Bossuat, p. 56.
69. Avicenna, *Liber de anima*, ed. van Riet, p. 25: "Saepe autem videt homo interpretationem sui somnii in somnio suo, et est illud vere recordatio: quia virtus cogitationis sicut mota est primum ab ipsa re ad conformationem propter comparationem quae est inter illas, similiter non est longe ut moveatur a conformatione ad ipsam rem." See also Averroes's suggestion that a man may envision the interpretation of an earlier dream in a subsequent one; Averroes, "Libri Aristoteles," ed. Shields and Blumberg, p. 118.
70. King Alfred's naming of the narrator's character in his translation, Mōd, is perhaps the first and best known of such equations, which owe a clear debt to the *Soliloquia*.
71. Piehler, *Visionary Landscape*, pp. 15, 21–30.
72. Ibid., p. 19.
73. Macrobius, *Commentary*, trans. Stahl, p. 90; Pascalis Romanus, *Liber thesauri occulti*, ed. Collin-Roset, p. 161.
74. Averroes, "Libri Aristoteles," ed. Shields and Blumberg, p. 116: "Propter quid vero sunt sompnia? Dicamus ergo propter sollicitudinem circa hominem: homo enim quia indiget cognitione et comprehensione in virtute cogitativa." I have consulted, though I do not quote directly, Blumberg's translation, *Epitome of Parva naturalia*, p. 49.
75. Alain de Lille, *Distinctiones dictionum theologicalium*, *PL*, 210, 687B, quoted by Evans, *Alan of Lille*, p. 48: "ubi divina descendit excellentia ut humana ascendat intelligentia."
76. See Laporte, *Structures dynamiques*, pp. 24–47. For contemporary movements in the theology of grace, see also Taylor and Little's abridgment and translation of Chenu's study of twelfth-century theology, *Nature, Man and Society*, pp. 84–85, 202–3, 230, 288.
77. Hugh of St. Victor, *Didascalicon*, trans. Taylor, III.iv, pp. 87–88. Hugh of St. Victor, *Didascalicon*, ed. Buttimer, pp. 54–55: "Duo sunt, artes

et appendicia artium. . . . Ita ut quicumque ad scientiam pertingere cupit, si relicta veritate artium reliquis se implicare voluerit, materiam laboris, ut non dicam infinitam, plurimam inveniat et fructum exiguum."

78. This idea is explicit in Macrobius, *Commentary*, trans. Stahl, p. 86: "But in treating of the other gods and the Soul, as I have said, philosophers make use of fabulous narratives; not without a purpose, however, nor merely to entertain, but because they realize that a frank, open exposition of herself is distasteful to Nature, who, just as she has withheld an understanding of herself from the uncouth senses of men by enveloping herself in variegated garments, has also desired to have her secrets handled by more prudent individuals through fabulous narratives."

79. See also Dwyer, *Boethian Fictions*, pp. 20–23.

80. Macrobius, *Commentary*, trans. Stahl, p. 85.

81. Pascalis Romanus, *Liber thesauri occulti*, ed. Collin-Roset, pp. 160–61. *Fantasia* becomes equivalent to *fabula*; *insompnium* to *proverbium* or *parabola*.

82. Dronke, *Fabula*, pp. 13–78.

83. Pascalis Romanus, *Liber thesauri occulti*, p. 160.

84. John of Salisbury, *Frivolities of Courtiers*, trans. Pike, p. 81; and *Policraticus*, ed. Webb, p. 94. Also, John's discussion of dreams grows initially out of a treatment of sign. See *Frivolities of Courtiers*, p. 74; and *Policraticus*, p. 87.

85. This analogy is made explicit in Macrobius, *Commentary*, trans. Stahl, p. 92.

86. Newman, "*Somnium*," p. 135.

87. John of Salisbury, *Frivolities of Courtiers*, trans. Pike, p. 84. John of Salisbury, *Policraticus*, ed. Webb, p. 97: "Quisquis enim somniorum sequitur uanitatem, parum in lege Dei uigilans est, et dum fidei facit dispendium, perniciosissime dormit."

88. John of Salisbury, *Frivolities of Courtiers*, trans. Pike, p. 81. John of Salisbury, *Policraticus*, ed. Webb, p. 94: "Est itaque tam ad interpretationem somniorum quam ad reuelationem enigmatum et figurarum sollerter attendenda rerum significatio, quae tanto multiplicior est quam uocum, quanto ab operibus naturae opera uincuntur artificis imitantis naturam."

89. Trans. of Pascalis Romanus, *Liber thesauri occulti*, pp. 144–46: "littera occidit, spiritus autem vivificat"; "et significatam veritatem perscrutemur."

CHAPTER 3

1. Lewis, *Allegory of Love*, pp. 105–6. For convenience's sake, I will refer to the *De planctu*, as I did to the *De consolatione*, as a poem, even though its form is more properly *prosimetrum*.

2. Sheridan, introduction, *Plaint of Nature*, p. 33.

3. Moffat, preface, *Complaint of Nature*, p. 1. See also Raynaud de Lage, *Alain de Lille*, pp. 47, 95–96.

4. See Green, "Alan of Lille's *De Planctu Naturae*," pp. 649–74; Wetherbee, "Function of Poetry"; Wetherbee's discussion of the poem in *Platonism and Poetry*, pp. 188–211; and Economou, *Goddess Natura*, pp. 72–97.

5. See Wetherbee, "Function of Poetry." See also his discussion of the role of poetry in the *De planctu* in "Theme of Imagination," pp. 56–58.

6. See Piehler, *Visionary Landscape*; also Curtius, *European Literature*, pp. 118–19.

7. But see Piehler, *Visionary Landscape*, pp. 46–68; also Wetherbee, "Function of Poetry," pp. 101–7. Yet even these critics seem finally to leave the Dreamer behind in a way that Alain did not.

8. I take the phrase "moral allegory," of course, from the famous fourfold method of interpreting medieval texts. Indeed, what I am talking about is very precisely "moral allegory," which treats, as Dante announces in his *Letter to Can Grande*, "the conversion of the soul from the sorrow and misery of sin to a state of grace," in *Dantis Alagherii epistolae*, ed. and trans. Toynbee, p. 199. But what I will discuss is moral allegory in a very special sense, for this "allegory" signifies a moral conversion by imitating its sequence in an individual psychology.

9. Alain de Lille, *De planctu*, ed. Häring, XVI.38–42, p. 866. Further references to this work appear in the text. All quotations will be taken from this edition, and all translations will be my own unless otherwise acknowledged. I have, however, benefited greatly from consulting both Moffat's and Sheridan's excellent translations, whose numbering of the prose and metrical sections I follow in my own text as more convenient and conventional than Häring's.

10. Piehler, *Visionary Landscape*, p. 85.

11. Wetherbee, "Function of Poetry," p. 107.

12. Ibid., p. 109.

13. Ibid.; Economou, *Goddess Natura*, pp. 86–88.

14. This is what I take the opening lines of Prose V to indicate. See Alain de Lille, *De planctu*, ed. Häring, X.1–2, p. 845: "Iam ex hoc mee doctrine artificio tibi cupidinarie artis elucescit theorica. Per librum uero experientie tibi practicam poteris conparare."

15. See, for example, Sheridan, introduction, *Plaint of Nature*, pp. 33–34; Raynaud de Lage, *Alain de Lille*, pp. 43–45.

16. Piehler, *Visionary Landscape*, p. 52.

17. Dronke, *Fabula*, p. 145. See also Trout, *Voyage of Prudence*, pp. 76–79.

18. Evans, *Alan of Lille*, pp. 21–80.

19. This is not a simple point. The dream is not explicitly framed, as it would be in later vision poems. We do not know for sure the status of the vision until the work's final lines, which are themselves open to question. Häring's edition, based on a collation of manuscripts, reads, "Huius igitur imaginarie uisionis subtracto speculo, me ab extasis excitatum insompnio prior mistice apparitionis dereliquit aspectus" (XVIII.164–65, p. 879), sug-

gesting merely that the dream is over; the *PL* (210, 482C), which bases its text on the seventeenth-century edition of C. de Visch, reads, "Hujus imaginariae visionis subtracto speculo, me ab exstasi excitatum in somno, prior mysticae apparitionis dereliquit aspectus," indicating that once his visionary sight is taken from him, the Dreamer falls into a different kind of sleep, as the lights of the tapers—in both editions—had fallen asleep ("defectae sopore"). As in n. 62 below, I prefer the *PL* reading. But in either case, the ending of the poem makes clear that the work has recorded a dream.

20. For example, in Prose II, when all the elements renew their natures at her coming; or more obviously, in her appearance as she represents in a visual form all of creation. This multivalence in her symbolic dimension is acceptable medieval practice. See *Commentary on the Aeneid*, ed. Jones and Jones, p. 9: "Notandum est vero in hoc loco, quemadmodum in aliis misticis voluminibus, ita et in hoc equivocationes et multivocationes esse et integumenta ad diversa respicere."

21. X.44, p. 846. See also VI.190–91, where "humane nature" is clearly equivalent in man to the reasoning principle. Similarly, VIII.19–21, p. 833.

22. Alain de Lille, *Distinctiones dictionum theologicalium*, *PL*, 210, 871D. Stock, in *Myth and Science*, p. 164, notes that the figure could be used in Bernardus to denote "rational curiosity." This usage has precedent in classical meanings of *natura*. See Economou, *Goddess Natura*, pp. 2–27, where he indicates that one of the most important meanings of the term was the essence of an object, which in man's case would certainly be rational. The late medieval commentator on *Les Echecs amoureux* calls this the Aristotelian definition and applies it first in his allegorization of the goddess Nature; "*Chess of Love*," trans. Jones, pp. 36–37.

23. Both Natura and the vision itself are named repeatedly in the work as mirrors; see, for example, XVI.190, p. 871; or XVIII.164, p. 879.

24. Trans. of Raynaud de Lage, *Alain de Lille*, p. 44.

25. In VI.94–96, p. 828, Alain makes clear that these powers are the same ones we have studied earlier, inhabiting the different chambers of the head, "diuersis capitis thalamis habitantes."

26. Alain de Lille, *Sermo de sphaera intelligibili*, in his *Textes inédits*, ed. d'Alverny, p. 301.

27. Wetherbee, "Function of Poetry," p. 107. Later in his discussion, Wetherbee does seem to retreat somewhat from this position, although not in a way that would negate his earlier insight; see pp. 121–25 of this same article.

28. See, for example, Johannes Scotus, *De divisione naturae*, V.xxxvi, 975D, quoted by Green, "Alan of Lille's *De Planctu Naturae*," p. 669.

29. For example, in the *Sermo de sphaera intelligibili*, in Alain de Lille, *Textes inédits*, ed. d'Alverny, p. 300.

30. "Apocalypse of Paul," trans. James, p. 543; see also p. 546.

31. The Dreamer's development, thus, is much like Dante's as he progresses through the *Inferno* and the *Purgatorio* in a journey that I will show in Chapter 4 is much like Alain's in other ways as well. One of Dante's pri-

mary limitations in the *Inferno* is too much sympathy with the damned (see *Inf.*XX), a problem that his behavior near the end of the canticle shows he has overcome. In the *Purgatorio*, then, Pride becomes his besetting sin (see *Purg.*XI and XIII.136–38), which he begins to conquer by the posture of humility he copies from those on the first terrace.

32. Bernardus Silvestris, *Cosmographia*, trans. Wetherbee, p. 96. For the Latin, see Dronke's edition, p. 125: "Illic Oyarses idem erat et Genius, in artem et officium pictoris et figurantis addictus."

33. For Bernardus's debt to Apuleius, see Baker, "Priesthood of Genius." For Genius's origins in Claudian, see Knowlton, "Allegorical Figure Genius." Nitzsche discusses both these traditions in *Genius Figure*; see, for example, pp. 17, 72.

34. In addition to the works by Nitzsche, Baker, and Knowlton quoted in n. 33, see Knowlton, "Genius as an Allegorical Figure," in which he compares earlier uses to fifteenth-century references to the figure; Woolsey, "Bernard Silvester," in which he traces Pantomorphos to that work; Raynaud de Lage's chapter on Genius in *Alain de Lille*, pp. 89–93; Brumble, "Genius in the *De planctu*"; Economou, "Genius"; also Economou's discussion of Genius in *Goddess Natura*, esp. pp. 37, 90–97; Schueler, "Gower's Characterization of Genius," which, although it is not explicitly about a twelfth-century work, shows Genius as a "mediator between man's natural self and the divine will" (p. 245); and Wetherbee's "Theme of Imagination."

35. Nitzsche, *Genius Figure*, pp. 7–20.

36. Baker, "Priesthood of Genius," pp. 277–84; see also Nitzsche's discussion of the universal Genius in Augustine, in *Genius Figure*, pp. 25–30; and Lewis, "Genius and Genius."

37. Bernardus Silvestris, *Cosmographia*, trans. Wetherbee, pp. 107, 126; and *Cosmographia*, ed. Dronke, pp. 135–36, 154. In the first reference quoted here, he speaks of that "Genius, qui, de nascendi principiis homini copulatus, vitanda illi discrimina vel mentis presagio, vel soporis ymagine, vel prodigioso rerum spectaculo configurat."

38. Wetherbee, "Function of Poetry," pp. 112–13; Baker calls Wetherbee into question here in "Priesthood of Genius," pp. 281–82.

39. Trans. of Raynaud de Lage, *Alain de Lille*, p. 91.

40. Ibid., p. 92.

41. Brumble, "Genius in the *De Planctu*," p. 313.

42. Nitzsche, *Genius Figure*, pp. 88–92.

43. Economou, *Goddess Natura*, p. 92. See Wetherbee, "Function of Poetry," pp. 114–18.

44. This impersonal quality of intellect is borne out by commentary on the Aristotelian "active intellect" made by certain Arabic writers, notably Averroes. A natural outgrowth of the belief in such an undifferentiated intellect was doubt about personal immortality, a heresy of which Averroes has been accused, so most philosophers found various ways around admitting the doctrine's full implications. For a brief, introductory discussion of some of these issues as they relate to Averroes and other Islamic philoso-

phers, see ch. 8 of Copleston's *History of Medieval Philosophy*, esp. pp. 121–24.

45. Wetherbee, "Theme of Imagination," p. 57.
46. Both words derive ultimately from *gignere*, meaning "to bring forth" or "engender."
47. Nitzsche, *Genius Figure*, p. 46.
48. This idea is explored at length by Nitzsche in her chapter on Bernardus Silvestris, ibid., pp. 65–87.
49. Horace, *Epistles*, II.ii.187–89, in his *Satires, Epistles and Ars Poetica*, ed. and trans. Fairclough, p. 439: "naturae deus humanae, mortalis in unum / quodque caput, voltu mutabilis, albus et ater."
50. Wetherbee, *Platonism and Poetry*, p. 94.
51. Ibid., p. 97.
52. Interpretations of this myth vary, but such identifications are at least implied by Remigius of Auxerre who sees Eurydice as *inventio* and Orpheus, after she has disappeared, as *vox* lacking *ratio*. For a description of Remigius's interpretation, see Nitzsche, *Genius Figure*, p. 61. Even more suggestive, though, is Guillaume de Conches's reading of the myth in his commentary on the *De consolatione*, in "Commentaires inédits," ed. Jourdain, vol. 20, pt. 2, p. 81. In this interpretation, Eurydice is *genius*; "Genius est naturalis concupiscentia; sed haec naturalis concupiscentia merito dicitur Euridice, id est boni judicatio." In his descent to rescue her, Orpheus becomes the *sapiens* who comes down to earth to reorient his *genius* or concupiscence toward a higher truth. A similar meaning is attached to the myth by the author of the twelfth-century *Commentary on the Aeneid*, ed. Jones and Jones, pp. 53–55; in this analysis of the myth, Eurydice is again *genius*, and Orpheus in his song exercises "sapientiam et eloquentiam" (p. 55).
53. Nitzsche, *Genius Figure*, pp. 2, 5, 57–58.
54. Mythographus Tertius, "De diis gentium et illorum allegoriis," ed. Bode, p. 242.
55. Augustine, *City of God*, trans. Green, p. 422; "Et cum alio loco genium dicit esse uniuscuiusque animum rationalem et ideo esse singulos singulorum, talem autem mundi animum Deum esse, ad hoc idem utique revocat ut tamquam universalis genius ipse mundi animus esse credatur. Hic est igitur quem appellant Iovem. Nam si omnis genius deus et omnis viri animus genius, sequitur ut sit omnis viri animus deus; quod si et ipsos abhorrere absurditas ipsa compellit, restat ut eum singulariter et excellenter dicant deum Genium, quem dicunt mundi animum ac per hoc Iovem."
56. See, for example, Bernardus in the *Cosmographia*, ed. Dronke, p. 102. The term also occurs in Martianus, *De nuptiis*, VI.567.
57. Alain de Lille, *Textes inédits*, p. 228: "Per substantificos genios, id est per substantiales naturas. Genius enim natura vel Deus nature dicitur. Haec autem manifestatio pertinet ad naturalem philosophiam que de rerum natura pertractat."
58. Ibid.: "Scientia autem non habetur de Deo per substantiales naturas."

59. Ibid., p. 301; here *ingenium* is described as "rerum proprietates circumuolans, caducas vix earum valet sompniare naturas. Ibi ad unitatem pluralitas, ad identitatem diuersitas, ad consonantiam dissonantia, ad concordiam discordia proprietatum reuertitur."

60. Lévi-Strauss, "The Structural Study of Myth," p. 227.

61. In following Lévi-Strauss's formal analysis here, I do not intend to imply agreement with his special valuing of this process in myth over ritual or the severing of language and referent that emerges as its result; see Girard, "Differentiation and Reciprocity."

62. It is not possible to tell from Häring's apparatus precisely how much support for either reading the manuscripts he used provide. Sheridan writes, "Antigenius, not Antigamus, is the reading supported by the best manuscripts" (Alain de Lille, *Plaint*, trans. Sheridan, p. 163n). But presumably the Cysoing manuscript upon which de Visch relied when making the edition for the *PL* reads "Antigamus," since no variant readings are reported there, and this manuscript, according to Häring, was complete and praiseworthy, at least when de Visch used it; it is now preserved at Lille and is in fact one of the manuscripts followed by Häring as well (Alain de Lille, *De planctu*, ed. Häring, p. 799). It is extremely doubtful that works by critics who have recently made the argument in favor of Antigenius had anything to do with Häring's editorial decision here, but the number of these had become impressive even before Häring's edition, including Green's "Alan of Lille's *De planctu naturae*" (p. 671n), Brumble's "Genius in the *De planctu*" (p. 317n), and Nitzsche's *Genius Figure* (p. 89). In any case, I suggest that the correct reading remain an open subject.

63. Here I follow Moffat's translation (*Complaint of Nature*), pp. 90–91.

64. Dronke, *Fabula*, p. 151.

65. Lévi-Strauss, "The Structural Study of Myth," p. 224.

66. Evans, *Alan of Lille*, p. 73.

67. See Boethius, *Philosophiae consolatio*, ed. Biehler, Book V, Prose 4–Meter 5.

68. Wetherbee, *Platonism and Poetry*, p. 82. See also my discussion of this work in Ch. 2.

69. Boethius, *Consolation of Philosophy*, trans. Green, pp. 79–80. Boethius, *Philosophiae consolatio*, ed. Biehler, Book IV, Prose 2.33: "Quod quidem cuipiam mirum forte uideatur, ut malos, qui plures hominum sunt, eosdem non esse dicamus; sed ita sese res habet. Nam qui mali sunt eos malos esse non abnuo; sed eosdem esse pure atque simpliciter nego."

70. This point is also made by Brumble, "Genius in the *De planctu*," pp. 222–23, who quotes Augustine (*City of God*, XII.2) for authority rather than Boethius.

71. The quest for this tertium quid has been one of the leitmotifs in criticism of Alain's work. The term was first introduced by Lewis, *Allegory of Love*, pp. 101–5. It is rejected, however, by Green, "Alan of Lille's *De*

planctu naturae," p. 674; then reintroduced by Wetherbee in "Function of Poetry," p. 125.
72. Green, "Alan of Lille's *De planctu naturae*," p. 674.
73. Wetherbee, "Function of Poetry," pp. 110, 120.
74. Most critics find this work rather more insistent on the unity of nature and grace; see Raynaud de Lage, *Alain de Lille*, p. 95; Lewis, *Allegory of Love*, pp. 101–5; or Wetherbee, "Function of Poetry," pp. 123–24. Green, however, reads both as tentative about this unity; see "Alan of Lille's *Anticlaudianus*," p. 7.
75. Alain de Lille, *Anticlaudianus*, trans. Sheridan, p. 157. For the Latin, see Bossuat's edition, p. 142:
>In quo discordes Natura Fidesque duellum
>Exercent unamque trahunt in dissona mentem;
>Nam Natura docet genitorem parcere nato.
>Econtra stat firma Fides que spernere natum
>Imperat, ut summo faueat Natura parenti.
>Quod non uult cupit ergo pater; nunc parcere temptans,
>Nunc offerre uolens, tandem negat ipse quod optat.
>Ergo succumbit Fidei Natura dolensque
>Cedit uictrici, quod non uult uelle coacta.

76. Spearing, *Medieval Dream-Poetry*, p. 21.
77. Sheridan, introduction, *Plaint of Nature*, p. 53.

CHAPTER 4

1. In my presentation of thirteenth-century intellectual history, I am relying mainly on the following studies: Gilson, *History of Christian Philosophy*, pp. 387–427; Steenberghen, *Aristotle in the West*; Copleston, *History of Medieval Philosophy*, pp. 199–212; Weinberg, *Short History of Medieval Philosophy*, pp. 157–81; Knowles, *Evolution of Medieval Thought*, pp. 269–77; and though its emphasis is on the fourteenth century, Leff, *Medieval Outlook*, esp. pp. 1–31. An interesting account of the atmosphere of dissent and repression in the age—and the political and poetic strategies for avoiding persecution—is provided by Fortin, *Dissidence et philosophie*. For Southern's definition of medieval humanism, see my Ch. 1, n. 5.
2. Leff, *Medieval Outlook*, p. 25. See also my Introduction, n. 30.
3. Steenberghen, *Aristotle in the West*, pp. 219–20. In fact, Siger became increasingly orthodox in his beliefs, particularly in his psychology; see Steenberghen, *Siger de Brabant*. A brief summary of the terms of the debate over Siger's orthodoxy is provided by Knowles, *Evolution of Medieval Thought*, p. 270.
4. I am following the translation of these articles by Fortin and O'Neill in Lerner and Mahdi, eds., *Medieval Political Philosophy*, pp. 337–54. The quoted propositions are 180 (p. 352), 203 (p. 353), and 205 (p. 353). Fortin and O'Neill follow the order established by Mandonnet in his edition of the condemnation in *Siger de Brabant*, vol. 2, pp. 175–91. I will also in-

clude the Latin of quoted propositions in my notes, with the original numbering, taken from *Chartularium*, ed. Denifle and Chatelain, pp. 543–55. Proposition 180 is 175 in this text: "Quod lex christiana impedit addiscere." Proposition 203 is 179: "Quod non est confitendum, nisi ad apparentiam." Proposition 205 is 183: "Quod simplex fornicatio, utpote soluti cum soluta, non est peccatum." In my identification of the sources of doctrines and in my assessment of their orthodoxy, I am following the very useful recent study of the subject, Hissette's *Enquête sur les 219 articles*; see esp. his summary of conclusions, pp. 313–18. This book makes it possible for me to question (more than, for example, Gilson does) the real justification for the condemnation, in the interest of reconstructing Jean de Meun's possible reactions to the event. Further speculation about the issues and jurisdictional relationships between the arts and theology can be found in Grant, "Issues in Natural Philosophy."

5. The full sentence from Tempier reads as follows: "Dicunt enim ea esse vera secundum philosophiam, sed non secundum fidem catholicam, quasi sint due contrarie veritates, et quasi contra veritatem sacre scripture sit veritas in dictis gentilium dampnatorum, de quibus scriptum est: 'Perdam sapientiam sapientium,' quia vera sapientia perdit falsam sapientiam" (*Chartularium*, ed. Denifle and Chatelain, p. 543).

6. Knowles, *Evolution of Medieval Thought*, p. 277.

7. Trans. of Hissette, *Enquête sur les 219 articles*, p. 318.

8. Ibid., pp. 314–16.

9. For a translation of this statute, see Thorndike, *University Records*, pp. 85–88.

10. For this description of the intellectual life of the university and changes in the curriculum, and even more so, for my interpretation of these, I am most indebted to Hardison, "Medieval Literary Criticism"; see also his "Toward a History of Medieval Literary Criticism." I have also relied upon the accounts of the history of the university provided by Rashdall in *Universities of Europe*, vol. 1; by Schachner in *Medieval Universities*; and by Leff in *Paris and Oxford Universities*. For information about the arts curriculum in particular, I have consulted Paetow's *Arts Course at Medieval Universities*.

11. John of Salisbury, *Metalogicon*, trans. McGarry, p. 37. For the Latin, see *PL*, 199, 840A, where *grammatica* is designated as "totius philosophiae cunabulum."

12. Rashdall, *Universities of Europe*, p. 68.

13. See, for example, *Accessūs ad auctores*, ed. Huygens; see also the discussion of this classification by Allen, *Ethical Poetic*, pp. 3–66.

14. In, for example, the *De divisione philosophiae* of Dominicus Gundissalinus, ed. Baur; see Hardison, "Medieval Literary Criticism," pp. 274–75, 294–95. See also my Ch. 1, n. 10. My account of course provides a simplification of a highly diverse and complex movement; the precise influence of the Aristotelian tradition on the increasing classification of poetry as part

of logic, and the changing definition of its reach and proper object is traced by Dahan, "Poétique du moyen âge."

15. Dronke, *Fabula*, pp. 3–4; also Dahan, "Poétique du moyen âge," p. 192. See also Hardison, "Medieval Literary Criticism," p. 297.

16. For Dante's connection with the University of Bologna, see Robson, "Dante's Reading," p. 82. Although Paetow speaks briefly of this "healthy interest" in grammar at Bologna (*Arts Course at Medieval Universities*, p. 48), the evidence for it is rather sketchy and, as he also points out, grammar may have fared "almost as badly" here as at Paris (p. 49). A better understanding of the nature of the work in grammar done at Italian universities awaits further research.

17. Boccaccio, *Genealogie deorum gentilium libri*, ed. Romano, vol. 2, e.g., XIV.xviii, p. 735.

18. Fleming, *Roman de la rose*, pp. 18–20. Cp. Laurent de Premierfait, quoted by Martin, *Boccace de Jean Sans Peurs*, pp. 10–11: "Cestui poète Daut, qui, entre pluseurs volumes nouveaulx et proufitables estans lors à Paris, rencontra le noble livre de la *Rose*, en quoy Jehan Clopinel de Meung, homme d'engin celeste, peigny une vraye mapemonde de toutes choses celestes et terrienes; Daut donques, qui de Dieu et de nature avoit receu l'esperit de poétrie, advisa que ou livre de la *Rose* est souffisammant descript le paradis des bons et l'enfer des mauvais en langaige françois, voult en langaige florentin, soubz aultre manière de vers rimoiez, contrefaire au vif le beau livre de la *Rose*, en ensuyvant tel ordre comme fist le divin poète Virgile ou sixiesme livre que l'en nomme *Enéide*."

Although my argument in no way depends upon a direct and intentional relationship between the two poems, the tradition relied upon here and certain verbal and thematic echoes of the *Rose* in Dante suggest that such a relationship is not implausible. For the likelihood that Dante was familiar with the *Rose* at least before completion of the *Commedia* and for a summary of the debate over the relationship between the two works, see Richards, *Dante and the Roman de la rose*, pp. 71–108.

19. Kelly, "Li chastiaus," p. 61; Piehler, *Visionary Landscape*, p. 105.

20. Dahlberg, "Unity of the *Rose*," p. 580.

21. Roughly speaking, critics fall into two distinct camps: among proponents of the first, nonironic view are several French critics, who hold that Guillaume's idealism is subjected by his continuator to scholastic scrutiny and parodied, but ultimately only so that Jean can endorse a new, more overtly sexual, art of love. See Paré, *Idées et lettres*; Langlois, *Origines et sources*; Faral, "*Roman de la rose* et la pensée française"; and more recently Badel, *Roman de la rose au XIVe siècle*; and Poirion's analysis, *Roman de la rose*, and his edition of *Le Roman de la rose*. Also see Lecoy's edition of *Le Roman de la rose*, pp. xi–xxviii. In English, see Gunn, *Mirror of Love*, and his article "Teacher and Student in the *Roman de la rose*."

The second, Robertsonian or ironic, perspective is well represented by Robertson himself in "Doctrine of Charity" and *Preface to Chaucer*, esp. pp.

91–104. Also influential are Fleming's two books: *Roman de la rose* and his reformulation and defense of the position there presented, *Reason and the Lover*. For further references, the reader may consult the useful bibliographies provided by Gunn in *Mirror of Love*, pp. 525–44; by Dahlberg in his translation, *Romance of the Rose*, pp. 429–38; by Gunn and Dahlberg in "*Rose* Scholarship," pp. 68–77; and by Luria in *Reader's Guide*, pp. 225–65.

   22. Guillaume de Lorris, *Romance of the Rose*, trans. Dahlberg, p. 73. The passage in Old French from which this is taken reads:
> Sachiez, se la letre ne ment,
> que Dex la fist ou firmament
> a sa semblance et a s'image
> et li dona tel avantage
> qu'ele a pooir et seignorie
> de garder home de folie,
> por tant qu'il soit tex qu'il la croie.

I am following Lecoy's edition of the poem, vol. 1, ll. 2973–79. I will continue to use this translation and edition throughout, citing first page numbers from the English and subsequently line numbers from the French in my text.

   23. Criticism seems especially likely to polarize at this crux. Robertson and Fleming argue for the fountain's destructiveness; see Robertson's *Preface to Chaucer*, pp. 93–95; Robertson's "Doctrine of Charity," p. 42; and Fleming's *Roman de la rose*, pp. 94–97. An excellent summary of views is provided by Hill, "Narcissus"; also Hillman, "Mirror Perilous." Proponents of the fountain's positive moral qualities include Köhler, "Narcisse"; and Goldin, *Mirror of Narcissus*, pp. 25–59.

   24. The mirror as a means to moral refinement is studied by Goldin in *Mirror of Narcissus*. The various and ambiguous possibilities for this image are well documented by Grabes, *Mutable Glass*, esp. pp. 67–162. Fountains, of course, also suggest competing secular and spiritual possibilities, as do the fountains described by Genius in Jean de Meun's poem (ll. 20339–637).

   25. See, for example, Guillaume de Lorris, *Romance of the Rose*, trans. Dahlberg, pp. 31, 59, and 80; and *Le Roman de la rose*, ed. Lecoy, ll. 45–52, 2058–73, and 3470–75; also Vitz, "The *I* of the *Roman*."

   26. Muscatine, *Chaucer and the French Tradition*, p. 41; see also Stone, "Guillaume de Lorris," p. 168.

   27. Langlois, *Origines et sources*, pp. 93–102, 136–38, 148–50.

   28. The idea that Jean's poem might properly be designated an "anti-Guillaume" was suggested first by Faral in "*Roman de la rose* et la pensée française," p. 439; by Paré, *Idées et lettres*, pp. 320–21; and recently on more formal grounds by Zumthor, "Récit et anti-récit."

   29. The question of which character's voice has authority in the poem—or whether any voice does—has been a matter of warm debate in criticism. Genius and Nature have at various times been offered as substitutes, and some feel that none of Jean's spokesmen are without some limitation. For a

summary of this debate and reformulation of the grounds for Reason's authority, see Fleming, *Reason and the Lover*, pp. 3–63; for an opposing view, Hill, "Narcissus," esp. pp. 417–22.

30. Pearcy, "Modes of Signification," pp. 163–65. See also Poirion, "Mots et les choses."

31. See, for example, William of Ockham, *Ordinatio*, D.II.Q.viii, *prima redactio*; translated by Boehner in William of Ockham, *Philosophical Writings*, pp. 44–48. See William of Ockham, *Ordinatio*, ed. Brown and Gál, pp. 266–92.

32. Wetherbee, "Literal and the Allegorical," p. 269.

33. John of Salisbury, *Metalogicon*, trans. McGarry, p. 215. "Communes enim conceptiones, a singulorum inductione fidem sortiuntur" (*PL*, 199, 921A). This point receives added support from Lonergan's analysis of the stages of intellection, which ultimately involve a return to the singular; see his *Verbum*, pp. 144–81.

34. Fleming, *Reason and the Lover*, p. 36.

35. Tillman, "Scholastic and Averroistic Influences," p. 96. The classic statement on Jean's naturalism is offered by Paré, *Idées et lettres*.

36. Fleming, *Roman de la rose*, p. 214. Typical dismissals of the influence of Aristotelianism may be found in Robertson, *Preface to Chaucer*, pp. 100–101, and in Economou, *Goddess Natura*, p. 116.

37. Fleming, *Roman de la rose*, p. 218.

38. Tillman, "Scholastic and Averroistic Influences," p. 98. See also Paré, *Idées et lettres*, pp. 321–25. Cp. Friedman, "Jean de Meung."

39. Fleming, *Reason and the Lover*, p. 56.

40. For La Vielle's moralizing, see esp. Jean de Meun, *Romance of the Rose*, trans. Dahlberg, pp. 228–29, 232; for Genius, pp. 323–25, 329–30; and *Le Roman de la rose*, ed. Lecoy, ll. 13143–252, 13427–44, 19599–722, 20007–84. Orpheus, of course, should represent "the wise and eloquent man who seeks, having learned the emptiness of temporal life, to fix his desire on higher things" (Wetherbee, *Platonism and Poetry*, p. 96).

41. Lecoy, in Guillaume de Lorris Jean de Meun, *Le Roman de la rose*, pp. vii–viii.

42. Wetherbee, "Literal and the Allegorical," p. 276.

43. Cp. Galen, *Parts of the Body*, trans. May, pp. 107–8. For my discussion of the organization of Nature's speech here, I am indebted to conversations with my colleague Katharine Park (see also Ch. 1, n. 19).

44. In "Condemnation of 219 Propositions," p. 351, Fortin and O'Neill have made this Proposition 177. In *Chartularium*, ed. Denifle and Chatelain, it is Proposition 33: "Quod raptus et visiones non fiunt, nisi per naturam." Hissette, in *Enquête sur les 219 articles*, pp. 271–72, has suggested that this condemnation can only have been directed at Boetius of Dacia and, even then, depends upon reading his work out of context.

45. In "Condemnation of 219 Propositions," trans. Fortin and O'Neill, these are Propositions 205, 207, 208, 209, and 210. In *Chartularium*, ed. Denifle and Chatelain, they are 183, 172, 168, 181, and 169: "Quod simplex fornicatio . . . non est peccatum"; "Quod delectatio in actibus venereis non

impedit actum seu usum intellectus"; "Quod continentia non est essentialiter virtus"; "Quod castitas non est majus bonum, quam perfecta abstinentia"; and "Quod perfecta abstinentia ab actu carnis corrumpit virtutem et speciem."

46. Hissette, *Enquête sur les 219 articles*, pp. 294–300.

47. Jean's loyalties are made absolutely clear in his defense of Guillaume de St. Amour, whose mendicant opponents are explicitly identified with the followers of Faus Semblant; Jean de Meun, *Romance of the Rose*, trans. Dahlberg, pp. 200–202; and *Le Roman de la rose*, ed. Lecoy, ll. 11376–494.

48. Wetherbee, "Literal and the Allegorical," p. 286.

49. Tuve, *Allegorical Imagery*, p. 280.

50. This tendency in longer satires is noted by Lanham in a discussion of the *Metamorphoses*; see his *Motives of Eloquence*, p. 60.

51. Muscatine, *Chaucer and the French Tradition*, p. 76.

52. Ibid., p. 78.

53. Dane, "Parody and Satire," p. 150.

54. Muscatine, *Chaucer and the French Tradition*, p. 77.

55. Spearing, *Medieval Dream-Poetry*, p. 28.

56. Hanning, *Individual in Twelfth-Century Romance*, p. 108.

57. Spearing, *Medieval Dream-Poetry*, p. 40. See Jean de Meun, *Romance of the Rose*, trans. Dahlberg, pp. 187–89; and *Le Roman de la rose*, ed. Lecoy, ll. 10535–648.

58. For a discussion of the phrase's literary and philosophical contexts, see P. B. Taylor, "Chaucer's *Cosyn to the Dede*," where he also discusses the intriguing double meaning of the word "cousin": "Besides 'blood-relative,' *cousin* denotes a 'dupe' " (p. 324). See also David H. Abraham, "*Cosyn* and *Cosynage*."

CHAPTER 5

1. Regardless of Siger's actual orthodoxy or heterodoxy, he did represent for the age a "prince of pure philosophy"; see Gilson, *Dante and Philosophy*, pp. 256–57 and passim.

2. The physical differences between Hell and Purgatory are summarized in detail by Newman, "*Somnium*," pp. 351–54. This discussion forms part of a larger investigation of the tripartite structure of the work, pp. 338–57. See also his "Saint Augustine's Three Visions," pp. 56–78. Newman contends that the *Inferno* and the *Purgatorio* correspond respectively to the Augustinian modes of corporeal and spiritual vision—purely natural ways of seeing—and the *Paradiso* to the *visio intellectualis*, a mode of apprehension beyond images. Such an Augustinian division of the poem was first suggested by Bundy in *Theory of Imagination*, pp. 225–56, then independently elaborated by Newman. Dante, however, likely planned more than one complementary mental itinerary for his pilgrim. A slightly different way of dividing up the narrator's progress has been suggested by Singleton (see *Journey to Beatrice*), who argues that the movement of the poem is organized by the

three lights of Thomistic psychology (see esp. pp. 15–38). By the first of these, the soul sees naturally, with the aid of intellect; by the second light, it sees by faith, with the help of grace; the third light brings the soul to a state of blessedness. These three lights, according to Singleton, correspond to the pilgrim's three guides in the poem. Singleton is anticipated in his argument by Silverstein, "Dante and Vergil the Mystic," p. 78. On the other hand, Thompson, in *Dante's Epic Journeys*, pp. 201–6, offers a bipartite division of the poem. According to Thompson, the poet sees naturally during the first two canticles, then, as the verb *transumanar* suggests, transcends the natural in the *Paradiso*. Common to all these theories are two essential ideas: (1) that the *Inferno* and the *Purgatorio* belong together as realms where the pilgrim sees naturally; and (2) that Beatrice leads Dante to the kind of vision that transcends the natural and requires some special grace. For this point, see also Mazzeo, *Structure and Thought in the Paradiso*, pp. 84–110.

3. Villani, *Comento al primo Canto dell' Inferno*, ed. Cugnoni, p. 85, quoted by Newman, "Somnium," p. 344. See also Pietro Alighieri, *Super Dantis ipsius Genitoris Comoediam commentarium*, ed. Nannucci, pp. 24–29, 739, cited by Newman, "Somnium," pp. 342–43; see also Pietro Alighieri, *"Commentarium" di Pietro Alighieri*, ed. della Vedova and Silvotti, pp. 26–27, 34. A fine summary of the evidence for reading the poem as a vision is provided by Newman, "Somnium," pp. 338–47, but is ultimately rejected as inconclusive regarding the poet's intention.

4. In addition to Singleton's discussion of the three lights in *Journey to Beatrice*, see also his chapter on the three conversions of the will toward God and the three kinds of grace that these reflect, pp. 39–56.

5. Ibid., pp. 11–12.

6. Dante Alighieri, *Divine Comedy*, trans. Singleton.

7. Gilson, *Saint Thomas Aquinas*, trans. Bullough, p. 228, also p. 243.

8. Silverstein, "Dante and Vergil the Mystic"; on pp. 81–82, he discusses specifically Dante's debt for the wood of error. Thompson, in *Dante's Epic Journeys*, pp. 7–11, 21–28, and 81–82, and in "Dante and Bernard Silvestris," pp. 201–6, also discusses the relationship between Dante's poem and the *Aeneid* commentary, citing Padoan's "Tradizione e fortuna del commento all' 'Eneide' di Bernardo Silvestre," pp. 227–40, for evidence that Dante was acquainted with this commentary; see also Padoan, *Il pio Enea, l'empio Ulisse*, for a comprehensive discussion of Dante's debt to the moral and allegorical tradition of classical exegesis that this commentary represents.

9. *Commentary on the Aeneid*, trans. Schreiber and Maresca, p. 53. For the Latin, see *Commentary on the Aeneid*, ed. Jones and Jones, p. 53: "Quemadmodum enim nemora propter solis absentiam sunt obscura, ita propter deffectum rationis temporalia. Sicut nemora propter multitudinem varietatemque viarum sunt invia, ita temporalia propter varias vias que ad summum bonum ducere videntur, cum non ducant, invia sunt."

10. *Commentary on the Aeneid*, trans. Schreiber and Maresca, p. 106. *Commentary on the Aeneid*, ed. Jones and Jones, p. 114: "Menia ergo Ciclopum sunt celi que sunt naturales regiones spirituum."

11. Thompson, "Dante and Bernard Silvestris," p. 206.
12. In Dante Alighieri, *Dantis Alagherii epistolae*, ed. and trans. Toynbee, p. 202.
13. *Commentary on the Aeneid*, trans. Schreiber and Maresca, p. 13. *Commentary on the Aeneid*, ed. Jones and Jones, p. 12: "Hic occulos 'pictura pascit inani.' Quia enim tunc novus est mundus ei et ipse est in nebula, scilicet ignorantia nec naturam mundanam intelligit; ideo placent ei hec et in eis admirationem habet. Per oculos intelligimus sensus quorum quidam sunt veri, quidam falsi quia sicut oculorum alter est dexter, alter sinister, ita intelligimus quod quidam sunt veri, quidam falsi; per picturas vero bona temporalia que ideo picture dicuntur quia bona non sunt, sed videntur et ideo Boetius ea 'imagines veri boni' vocat. Atque ita occulos, id est sensus, saturat in picturis, id est in mundanis bonis."
14. For the medicinal association of the eagle with sight, see MacKinney, *Medical Illustrations in Medieval Manuscripts*, vol. 1, pp. 38–39, fig. 28: "The illustrator dramatized the eagle by having him hover over the patient as the physician applied the ointment with a rod." The explanatory text accompanying the illustration described here, taken from a thirteenth-century Italian manuscript, reads (in trans.), "For dimness of vision: It is said that the eagle, when he wishes to fly high to view the nature of things, eats wild lettuce. Anoint your eyes with juice of wild lettuce and its leaves macerated with Attic honey and you will attain the maximum of clear eyesight."
15. Dante makes clear that it is only "an imagined fire" ("lo 'ncendio imaginato") that scorches him (IX.32). For this interpretation of the first dream, see Bundy, *Theory of Imagination*, p. 242. I follow Bundy closely (pp. 241–44) in interpreting all three dreams in the *Purgatorio*.
16. See Dronke, "Dante's Earthly Paradise."
17. The involvement of intellect in the volitional act is made clear by Singleton in his commentary on *The Divine Comedy*, pp. 430–32, where he quotes extensively from Aquinas, *Summa theologiae*, I, Q.83, A.4, resp.
18. Aquinas, *De anima*, trans. Foster and Humphries, III.iii.664, p. 398.
19. Singleton, however, in his commentary on *The Divine Comedy*, pp. 451–52, interprets this dream slightly differently. The holy lady, in his reading, becomes the light of discernment and Virgil the will that acts upon that discernment.
20. Mazzeo, *Structure and Thought in the Paradiso*, p. 96.
21. The importance of this sleep was suggested to me by Hawkins, "Transfiguring the Text."
22. Various sources for the two rivers have been suggested, but no one, to my knowledge, has explained fully their precise function in the process of the visionary's redemption or their positioning at just this moment in the poem. Lethe, of course, derives from pagan tradition, but the addition of Eünoè remains a mystery. See Dronke's suggestion (in "Dante's Earthly Paradise," pp. 484–85) that Dante borrows Eünoè from the Sienese notary Bonaventura's *Livre de l'eschiele Mahomet*. Also see Singleton's argument that Dante has transformed the four rivers traditionally found in Eden to

stars, which thus signify the four infused cardinal virtues (*Journey to Beatrice*, pp. 159–83). Neither approach, however, completely accounts for the presence of these two specific rivers.

23. Aquinas, *De anima*, trans. Foster and Humphries, I.iv.165, p. 131.
24. Lorenzo de' Medici, *Scritti scelti*, ed. Bigi, pp. 314–15, quoted by Thompson, *Dante's Epic Journeys*, p. 1.
25. Bonaventure, *Itinerarium mentis in Deum*, trans. Boehner, pp. 64–65: "non solum habet *ab exteriori* formari per phantasmata, verum etiam *a superiori* suscipiendo et in se habendo simplices formas, quae non possunt introire per portas sensuum et sensibilium phantasias." Such a distinction between two kinds of memory was common. See Wolfson, "Internal Senses," esp. pp. 74–76.
26. Le Goff, *Birth of Purgatory*, p. 360.
27. Eliot, *Dante*, p. 36.
28. See Dante Alighieri, *Convivio*, trans. Jackson, III.iv, p. 136.
29. Freccero, "Infernal Irony," p. 772.

CHAPTER 6

1. For a summary of Gower's literary relations, conveniently divided by their origins in the penitential, sermon, belletristic, or political traditions, see Fisher's chapter on "Major Themes," in *John Gower*, esp. pp. 135–63.
2. This is immediately evident from a survey of the manuscripts, as described by Macaulay in the introduction to his critical edition of the poem; see Gower, *Complete Works*, cxxxviii–clxvii. By thus concentrating on the significance of the Nebuchadnezzar story as a dream, of course I do not mean to minimize its obvious importance in organizing many of the poem's political and social concerns.
3. See Gower, *Complete Works*, ed. Macaulay, I.121.
4. See the descriptions of Genius's appearances in the fifteenth and sixteenth centuries provided by Knowlton in "Genius as an Allegorical Figure." According to Knowlton (see pp. 91–92), Genius appears as "Sens Abesti" in Martin Franc's *Champion des Dames*, but when he gets his own name back in Jean Lemaire de Belges's *Concorde des deux langages* in 1511, it is in a poem that ends, as Gower's does, with the narrator's dream.
5. See Peck's introduction to his excellent abridgment of Gower's *Confessio Amantis*, pp. xi–xiv, and also his *Kingship and Common Profit*, pp. 25–27; Schueler, "Age of the Lover," p. 153; Nitzsche, *Genius Figure*, p. 135. A similar comment is made by Spearing in *Medieval Dream-Poetry*, p. 2.
6. *Vox Clamantis*, in Gower, *Complete Works*, ed. Macaulay, vol. 4, I.Prol.7–12:

> Ex Daniele patet quid sompnia significarunt,
> Nec fuit in sompnis visio vana Ioseph:
> Angelus immo bonus, qui custos interioris
> Est hominis, vigili semper amore fauet;

> Et licet exterius corpus sopor occupet, ille
> Visitat interius mentis et auget opem.

The English translation is taken from Gower, *Major Latin Works*, trans. Stockton, p. 49. Compare Gower's dream theory here with that prevalent in the twelfth and thirteenth centuries, as discussed in my Ch. 2.

7. Fisher, *John Gower*, pp. 74–75. However, an interesting discussion of Gower's debt to the lover's portrayal in the fourteenth-century French love vision can be found in Burrow's "Portrayal of Amans."

8. James Russell Lowell, quoted by Fisher in *John Gower*, p. 2.

9. See the useful bibliographies provided by Yeager, first in "Bibliography of John Gower Materials (1975)," then in *John Gower Materials (1979)*. The book-length studies of the poet by Fisher (*John Gower*) and Peck (*Kingship and Common Profit*) must be given credit for much of the new enthusiasm for the poet. Peck's accessible edition, *Confessio Amantis*, has made the *Confessio* available to a wider readership than ever before. And Gallacher's *Love, the Word, and Mercury*, discussed in greater detail in the text, has contributed its share to the current interest in Gower's craftsmanship. Also influential in Gower scholarship are the recent treatments of the poem in Burrow's *Ricardian Poetry*; Leonard's *Laughter in the Courts of Love*; Baker's "Priesthood of Genius," esp. pp. 286–91; and Middleton's "Idea of Public Poetry in the Reign of Richard II." Among the many articles on Gower alone that call for a reevaluation of the poet's skill, I have found particularly useful the following: McNally, "Penitential and Courtly Traditions"; Pearsall, "Gower's Narrative Art"; Schueler, "Age of the Lover"; and Olsson, "Rhetoric, Gower, and *Exemplum*." The John Gower Society was founded in 1982 by R. F. Yeager of Warren Wilson College and has since established a chapter at the University of Bristol headed by Alastair Minnis.

10. Lewis, *Allegory of Love*, pp. 198–222.

11. See Macaulay on the *Vox Clamantis* in Gower, *Complete Works*, vol. 4, pp. xxx–xxxiv, and, even more so, on the *Speculum Meditantis*, in Gower, *Complete Works*, vol. 1, pp. xi–xiii, xlvi–lvi. His favorable judgment has been recently reaffirmed by Olsson in "Cardinal Virtues," where the latter traces Gower's artistry in using the cardinal virtues as a unifying device in his overall scheme.

12. Fisher, *John Gower*, p. 135.

13. See, however, Yeager, "John Gower's Poetic"; also Minnis, "Moral Gower."

14. This view is particularly propounded by Cherniss in "Allegorical Figures." But it is also evident even in many of the more sympathetic treatments of the poem. See, for example, Fisher, *John Gower*, pp. 161–62; or Pearsall, "Gower's Narrative Art," p. 477.

15. Macaulay, in Gower, *Complete Works*, vol. 2, p. xix.

16. Macaulay prints the Fairfax manuscript of the colophon in vol. 3 of Gower, *Complete Works*, pp. 479–80. For purposes of tracing the poet's development through the various redactions of his trilogy, Fisher also provides the texts of Bodley 902 and Bodley 204, pp. 311–12. He also includes

a translation of Bodley 902 (representing the poet's first version, ca. 1390), pp. 88–89.

17. Baker, "Priesthood of Genius," p. 290. In its roughest form, this argument was first made by Knowlton in "Genius as an Allegorical Figure," and has been refined and repeated also by Economou in "Genius" and by Schueler in "Gower's Characterization of Genius."

18. Cherniss, "Allegorical Figures," p. 12. See n. 14, above.

19. Baker, "Priesthood of Genius," p. 288. This tale is frequently puzzled over in Gower criticism, as verging "in a direction opposite to the moral point being made," or as being somehow "curious" or "unsettling" (Leonard, *Laughter in the Courts of Love*, p. 68).

20. Another critic who argues for the primacy of the confession is Kinneavy, in "Gower's *Confessio Amantis*"; see also Braswell, *Medieval Sinner*, esp. pp. 69–70, 81–87.

21. Peck, in *Kingship and Common Profit* (p. 34), briefly suggests this possibility, but does not discuss it at length or investigate its implications for the poem.

22. Lewis, *Allegory of Love*, p. 220.

23. *Vox Clamantis*, IV.xiii. That Gower had some familiarity with a concept of *ingenium* as that part of the spirit which had access to a higher truth is also clear from the *Vox Clamantis*, I.xx.2134, as well as from the headnote to the *Confessio Amantis*, VII. The word *engin* (see *Confessio Amantis*, II.1956 and passim) was for Gower as for some French romancers a rather debased talent, useful primarily for getting ahead and creating illusion; see my Ch. 4. *Engin*, however, could have a more elevated role. By analyzing the *engin* of Solomon's wife in the *Lancelot-Graal*, which allows Solomon successfully to communicate with Galahad, Kelly demonstrates the existence of a poetic in which romance imagination or *engin*, though potentially tricky and oversubtle, can be corrected and redeemed by divine inspiration; see his "Invention dans les romans en prose."

24. Though Gower's referent for "wit" is slippery and hard to locate with any consistency, some evidence suggests it may at times be identified with imagination and *ingenium* through its physiological location. Along with reason (which is always assigned the middle ventricle), wit occupies one of the cells of the brain (V.1462–63; cp. Chaucer's trio of "memorye," "engyn," and "intellect" in "The Second Nun's Tale," l. 339). The two faculties wit and reason probably do not occupy the same cell, for Gower's usage elsewhere makes clear that wit is not equivalent to reason, as a modern reader might guess, but rather something separable from it, which may be governed by either will or reason (see VII.4558–71). Thus, we may draw a very tentative connection between wit and *engin* or *ingenium*, which also occupies this anterior cell. For further references, compare the usages of "engine," "genius," and "wit" during this time, cited by the *OED*.

25. Lewis's treatment (*Allegory of Love*) was revolutionary in this regard. But Pearsall in "Gower's Narrative Art" worked to refine further the reader's appreciation of the subtlety of the poet's skill as storyteller, among

other things by looking at the way he expands and suppresses allusions from his sources. This method of analyzing the *Confessio Amantis* has proved fruitful, forming the basis for several recent dissertations on the poem: Tague, "John Gower's *Confessio Amantis*"; Foster, "Medieval Mythography," discussed in greater detail in the text; Yeager, "John Gower's Poetic"; and Shaw, "*Confessio Amantis*." A related study of those medieval Ovidian sources Gower actually relied on can be found in Mainzer's "Gower's Use of the 'Mediaeval Ovid.'"

26. Fisher, *John Gower*, pp. 137–38; also Tentler, *Sin and Confession*, esp. pp. 95–104.
27. Bergson, *Laughter*, p. 10.
28. Pearsall, "Gower's Narrative Art," p. 483.
29. Fisher, *John Gower*, p. 194.
30. See Olsson, "Rhetoric, Gower, and *Exemplum*," p. 194; Peck, *Kingship and Common Profit*, p. 37; and Leonard, *Laughter in the Courts of Love*, p. 68.
31. Foster, "Medieval Mythography," p. 147.
32. Burrow, *Ricardian Poetry*, pp. 69–78.
33. Kolve, "Chaucer and the Visual Arts," p. 297; see also *Chaucer and the Imagery of Narrative*, esp. pp. 9–58.
34. Lewis, *Allegory of Love*, p. 205.
35. Burrow, *Ricardian Poetry*, p. 77.
36. Foster, "Medieval Mythography," pp. 182–83.
37. Ibid., p. 170.
38. Ibid. The Latin marginalia are in Gower, *Complete Works*, vol. 2, p. 262.
39. See Macaulay's comparison of the tale with its source in Gower, *Complete Works*, vol. 2, pp. 492–93.
40. Ibid., p. 230.
41. Cp. Yates's discussion of the techniques of artificial memory, in *Art of Memory*, esp. pp. 50–104.
42. Pearsall, "Gower's Narrative Art," p. 478. Also Peck, *Kingship and Common Profit*; for example, on Envy, see pp. 59–77.
43. See Burke, "Tale of King, Wine, Woman, and Truth." In Gower's primary source, the apocryphal book of 3 Esdras 3–4, wine is weakest, followed by kings, then women, and finally truth. This is also the order followed by Flavius Josephus in *Antiquitates Judaicae*, XI.iii.1–10, also probably known by Gower (Burke, "Tale of King, Wine, Woman, and Truth," p. 4). But instead, Gower followed Vincent of Beauvais in his *Speculum historiale*, III.xxix, and Petrus Comestor in his *Historia scholastica*, Libri Judith cap.iii, in altering the source to place kings lowest.
44. The importance of this image is also attested to by the very large arrow Cupid is about to thrust into Amans's heart in a manuscript illumination of this section of the text from the second half of the fifteenth century (New York, Morgan Library M.126, f.9v), a motif picked up on in other illuminations as well, such as the ones of Pyramus (f.59v) and Dido (f.68r).

45. Jean de Meun, *Le Roman de la rose*, ed. Lecoy, ll. 13144–80. Commentators on the Ovidian tradition, however, were often critical of Dido's "foolishness"; see the *accessus* quoted by Minnis in "Moral Gower," p. 57.
46. Hall, "Chaucer and the Dido-and-Aeneas Story."
47. *Commentary on the Aeneid*, ed. Jones and Jones, pp. 3, 24–25, 37–38, 95–96; *Commentary on the Aeneid*, trans. Schreiber and Maresca, pp. 4, 26–27, 39, 90–91.
48. Gower, *Major Latin Works*, trans. Stockton, p. 197; and in *Complete Works*, ed. Macaulay, vol. 4, V.i.29–36.
49. Schueler in "Age of the Lover" argues that it is obvious throughout that Amans is old; Burrow in "Portrayal of Amans" that it is not. One's position on this question depends on how much weight is given to various small clues, and even in the Middle Ages some readers may have arrived at the Lover's age sooner than others.
50. New York, Morgan Library M.126, f.20r.
51. Tentler, *Sin and Confession*, p. 99.
52. Peck, *Kingship and Common Profit*, p. 103.
53. Foster, "Medieval Mythography," p. 192.
54. Ibid., p. 173.
55. Ibid., p. 188.
56. Peck's translation of Reins as "kidneys" in his edition of the poem (*Confessio Amantis*, p. 483) is problematic. I follow here the word's broader significance as "loins"; see the citations in the *OED* (compact edition), p. 389. A division of the body similar to Gower's is presented by the twelfth-century *Aeneid* commentator, who likens the human body to a city, composed of a number of dwelling places; among them are wisdom's chambers in the head, the abode of the spirit (*animositas*) in the heart, and desire or cupidity's home "in renibus" (*Commentary on the Aeneid*, ed. Jones and Jones, pp. 15–16; *Commentary on the Aeneid*, trans. Schreiber and Maresca, pp. 17–18). In like fashion, the Third Vatican Mythographer gives Venus dominion of "renes et inguina"; see Mythographus Tertius, "De diis gentium et illorum allegoriis," ed. Bode, p. 241. See also Trevisa's translation of Bartholomaeus Anglicus's *On the Properties of Things*, vol. 1, V.43, pp. 254–55.
57. Lewis, *Allegory of Love*, p. 218.
58. However, see Leonard, *Laughter in the Courts of Love*, pp. 63–65.
59. Lewis, *Allegory of Love*, p. 218; see also p. 211, where he claims that Gower has no "real grasp of conceptual thought." For a rebuttal to this charge, see Bennett, "Gower's Honeste Love," esp. p. 117.
60. Cherniss, "Allegorical Figures," p. 18.
61. Lewis, *Allegory of Love*, p. 218.
62. Green, "Dante's Allegory of Poets," p. 124.
63. Burrow discusses this unheroic image of man in *Ricardian Poetry*, pp. 93–129; see also his treatment of its specific realization in Gower in "Portrayal of Amans."

64. See, for example, Day, *Intuitive Cognition*. For a more recent discussion and corrective to certain of Day's interpretations, see Boler, "Intuitive and Abstractive Cognition."

65. For example, in John Lydgate's translation of this poem, *Pilgrimage*, vol. 1, ed. Furnivall, ll. 3768–73.

66. For example, Burke, in her essay on the tale "King, Wine, Woman, and Truth," suggests that the major effect of Gower's changes in his source was to stress, not the opposition between truth or God and the earthly goods named, as was usual in redactions of this tale, but their potential value.

67. Gallacher, *Love, the Word, and Mercury*, pp. 44–76.

68. Lewis, *Allegory of Love*, p. 221. See also Middleton, "Idea of Public Poetry in the Reign of Richard II," p. 111.

69. For this insight into the poet's reluctance to leave his subject matter, I am indebted to the comments of Winthrop Wetherbee.

70. In Gower, *Complete Works*, vol. 2, p. 37.

71. Tuve, *Allegorical Imagery*, p. 40. (Her discussion here does not specifically focus on Gower.)

WORKS CITED

Abelard, Peter. *Expositio in Hexaemeron*. *PL*, 178, 729–84.
Abraham, David H. "*Cosyn* and *Cosynage*: Pun and Structure in the *Shipman's Tale*." *Chaucer Review*, 11 (1977): 319–27.
Accessūs ad auctores. Ed. R. B. C. Huygens. 2d ed. Leiden, 1970.
Adelard of Bath. *Questiones naturales*. In Martin Müller, ed., *Beiträge zur Geschichte der Philosophie des Mittelalters*, 31. Münster, 1934.
Alain de Lille. *Anticlaudianus*. Ed. R. Bossuat. Paris, 1955.
———. *Anticlaudianus or the Good and Perfect Man*. Trans. James J. Sheridan. Toronto, 1973.
———. *De planctu naturae*. *PL*, 210, 429–82.
———. *De planctu naturae*. Ed. Nikolaus M. Häring. *Studi Medievali*, series 3, 19 (1978): 797–879.
———. *The Complaint of Nature*. Trans. Douglas Moffat. 1908; repr. Hamden, Conn., 1972.
———. *The Plaint of Nature*. Trans. James J. Sheridan. Toronto, 1980.
———. *Distinctiones dictionum theologicalium*. *PL*, 210, 687–1012.
———. *Summa de arte praedicatoria*. *PL*, 210, 109–98.
———. *Textes inédits*. Ed. Marie-Thérèse d'Alverny. Paris, 1965.
Alcher de Clairvaux. *De spiritu et anima*. *PL*, 40, 779–832.
Alcuin. *De animae ratione*. *PL*, 101, 639–50.
Alford, John A. "The Grammatical Metaphor: A Survey of Its Use in the Middle Ages." *Speculum*, 57 (1982): 728–60.
Allen, Judson Boyce. *The Ethical Poetic of the Later Middle Ages: A Decorum of Convenient Distinction*. Toronto, 1982.
"The Apocalypse of Paul." In M. R. James, trans., *The Apocryphal New Testament*, pp. 525–55. Oxford, 1924.
Aquinas, St. Thomas. *De anima in the Version of William of Moerbeke and*

the *Commentary of Saint Thomas Aquinas*. Trans. Kenelm Foster and Silvester Humphries. New Haven, 1951.

———. *Sancti Thomae Aquinatis in Aristotelis librum de anima commentarium*. Ed. Angelo M. Pirotta. Turin, 1925.

———. *Introduction to Saint Thomas Aquinas*. Ed. Anton C. Pegis. New York, 1945.

———. *Summa theologiae*. Blackfriars ed. and trans. 60 vols. New York, 1964–76.

Aristotle. See Aquinas, *De anima* . . .

Asclepius. 2d ed. Trans. A.-J. Festugière. Ed. A. D. Nock. *Corpus Hermeticum*, 2. Paris, 1960.

St. Augustine. *De Genesi ad litteram. CSEL*, 27.1.

———. *Soliloquia. PL*, 32, 867–904.

———. *City of God*. Trans. William M. Green. Loeb Classical Library. Cambridge, Mass., 1963.

Averroes. "Averrois Cordubensis Commentarium medium in Aristotelis poetriam." Ed. William Franklin Boggess. Ph.D. diss., University of North Carolina, 1965.

———. "The Middle Commentary of Averroes of Cordova on the *Poetics* of Aristotle." Trans. O. B. Hardison, Jr. In Alex Preminger, O. B. Hardison, Jr., and Kevin Kerrane, eds., *Classical and Medieval Literary Criticism: Translations and Interpretations*, pp. 349–82. New York, 1974.

———. "Libri Aristoteles de sompno et vigilia." In Emilia Shields and Harry Blumberg, eds., *Compendia librorum Aristotelis qui parva naturalia vocantur*, pp. 75–125. Cambridge, Mass., 1949.

———. *Epitome of Parva naturalia*. Trans. Harry Blumberg. Cambridge, Mass., 1961.

Avicenna. *Liber de anima, seu sextus de naturalibus*. Ed. S. van Riet. Louvain, 1968.

Badel, Pierre-Yves. *Le Roman de la rose au XIVe siècle: Etude de la reception de l'oeuvre*. Geneva, 1980.

Baker, Denise. "The Priesthood of Genius: A Study of the Medieval Tradition." *Speculum*, 51 (1976): 277–91.

Bartholomaeus Anglicus. *On the Properties of Things*. Trans. John Trevisa. Ed. M. C. Seymour et al. 2 vols. Oxford, 1975.

Bede. *A History of the English Church and People*. Trans. Leo Sherley-Price. Rev. ed. Harmondsworth, 1968.

Bennett, J. A. W. "Gower's Honeste Love." In John Lawlor, ed., *Patterns of Love and Courtesy: Essays in Memory of C. S. Lewis*, pp. 107–21. Evanston, 1966.

Bergson, Henri. *Laughter*. New York, 1912.

Bernardus Silvestris. *Cosmographia*. Ed. Peter Dronke. Leiden, 1978.

———. *The Cosmographia of Bernardus Silvestris*. Trans. Winthrop Wetherbee. New York, 1973.

Bloch, Marc. *Feudal Society*. Trans. L. A. Manyon. London, 1961.

Bloomfield, Morton W. *Piers Plowman as a Fourteenth-Century Apocalypse.* New Brunswick, N.J., 1961.
Boccaccio, Giovanni. *Genealogie deorum gentilium libri.* Ed. Vincenzo Romano. 2 vols. Bari, 1951.
Boethius. *De interpretatione.* PL, 64, 293–640.
———. *Philosophiae consolatio.* Ed. Ludwig Biehler. *Corpus Christianorum,* 94. Turnholt, 1957.
———. *The Consolation of Philosophy.* Trans. Richard Green. Indianapolis, 1962.
Boler, John F. "Intuitive and Abstractive Cognition." In Norman Kretzmann, Anthony Kenny, and Jan Pinborg, eds., *The Cambridge History of Later Medieval Philosophy,* pp. 460–78. Cambridge, 1982.
St. Bonaventure. *Itinerarium mentis in Deum.* Trans. Philotheus Boehner. Saint Bonaventure, N.Y., 1956.
Braswell, Mary Flowers. *The Medieval Sinner: Characterization and Confession in the Literature of the English Middle Ages.* London, 1983.
Brink, C. O. *Horace on Poetry: The 'Ars Poetica.'* Cambridge, 1971.
———. *Horace on Poetry: Prolegomena to the Literary Epistles.* Cambridge, 1963.
Brumble, H. David. "The Role of Genius in the *De planctu naturae* of Alanus de Insulis." *Classica et Mediaevalia,* 31 (1970): 306–23.
Bundy, Murray Wright. *The Theory of Imagination in Classical and Mediaeval Thought.* University of Illinois Studies in Language and Literature, 12, nos. 2, 3 (1927).
Burke, Linda Barney. "The Sources and Significance of the 'Tale of King, Wine, Woman, and Truth' in John Gower's *Confessio Amantis.*" *Greyfriar,* 21 (1980): 3–15.
Burrow, J. A. "The Portrayal of Amans in *Confessio Amantis.*" In Alastair J. Minnis, ed., *Gower's Confessio Amantis: Responses and Reassessments,* pp. 5–24. Cambridge, 1983.
———. *Ricardian Poetry: Chaucer, Gower, Langland and the Gawain Poet.* London, 1971.
Chadwick, Henry. *Boethius: The Consolations of Music, Logic, Theology and Philosophy.* Oxford, 1981.
Chartularium universitatis Parisiensis. Ed. H. Denifle and E. Chatelain. Vol. 1. Paris, 1889.
Chenu, Marie-Dominique. "*Imaginatio*: Note de lexicographie philosophique médiévale." *Studi e Testi,* 122 (1946): 593–602.
———. *La Théologie au douzième siècle.* Paris, 1957.
———. *Nature, Man and Society in the Twelfth Century: Essays on New Theological Perspectives in the Latin West.* Trans. and abridged Jerome Taylor and Lester K. Little. Chicago, 1968.
Cherniss, Michael D. "The Allegorical Figures in Gower's *Confessio Amantis.*" *Res Publica Litterarum,* 1 (1978): 7–20.
———. *Boethian Apocalypse: Studies in Middle English Vision Poetry.* Norman, Okla., 1987.

"*The Chess of Love*: Old French Text with Translation and Commentary." Trans. Joan Martin Jones. Ph.D. diss., University of Nebraska, 1968.
Cicero. *De re publica, De legibus*. Trans. C. W. Keyes. Loeb Classical Library. London, 1928.
Clarke, Edwin, and Kenneth Dewhurst. *An Illustrated History of Brain Function*. Oxford, 1972.
The Commentary on the First Six Books of the Aeneid of Vergil Commonly Attributed to Bernardus Silvestris. Ed. Julian Ward Jones and Elizabeth Frances Jones. Lincoln, Nebr., 1977.
Commentary on the First Six Books of Virgil's Aeneid. Trans. Earl G. Schreiber and Thomas E. Maresca. Lincoln, Nebr., 1979.
"Condemnation of 219 Propositions." Trans. Ernest L. Fortin and Peter D. O'Neill. In Ralph Lerner and Mushin Mahdi, eds., *Medieval Political Philosophy: A Sourcebook*, pp. 335–54. Toronto, 1963.
Congresso Internazionale di Studi Boeziani (1980, Pavia). *Atti*. Rome, 1981.
Copleston, F. C. *A History of Medieval Philosophy*. 1972; repr. New York, 1974.
Courcelle, Pierre. *La Consolation de philosophie dans la tradition littéraire: Antécédents et postérité de Boèce*. Paris, 1967.
———. *Les Lettres grecques en occident de Macrobe à Cassiodore*. Paris, 1948.
———. "Le Personnage de Philosophie dans la littérature latine." *Journal des Savants* (1970): 209–52.
Courtenay, William J. "Nominalism and Late Medieval Religion." In Charles Trinkaus, ed., with Heiko A. Oberman, *The Pursuit of Holiness in Late Medieval and Renaissance Religion*, pp. 26–59. Studies in Medieval and Reformation Thought, 10. Leiden, 1974.
Curtius, Ernst Robert. *European Literature and the Latin Middle Ages*. Trans. Willard R. Trask. Bollingen, 36. Princeton, 1953.
Dahan, Gilbert. "Notes et textes sur la poétique du moyen âge." *Archives d'histoire doctrinale et littéraire du moyen âge*, 47 (1980): 171–93.
Dahlberg, Charles. "Macrobius and the Unity of the *Roman de la rose*." *Studies in Philology*, 58 (1961): 573–82.
Dane, Joseph A. "Parody and Satire: A Theoretical Model." *Genre*, 13 (1980): 145–60.
Dante Alighieri. *Dante's Convivio*. Trans. William Walrond Jackson. Oxford, 1909.
———. *Dantis Alagherii epistolae*. Ed. and trans. Paget Toynbee. Oxford, 1920.
———. *The Divine Comedy*. Ed. and trans. Charles S. Singleton. 3 vols., 6 parts. Princeton, 1970–75.
———. *De vulgari eloquentia*. Ed. Aristide Marigo. Florence, 1948.
Day, Sebastian J. *Intuitive Cognition: A Key to the Significance of the Later Scholastics*. New York, 1947.

Delany, Sheila. *Chaucer's House of Fame: The Poetics of Skeptical Fideism.* Chicago, 1972.
Dinzelbacher, Peter. *Vision und Visionsliteratur im Mittelalter.* Stuttgart, 1981.
Dominicus Gundissalinus. *De divisione philosophiae.* Ed. Ludwig Baur. Münster, 1903.
Dronke, Peter. "Dante's Earthly Paradise: Towards an Interpretation of *Purgatorio* XXVIII." *Romanische Forschungen,* 82 (1970): 467–87.
———. *Fabula: Explorations into the Uses of Myth in Medieval Platonism.* Leiden, 1974.
———. "New Approaches to the School of Chartres." *Annuario de estudios medievales,* 6 (1971): 117–40.
Dwyer, Richard A. *Boethian Fictions: Narratives in the Medieval French Versions of the Consolatio Philosophiae.* Cambridge, Mass., 1976.
Economou, George D. "The Character Genius in Alan de Lille, Jean de Meun, and John Gower." *Chaucer Review,* 4 (1970): 203–10.
———. *The Goddess Natura in Medieval Literature.* Cambridge, Mass., 1972.
Edelstein, Emma, and Ludwig Edelstein. *Asclepius: Collection and Interpretation of the Testimonies.* Baltimore, 1945.
Eliot, T. S. *Dante.* London, 1930.
Evans, G. R. *Alan of Lille: The Frontiers of Theology in the Later Twelfth Century.* Cambridge, 1983.
Faral, Edmond. "*Le Roman de la rose* et la pensée française au XIIIe siècle." *Revue des Deux Mondes,* Sept. 15, 1926, pp. 430–58.
Fisher, John H. *John Gower: Moral Philosopher and Friend of Chaucer.* New York, 1964.
Flacelière, Robert. *Greek Oracles.* Trans. Douglas Garman. London, 1965.
Fleming, John V. *Reason and the Lover.* Princeton, 1984.
———. *The Roman de la rose: A Study in Allegory and Iconography.* Princeton, 1969.
Fletcher, Angus. *Allegory: The Theory of a Symbolic Mode.* Ithaca, 1964.
Fortin, E. L. *Dissidence et philosophie au moyen âge: Dante et ses antécédents.* Montreal, 1981.
Foster, James Joseph. "The Influence of Medieval Mythography on John Gower's *Confessio Amantis.*" Ph.D. diss., Duke University, 1973.
Fowler, Alastair. *Kinds of Literature: An Introduction to the Theory of Genres and Modes.* Cambridge, Mass., 1982.
Freccero, John. "Infernal Irony: The Gates of Hell." *MLN,* 99 (1984): 769–86.
Friedman, Lionel J. "'Jean de Meung,' Antifeminism, and 'Bourgeois Realism.'" *Modern Philology,* 57 (1959): 13–23.
Frye, Northrop. *Anatomy of Criticism: Four Essays.* Princeton, 1957.
Fulgentius, Fabius Planciades. *Fabii Planciadis Fulgentii opera.* Ed. R. Helms. Leipzig, 1898.

---. "The Exposition of the Content of Virgil According to Moral Philosophy." In Leslie George Whitbread, trans., *Fulgentius the Mythographer*, pp. 119–35. Columbus, 1971.

Galen. *On the Usefulness of the Parts of the Body*. Trans. Margaret Tallmadge May. Vol. 1. Ithaca, 1968.

Gallacher, Patrick. *Love, the Word, and Mercury: A Reading of John Gower's Confessio Amantis*. Albuquerque, 1975.

Gallo, Ernest. *The Poetria nova and Its Sources in Early Rhetorical Doctrine*. The Hague, 1971.

---. "The *Poetria nova* of Geoffrey of Vinsauf." In James J. Murphy, ed., *Medieval Eloquence: Studies in the Theory and Practice of Medieval Rhetoric*, pp. 68–84. Berkeley, 1978.

Gennep, Arnold van. *The Rites of Passage*. Trans. Monika B. Vizedom and Gabrielle L. Caffee. Chicago, 1960.

Geoffrey of Vinsauf. *Poetria nova*. In Edmond Faral, ed., *Les Arts poétiques du XIIe et du XIIIe siècle*, pp. 194–262. Paris, 1924.

---. *Poetria nova*. Trans. Margaret F. Nims. Toronto, 1967.

Giacone, R. "Masters, Books and the Library at Chartres." *Vivarium*, 12 (1974): 30–51.

Gibson, Margaret, ed. *Boethius: His Life, Thought and Influence*. Oxford, 1981.

Gilson, Etienne. *Dante and Philosophy*. Trans. David Moore. 1949; repr. Gloucester, Mass., 1968.

---. *History of Christian Philosophy in the Middle Ages*. New York, 1955.

---. *The Philosophy of Saint Thomas Aquinas*. Trans. Edward Bullough. Cambridge, 1924.

Girard, René. "Differentiation and Reciprocity in Lévi-Strauss and Contemporary Theory." In his *"To Double Business Bound": Essays on Literature, Mimesis, and Anthropology*, pp. 155–77. Baltimore, 1978.

Goichon, A. M. *Philosophy of Avicenna*. Trans. M. S. Khan. Delhi, 1969.

Goldin, Frederick. *The Mirror of Narcissus in the Courtly Love Lyric*. Ithaca, 1967.

Gower, John. *The Complete Works of John Gower*. Ed. G. C. Macaulay. 4 vols. Oxford, 1899-1902.

---. *Confessio Amantis*. Ed. and abridged Russell A. Peck. New York, 1968.

---. *The Major Latin Works of John Gower*. Trans. Eric W. Stockton. Seattle, 1962.

Grabes, Herbert. *The Mutable Glass: Mirror-Imagery in Titles and Texts of the Middle Ages and English Renaissance*. Trans. Gordon Collier. Cambridge, 1982.

Grant, Edward. "Issues in Natural Philosophy at Paris in the Late Thirteenth Century." *Medievalia et Humanistica*, n.s. 13 (1985): 75–94.

Green, Richard Hamilton. "Alan of Lille's *Anticlaudianus: Ascensus mentis in Deum*." *Annuale Mediaevale*, 8 (1967): 3–16.

―――. "Alan of Lille's *De planctu naturae*." *Speculum*, 31 (1956): 649–74.
―――. "Dante's Allegory of Poets and the Mediaeval Theory of Poetic Fiction." *Comparative Literature*, 9 (1957): 118–28.
Guillaume de Conches. *De philosophia mundi*. PL, 172, 39–102.
―――. "Des commentaires inédits de Guillaume de Conches et de Nicolas Triveth sur la Consolation de la philosophie de Boèce." Ed. Charles M. G. B. Jourdain. *Notices et extraits des manuscrits de la Bibliothèque Impériale*, 20, pt. 2 (1862): 40–82.
―――. *Glosae super Platonem*. Ed. Edouard Jeauneau. Paris, 1965.
―――. "Les Gloses de Guillaume de Conches sur le Timée." In J. M. Parent, ed., *La Doctrine de la création dans l'école de Chartres*, pp. 137–77. Publications de l'Institut Médiévales d'Ottawa, 8. Paris, 1938.
Guillaume de Lorris and Jean de Meun. *Le Roman de la rose*. Ed. Félix Lecoy. 3 vols. Paris, 1965–70.
―――. *Le Roman de la rose*. Ed. Daniel Poirion. Paris, 1974.
―――. *The Romance of the Rose*. Trans. Charles Dahlberg. Princeton, 1971.
Gunn, Alan M. F. *The Mirror of Love*. Lubbock, Texas, 1952.
―――. "Teacher and Student in the *Roman de la rose*." *L'Esprit Créateur*, 2 (1962): 126–34.
Gunn, Alan M. F., and Charles Dahlberg. "*Rose* Scholarship, 1970–1973, et al." *Encomia*, 1, no. 2 (1976): 68–77.
Hall, Louis Brewer. "Chaucer and the Dido-and-Aeneas Story." *Mediaeval Studies*, 25 (1963): 148–59.
Hamilton, Mary. *Incubation or The Cure of Disease in Pagan Temples and Christian Churches*. London, 1906.
Hanning, Robert W. *The Individual in Twelfth-Century Romance*. New Haven, 1977.
Hardison, O. B., Jr. "Medieval Literary Criticism: General Introduction." In Alex Preminger, O. B. Hardison, Jr., and Kevin Kerrane, eds., *Classical and Medieval Literary Criticism: Translations and Interpretations*, pp. 263–98. New York, 1974.
―――. "Toward a History of Medieval Literary Criticism." *Medievalia et Humanistica*, n.s. 7 (1976): 1–12.
Häring, Nikolaus M. "Chartres and Paris Revisited." In J. Reginald O'Donnell, ed., *Essays in Honor of Anton Pegis*, pp. 268–327. Toronto, 1974.
Harvey, E. Ruth. *The Inward Wits: Psychological Theory in the Middle Ages and the Renaissance*. Warburg Institute Surveys, 6. London, 1975.
Hawkins, Peter. "Transfiguring the Text: Biblical Allusion in *Purgatorio* XXXII." Paper presented at the Nineteenth International Congress on Medieval Studies, sponsored by the Medieval Institute, Kalamazoo, Mich., May 12, 1984.
Henri d'Andeli. *The Battle of the Seven Liberal Arts*. Ed. and trans. Louis John Paetow. Berkeley, 1914.
Hernadi, Paul. *Beyond Genre: New Directions in Literary Classification*. Ithaca, 1972.

Hieatt, Constance B. *The Realism of Dream Visions: The Poetic Exploitation of the Dream-Experience in Chaucer and His Contemporaries.* Paris, 1967.
Hill, Thomas D. "Narcissus, Pygmalion, and the Castration of Saturn." *Studies in Philology,* 71 (1974): 404–26.
Hillman, Larry. "Another Look into the Mirror Perilous: The Role of the Crystals in the *Roman de la rose.*" *Romania,* 101 (1980): 225–38.
Hirsch, E. D., Jr. *Validity in Interpretation.* New Haven, 1967.
Hissette, Roland. *Enquête sur les 219 articles condamnés à Paris le 7 Mars 1277.* Louvain, 1977.
Holub, Robert C. *Reception Theory: A Critical Introduction.* London, 1984.
———. "Trends in Literary Theory: The American Reception of Reception Theory." *The German Quarterly,* 55 (1982): 80–96.
Horace. *Satires, Epistles and Ars Poetica.* Ed. and trans. H. Rushton Fairclough. Loeb Classical Library. Cambridge, Mass., 1926.
Hugh of St. Victor. *De unione corporis et spiritus. PL,* 177, 285–94.
———. *Didascalicon.* Ed. Charles Henry Buttimer. Catholic University of America Studies in Medieval and Renaissance Latin, 10. Washington, D. C., 1939.
———. *The Didascalicon of Hugh of St. Victor.* Trans. Jerome Taylor. New York, 1961.
Isidore of Seville. *Etymologiae.* Ed. W. M. Lindsay. 2 vols. Oxford, 1911.
Jauss, Hans Robert. *Aesthetic Experience and Literary Hermeneutics.* Trans. Michael Shaw. Minneapolis, 1982.
———. "Literary History as a Challenge to Literary Theory." In his *Toward an Aesthetic of Reception,* pp. 3–45. Trans. Timothy Bahti. Minneapolis, 1982.
———. "Theory of Genres and Medieval Literature." In his *Toward an Aesthetic of Reception,* pp. 76–109. Trans. Timothy Bahti. Minneapolis, 1982.
Jean de Meun. See Guillaume de Lorris and Jean de Meun.
John of Salisbury. *Metalogicus. PL,* 199, 823–946.
———. *The Metalogicon: A Twelfth-Century Defense of the Verbal and Logical Arts of the Trivium.* Trans. Daniel D. McGarry. 1955; repr. Gloucester, Mass., 1971.
———. *Policraticus, sive de nugis curalium et vestigiis philosophorum libri VIII.* Ed. C. C. J. Webb. 2 vols. Oxford, 1909.
———. *Frivolities of Courtiers and Footprints of Philosophers: Being a Translation of the First, Second, and Third Books and Selections from the Seventh and Eighth Books of the Policraticus of John of Salisbury.* Trans. Joseph B. Pike. Minneapolis, 1938.
Kelly, Douglas. "'Li chastiaus . . . Qu'Amors prist puis par ses esforz': The Conclusion of Guillaume de Lorris' *Rose.*" In Norris Lacy, ed., *A Medieval French Miscellany: Papers of the 1970 Kansas Conference on Medi-*

eval French Literature, pp. 61–78. University of Kansas Humanistic Studies, 42 (1972).
———. "L'Invention dans les romans en prose." In Leigh Arrathoon, ed., The Craft of Fiction: Essays in Medieval Poetics, pp. 119–42. Rochester, Mich., 1984.
———. Medieval Imagination: Rhetoric and the Poetry of Courtly Love. Madison, 1978.
Kerenyi, C. Asklepios: Archetypal Image of the Physician's Existence. Trans. Ralph Manheim. New York, 1959.
Kinneavy, Gerald. "Gower's Confessio Amantis and the Penitentials." Chaucer Review, 19 (1984): 144–61.
Kiser, Lisa J. Telling Classical Tales: Chaucer and the Legend of Good Women. Ithaca, 1983.
Knowles, David. The Evolution of Medieval Thought. New York, 1962.
Knowlton, E. C. "The Allegorical Figure Genius." Classical Philology, 15 (1920): 380–84.
———. "Genius as an Allegorical Figure." Modern Language Notes, 39 (1924): 89–95.
Köhler, Erich. "Narcisse, La Fontaine d'Amour, et Guillaume de Lorris." Journal des Savants (1963): 86–103.
Kolve, V. A. Chaucer and the Imagery of Narrative: The First Five Canterbury Tales. Stanford, 1984.
———. "Chaucer and the Visual Arts." In Derek Brewer, ed., Geoffrey Chaucer: Writers and Their Background, pp. 290–320. Athens, Ohio, 1975.
Kuhn, Thomas S. The Structure of Scientific Revolutions. 2d ed. Chicago, 1970.
Langlois, Ernest. Origines et sources du Roman de la rose. 1890; repr. Geneva, 1973.
Lanham, Richard. The Motives of Eloquence: Literary Rhetoric in the Renaissance. New Haven, 1976.
Laporte, Jean-Marc. Les Structures dynamiques de la grâce: Grâce médicinale et grâce élevante selon Thomas d'Aquin. Montreal, 1973.
Latini, Brunetto. Il Tesoretto. Ed. and trans. Julia Bolton Holloway. New York, 1981.
Leff, Gordon. The Dissolution of the Medieval Outlook: An Essay on Intellectual and Spiritual Change in the Fourteenth Century. New York, 1976.
———. Paris and Oxford Universities in the Thirteenth and Fourteenth Centuries: An Institutional and Intellectual History. New York, 1968.
———. "Seeds of Reformation." Review of Steven Ozment, The Age of Reform 1250–1550: An Intellectual and Religious History of Late Medieval and Reformation Europe. TLS, Oct. 31, 1980, p. 1232.
Le Goff, Jacques. The Birth of Purgatory. Trans. Arthur Goldhammer. Chicago, 1984.

Leonard, Frances McNeely. *Laughter in the Courts of Love: Comedy in Allegory, from Chaucer to Spenser*. Norman, Okla. 1981.

Lerer, Seth. *Boethius and Dialogue: Literary Method in the Consolation of Philosophy*. Princeton, 1985.

Lerner, Ralph, and Mushin Mahdi, eds. *Medieval Political Philosophy: A Sourcebook*. Toronto, 1963.

Lévi-Strauss, Claude. "The Structural Study of Myth." In his *Structural Anthropology*, pp. 206–31. Trans. Claire Jacobson and Brooke Grundfest Schoepf. New York, 1963.

Lewis, C. S. *The Allegory of Love: A Study in Medieval Tradition*. 1936; repr. Oxford, 1977.

―――. "Genius and Genius." *Review of English Studies*, 12 (1936): 189–94; repr. in his *Studies in Medieval and Renaissance Literature*, pp. 169–74. Cambridge, 1966.

Little, Lester K. *Religious Poverty and the Profit Economy in Medieval Europe*. Ithaca, 1978.

Lonergan, Bernard. *Verbum: Word and Idea in Aquinas*. Ed. David B. Burrell. Notre Dame, 1967.

Luca, Costa ben. *De differentiis animae et spiritus*. Ed. Carl Sigmund Barach. 1878; repr. Frankfurt, 1968.

Luria, Maxwell. *A Reader's Guide to the Roman de la rose*. Hamden, Conn., 1982.

Lydgate, John, trans. *The Pilgrimage of the Life of Man, by Guillaume de Deguileville*. Ed. F. J. Furnivall. Vol. 1. Early English Text Society, e.s. 77. London, 1899.

McKeon, R. P. "Medicine and Philosophy in the Eleventh and Twelfth Centuries: The Problem of the Elements." *The Thomist*, 24 (1961): 211–56.

MacKinney, Loren. *Medical Illustrations in Medieval Manuscripts*. London, 1965.

McNally, John J. "The Penitential and Courtly Traditions in Gower's *Confessio Amantis*." In John R. Sommerfeldt, ed., *Studies in Medieval Culture*, pp. 74–94. Kalamazoo, Mich., 1964.

Macrobius. *Commentary on the Dream of Scipio*. Trans. William Harris Stahl. New York, 1952.

―――. *Saturnalia*. Ed. Jacob Willis. Leipzig, 1970.

Mainzer, Conrad. "John Gower's Use of the 'Mediaeval Ovid' in the *Confessio Amantis*." *Medium Aevum*, 41 (1972): 215–29.

Majno, Guido. *The Healing Hand: Man and Wound in the Ancient World*. Cambridge, Mass., 1975.

Mandonnet, Pierre. *Siger de Brabant et l'averroisme latin au XIIIme siècle*. 2d ed. Louvain, 1908.

Martianus Capella. *De nuptiis Philologiae et Mercurii*. Ed. Adolph Dick. Leipzig, 1925.

Martin, Henry. *Le Boccace de Jean Sans Peur*. Brussels, 1911.

Mazzeo, Joseph Anthony. *Structure and Thought in the Paradiso*. Ithaca, 1958.

Means, Michael H. *The Consolatio Genre in Medieval English Literature*. Gainesville, Fla., 1972.
Medici, Lorenzo de'. *Scritti scelti*. 2d ed. Ed. Emilio Bigi. Turin, 1965.
Meerson, Daniel Carl. "The Ground and Nature of Literary Theory in Bernard Silvester's Twelfth-Century Commentary on the *Aeneid*." Ph.D. diss., University of Chicago, 1967.
Michaud-Quantin, Pierre. "La Classification des puissances de l'âme au XIIe siècle." *Revue du Moyen Age Latin*, 5 (1949): 15–34.
Middleton, Anne. "The Idea of Public Poetry in the Reign of Richard II." *Speculum*, 53 (1978):94–114.
Minnis, Alastair J. "Literary Theory in Discussions of *Forma Tractandi* by Medieval Theologians." *New Literary History*, 11 (1979): 133–45.
———. "'Moral Gower' and Medieval Literary Theory." In Alastair J. Minnis, ed., *Gower's Confessio Amantis: Responses and Reassessments*, pp. 50–78. Cambridge, 1983.
Moffat, Douglas. Preface. In Alain de Lille, *The Complaint of Nature*. Trans. Douglas Moffat. 1908; repr. Hamden, Conn., 1972.
Muscatine, Charles. *Chaucer and the French Tradition: A Study in Style and Meaning*. Berkeley, 1957.
Mythographus Tertius [Albericus]. "De diis gentium et illorum allegoriis." In George Bode, ed., *Scriptores rerum mythicarum latini tres romae nuper reperti*, pp. 152–256. 1834; repr. Hildesheim, 1968.
Newman, Francis X. "Saint Augustine's Three Visions and the Structure of the *Commedia*." *Modern Language Notes*, 82 (1967): 56–78.
———. "*Somnium*: Medieval Theories of Dreaming and the Form of Vision Poetry." Ph.D. diss., Princeton University, 1962.
Nitzsche, Jane Chance. *The Genius Figure in Antiquity and the Middle Ages*. New York, 1975.
Nolan, Barbara. *The Gothic Visionary Perspective*. Princeton, 1977.
Oberman, Heiko A. "Fourteenth-Century Religious Thought: A Premature Profile." *Speculum*, 53 (1978): 80–93.
Olson, Glending. *Literature as Recreation in the Later Middle Ages*. Ithaca, 1982.
Olsson, Kurt O. "The Cardinal Virtues and the Structure of John Gower's *Speculum Meditantis*." *The Journal of Medieval and Renaissance Studies*, 7 (1977): 113–48.
———. "Rhetoric, John Gower, and the Late Medieval *Exemplum*." *Medievalia et Humanistica*, n.s. 8 (1977): 185–200.
Owen, D. D. R. *The Vision of Hell: Infernal Journeys in Medieval Literature*. Edinburgh, 1970.
Padoan, Giorgio. *Il pio Enea, l'empio Ulisse*. Ravenna, 1977.
———. "Tradizione e fortuna del commento all' 'Eneide' di Bernardo Silvestre." *Italica medioevale e umanistica*, 3 (1960): 227–40.
Paetow, Louis J. *The Arts Course at Medieval Universities with Special Reference to Grammar and Rhetoric*. University of Illinois, The University Studies, 3, no. 7. Urbana, 1910.

Paré, Gérard. *Les Idées et les lettres au XIIIe siècle: Le Roman de la rose.* Paris, 1947.
Pascalis Romanus. *Liber thesauri occulti.* Ed. S. Collin-Roset. *Archives d'histoire doctrinale et littéraire du Moyen Age,* 30 (1963): 112–98.
Patch, Howard Rollin. *The Other World According to Descriptions in Medieval Literature.* Cambridge, Mass., 1950.
_____. *The Tradition of Boethius: A Study of His Importance in Medieval Culture.* New York, 1935.
Payne, F. Anne. *Chaucer and Menippean Satire.* Madison, 1981.
Pearcy, Roy J. "Modes of Signification and the Humor of Obscene Diction in the Fabliaux." In Thomas D. Cooke and Benjamin Honeycutt, eds., *The Humor of the Fabliaux,* pp. 163–96. Columbia, 1974.
Pearsall, Derek. "Gower's Narrative Art." *PMLA,* 81 (1966): 475–84.
Peck, Russell A. "Chaucer and the Nominalist Questions." *Speculum,* 53 (1978): 745–60.
_____. Introduction. In John Gower, *Confessio Amantis.* Ed. Russell A. Peck. New York, 1968.
_____. *Kingship and Common Profit in Gower's Confessio Amantis.* Carbondale, Ill., 1978.
Petrarch, Francesco. *Secretum.* Ed. Enrico Carrara. Milan, 1955.
Piehler, Paul. *The Visionary Landscape: A Study in Medieval Allegory.* London, 1971.
Pietro Alighieri. *Il "Commentarium" di Pietro Alighieri nelle redazione Ashburnhamiana e Ottoboniana.* Ed. Roberto della Vedova and Maria Teresa Silvotti. Florence, 1978.
_____. *Super Dantis ipsius Genitoris Comoediam commentarium.* Ed. Vincentio Nannucci. Florence, 1845.
Poirion, Daniel. "Les Mots et les choses selon Jean de Meun." *L'Information littéraire,* 26 (1974): 7–11.
_____. *Le Roman de la rose.* Paris, 1973.
Quadlbauer, Franz. "Lukan im Schema des Ordo naturalis/artificialis." *Grazer Beiträge,* 9 (1977): 67–105.
Quintilian. *Institutio oratoria.* Trans. H. E. Butler. 4 vols. Loeb Classical Library. Cambridge, Mass., 1921–22.
Rashdall, Hastings. *The Universities of Europe in the Middle Ages.* Oxford, 1895.
Raynaud de Lage, G. *Alain de Lille, poète du XIIe siècle.* Montreal, 1951.
Reichert, John. "More than Kin and Less than Kind: The Limits of Genre Theory." In Joseph P. Strelka, ed., *Theories of Literary Genre,* pp. 57–79. University Park, Penn., 1978.
Reiss, Edmund. *Boethius.* Boston, 1981.
Richards, Earl Jeffrey. *Dante and the Roman de la rose.* Tübingen, 1981.
Robertson, D. W., Jr. "The Doctrine of Charity in Mediaeval Literary Gardens: A Topical Approach Through Symbolism and Allegory." *Speculum,* 26 (1951): 24–49.

———. *A Preface to Chaucer: Studies in Medieval Perspectives.* Princeton, 1962.
Robson, Alan. "Dante's Reading of the Latin Poets and the Structure of the *Commedia*." In Cecil Grayson, ed., *The World of Dante: Essays on Dante and His Times*, pp. 81–121. Oxford, 1980.
Schachner, Nathan. *The Medieval Universities.* New York, 1938.
Schmidt-Kohl, Volker. *Die neuplatonische Seelenlehre in der Consolatio Philosophiae des Boethius.* Meisenheim an Glan, 1965.
Schouten, J. *The God and Serpent of Asklepios: Symbol of Medicine.* New York, 1967.
Schueler, Donald G. "The Age of the Lover in Gower's *Confessio Amantis*." *Medium Aevum*, 36 (1967): 152–58.
———. "Gower's Characterization of Genius in the *Confessio Amantis*." *Modern Language Quarterly*, 33 (1972): 240–56.
Schupbach, William. *The Paradox of Rembrandt's 'Anatomy of Dr. Tulp.'* Medical History, Supplement 2. London, 1982.
Servius Grammaticus. *In Vergilii carmina commentarii.* Ed. George Thilo and Harman Hagen. 2 vols. Leipzig, 1884.
Shaw, Judith Davis. "*Confessio Amantis*: Gower's Art in Transforming His Sources into *Exempla* of the Seven Deadly Sins." *Dissertation Abstracts International*, 38 (1977): 6809A.
Sheridan, James J. Introduction. In Alain de Lille, *The Plaint of Nature.* Trans. James J. Sheridan. Toronto, 1980.
Silk, Edmund T. "Boethius's Consolatio Philosophiae as a Sequel to Augustine's Dialogues and Soliloquia." *Harvard Theological Review*, 32 (1939): 19–39.
Silverstein, H. Theodore. "Dante and Vergil the Mystic." *Harvard Studies and Notes in Philology and Literature*, 14 (1932): 51–82.
———. "The Fabulous Cosmogony of Bernardus Silvestris." *Modern Philology*, 46 (1948): 92–116.
Singleton, Charles S. Commentary. In Dante Alighieri, *The Divine Comedy.* Ed. and trans. Charles S. Singleton. 3 vols., 6 parts. Princeton, 1970–75.
———. *Journey to Beatrice.* Cambridge, Mass., 1958.
Southern, R. W. *Medieval Humanism and Other Studies.* New York, 1970.
———. *Platonism, Scholastic Method, and the School of Chartres.* Reading, Eng., 1978.
———. "The Schools of Paris and the School of Chartres." In Robert L. Benson and Giles Constable, eds., *Renaissance and Renewal in the Twelfth Century*, pp. 113–37. Cambridge, Mass., 1982.
Spearing, A. C. *Medieval Dream-Poetry.* Cambridge, 1976.
Steenberghen, Fernand van. *Aristotle in the West: The Origins of Latin Aristotelianism.* Trans. Leonard Johnston. Louvain, 1955.
———. *Les Oeuvres et la doctrine de Siger de Brabant.* Brussels, 1938.
Stock, Brian. *The Implications of Literacy: Written Language and Models of Interpretation in the Eleventh and Twelfth Centuries.* Princeton, 1983.

———. *Myth and Science in the Twelfth Century: A Study of Bernard Silvester*. Princeton, 1972.
Stone, Donald. "Old and New Thoughts on Guillaume de Lorris." *Australian Journal of French Studies*, 2 (1965): 157–70.
Synesius of Cyrene. *De insomniis*. PG, 66, 1281–1320.
———. *The Essays and Hymns of Synesius of Cyrene*. Trans. Augustine Fitzgerald. Oxford, 1930.
Tague, Wilma Long. "John Gower's *Confessio Amantis*: An Hypothesis of Structure." *Dissertation Abstracts International*, 33 (1972): 3604A.
Taylor, P. B. "Chaucer's *Cosyn to the Dede*." *Speculum*, 57 (1982): 315–27.
Tentler, Thomas N. *Sin and Confession on the Eve of the Reformation*. Princeton, 1977.
Thompson, David. "Dante and Bernard Silvestris." *Viator*, 1 (1970): 201–6.
———. *Dante's Epic Journeys*. Baltimore, 1974.
Thorndike, Lynn. *University Records and Life in the Middle Ages*. New York, 1944.
Tillman, Mary Katherine. "Scholastic and Averroistic Influences on the *Roman de la rose*." *Annuale Mediaevale*, 11 (1970): 89–106.
Trout, J. M. *The Voyage of Prudence: The World View of Alan of Lille*. Washington, D.C., 1979.
Turner, Victor, and Edith Turner. *Image and Pilgrimage in Christian Culture*. New York, 1978.
Tuve, Rosemond. *Allegorical Imagery: Some Mediaeval Books and Their Posterity*. Princeton, 1966.
Villani, Filippo. *Il Comento al primo Canto dell' Inferno*. Ed. Giuseppe Cugnoni. Collezione di opusculi danteschi inediti o rari, 31–32. Città di Castello, 1896.
Vitz, E. B. "The *I* of the *Roman de la rose*." Trans. Barbara di Stefano. *Genre*, 6 (1973): 49–75.
Vogel, C. J. de. "Boethiana I." *Vivarium*, 9 (1971): 49–66.
Walahfrid Strabo's Visio Wettini: Text, Translation, and Commentary. Ed. and trans. David A. Traill. Frankfurt, 1974.
Walton, Alice. *The Cult of Asklepios*. 1894; repr. New York, 1965.
Weinberg, Julius. *A Short History of Medieval Philosophy*. Princeton, 1964.
Wetherbee, Winthrop. "The Function of Poetry in the 'De planctu naturae' of Alain de Lille." *Traditio*, 25 (1969): 87–125.
———. Introduction. In Bernardus Silvestris, *The Cosmographia of Bernardus Silvestris*. Trans. Winthrop Wetherbee. New York, 1973.
———. "The Literal and the Allegorical: Jean de Meun and the 'De planctu naturae.'" *Mediaeval Studies*, 33 (1971): 264–91.
———. *Platonism and Poetry in the Twelfth Century: The Literary Influence of the School of Chartres*. Princeton, 1972.
———. "The Theme of Imagination in Medieval Poetry and the Allegorical Figure 'Genius.'" *Medievalia et Humanistica*, n.s. 7 (1976): 45–64.

William of Ockham. *Scriptum in librum primum sententiarum ordinatio.* Ed. Stephano Brown and Gedeon Gál. *Opera theologica*, vol. 2. St. Bonaventure, N.Y., 1970.

———. *Philosophical Writings: A Selection.* Trans. Philotheus Boehner. 1957; repr. Indianapolis, 1964.

Wolfson, Harry Austryn. "The Internal Senses in Latin, Arabic, and Hebrew Philosophic Texts." *Harvard Theological Review*, 28 (1935): 69–133.

Woolsey, Robert. "Bernard Silvester and the Hermetic Asclepius." *Traditio*, 6 (1948): 340–44.

Yates, Frances A. *The Art of Memory.* Chicago, 1966.

———. *Giordano Bruno and the Hermetic Tradition.* Chicago, 1974.

Yeager, R. F. "A Bibliography of John Gower Materials Through 1975." *Mediaevalia*, 3 (1977): 261–306.

———. *John Gower Materials: A Bibliography Through 1979.* New York, 1981.

———. "John Gower's Poetic." *Dissertation Abstracts International*, 37 (1976): 4345A.

Zumthor, Paul. "Récit et anti-récit: *Le Roman de la rose.*" *Medioevo Romanzo*, 1 (1974): 5–24.

INDEX

In this index an "f" after a number indicates a separate reference on the next page, and an "ff" indicates separate references on the next two pages. A continuous discussion over two or more pages is indicated by a span of page numbers, e.g., "pp. 57–58." *Passim* is used for a cluster of references in close but not consecutive sequence.

Abbas, Haly ('Alī ibn al-'Abbās al-Majūsī), 29
Abelard, Peter, 45, 116, 210
Absolution, 22, 153, 159f, 189. *See also* Confession motif
Abstraction, theory of: described, 16, 28–34 *passim*, 59–60, 204ff; poetry informed by, 45, 70, 82, 87–88, 100, 105, 182, 194
Accessus ad auctores, 43, 118, 235
Adelard of Bath, 35, 207
Aeneid, Book Six, 44–45, 62–63, 119f, 147, 214. *See also Commentary on the First Six Books of Virgil's Aeneid*
Alain de Lille, 4, 15, 23, 33, 46, 60, 76, 114, 191–95 *passim*; *Distinctiones dictionum theologicalium*, 51, 70, 83, 211, 216; *Quoniam homines*, 99, 221; *Sermo de sphaera intelligibili*, 82, 85, 91–92, 99–100, 103, 222; *Summa de arte praedicatoria*, 50
—*Anticlaudianus*, 36, 39f, 67, 138, 191, 208f; compared with *De planctu naturae*, 17, 77f, 83, 107–8, 223
—*De planctu naturae*, 13, 17, 42f, 77–112, 209, 217ff; use of *De consolatione philosophiae* in, 7, 17, 55, 72, 79–83, 87f, 103–7, 123f, 222; *Roman de la rose* compared with, 120–42 *passim*; *Commedia* compared with, 147, 155, 159, 162; *Confessio Amantis* compared with, 169f, 183, 190, 195
Albericus, 98, 213, 235
Albertus Magnus, 12, 27
Alcher de Clairvaux, 36, 50, 207, 211
Alcuin, 216

Alfred, king of Wessex, 53, 216
Alighieri, Dante, *see* Dante Alighieri
Alighieri, Pietro, 147
Allegory, high medieval theory of, 41–42, 74–75; moral allegory defined, 79, 218
Allen, Judson Boyce, 204, 209, 224
Andreas Capellanus, 137
Anglicus, Bartholomaeus, 235
Antigamus, 101, 222
Apocalypse, 52, 165
"Apocalypse of Paul," 46, 92, 151, 161
Apuleius of Madaura, 93
Aquinas, St. Thomas, 12, 25, 46, 50, 114, 116, 146; on creativity, 13–14, 118, 203; psychology of, 27–33 *passim*, 148, 155–60 *passim*, 204ff, 211, 228ff; on hands, 39–40, 208; on dreams, 66, 215; on grace, 70
Aristotle, 111, 143, 185; medieval commentary on, 16, 39, 114; psychology or epistemology of, 17, 26–30 *passim*, 54–60 *passim*, 70, 220; availability of works of, in West, 24, 26, 28, 113–18 *passim*, 215; spirit of philosophy of, 26f, 49–50, 113; on hands, 39–40, 156, 208; on dreams, 54, 65. *See also* Condemnations of 1277
Ars memorandi, 177
Artes poeticae and *rhetoricae*, 38f. *See also individual authors by name*
Arts programs at medieval universities, 117–18, 131, 138, 224
Asclepius, 209
Augustine of Hippo, St., 26f, 44, 68, 78, 121, 194, 210; and solution to problem of evil, 17, 222; and theory of three levels of vision, 50–51, 64f, 147, 211, 228; *Soliloquia*, 51f, 53–54, 60, 67, 123, 211–12, 216; on *genius*, 94, 99, 220f. *See also visio spiritualis*
Averroes (Ibn Rushd), 129, 220; commentary of, on Aristotle's *Poetics*, 24, 34, 204, 209; on dreams and visions, 51, 70, 134, 215f, 220. *See also* Condemnations of 1277
Avicenna (Ibn Sina): on dreams and visions, 16–17, 51, 65–69 *passim*, 88, 98, 134, 211, 215–16; on imagination, 28–29, 85

Badel, Pierre-Yves, 225
Baker, Denise, 94, 169f, 220, 232
Bartholomaeus Anglicus, 235
Beatrice, 18, 48, 147–53 *passim*, 158–62 *passim*, 229
Bede, St. (the Venerable Bede): and vision of Drycthelm, 47–49, 51, 70, 161
Bergson, Henri, 172
Bernard of Chartres, 35f
Bernard of Clairvaux, St., 116
Bernardus Silvestris, 23, 25, 33; *Cosmographia*, 39–42, 93–98 *passim*, 156, 208f, 220f
Bersuire, Pierre, 175
Bloch, Marc, 22, 203
Bloomfield, Morton W., 34, 216
Boccaccio, Giovanni, 118
Boethian vision, *see* Philosophical vision
Boethius, 4, 13, 78, 108, 189, 192, 195, 212; medieval commentary on, 23–24, 35, 60–61; Platonism of, 26, 57
—*De consolatione philosophiae*, 48, 132, 211; as model for vision poems, vii-viii, 7, 15, 51–52, 61, 68; psychological or epistemological structure of, 17, 44, 53–63 *passim*, 67–70 *passim*, 87, 210, 213, 215; Platonism of, 17, 53–61, 68, 70, 103–4; poetic authority in, 72–74, 88, 162; as

Index   255

model for *Roman de la rose*, 120–26 *passim*; as model for *Purgatorio*, 147, 162; as model for *Confessio Amantis*, 166, 190. See also Alain de Lille, *De planctu naturae*; Philosophy, personification of
Bologna, University of, 118, 225
Bonaventure, St., 12, 30, 160, 204f, 231
Brink, C. O., 208
Brumble, H. David, 95, 220, 222
Brunetto Latini, vii, 12, 83
Bundy, Murray Wright, 32–33, 206, 211, 228, 230
Burke, Linda Barney, 234, 236
Burrow, J. A., 173, 175, 232, 235

Capella, Martianus, *see* Martianus Capella
Capellanus, Andreas, 137
Castor and Pollux myth, 62
Catharists, 78
Change, continuous and discontinuous, 11–18 *passim*, 22, 25, 31, 116, 141–42, 192
Chartres, School of: approach of, to philosophy, 25, 28, 80–81, 107; Chartrian Nature, 169; Bernard of, 35f
Chaucer, Geoffrey, vii, 1, 4, 19, 55, 163, 166, 198; *Book of the Duchess*, 166; *Canterbury Tales*, 136, 145, 169, 176, 180, 233; *House of Fame*, 12f, 19, 179, 193; *Legend of Good Women*, 12f, 179; *Parliament of Fowls*, 77, 86; *Troilus and Criseyde*, 53
Chenu, Marie-Dominique, 26–27, 216
Cherniss, Michael D., viii, 169f, 191, 232
Cicero, Marcus Tullius, 111; *De inventione*, 45, 208; *Somnium Scipionis*, 51–60 *passim*, 90, 152, 212

Claudian, 93, 220
Commentary on *Les Echecs amoureux*, 40, 219
Commentary on the First Six Books of Virgil's Aeneid (commonly attributed to Bernardus Silvestris), 179, 203, 221, 235; poetic theory of, 23–24, 37–38, 44–45, 210, 219; psychological or epistemological theory of, 35, 37–38, 60–63, 64, 214f; on dreams, 64, 215; influence of, on Dante, 149–52, 229f; quoted, 21
Common sense, in medieval psychology, 28, 31, 65f, 147
Complaint motif (or "lament"), 79–80, 88–89, 91, 95, 122, 139, 164, 186–87
Condemnations of 1277, 11, 18, 114–17, 129, 131, 136–37, 202, 223–24, 227–28. *See also* Tempier, Bishop Stephen
Confession motif, 153, 164, 167–71, 182
Constantine the African, 61
Continuous change, *see* Change
Copleston, F. C., 202, 220–21, 223
Costa ben Luca (Qusṭā ibn Lūqā), 205
Courcelle, Pierre, 58, 212f
Creation, three levels of, 34, 142, 144
Croce, Benedetto, 5
Croesus and Phanie myth, 130, 134
Cupid, *see* God of Love
Curtius, Ernst Robert, 208, 218

Dahan, Gilbert, 224–25
Dahlberg, Charles, 119, 226
Damian, St. Peter, 43, 209–10
Dane, Joseph A., 140
Dante Alighieri, 4, 25, 37, 39, 46, 60, 76f, 118f, 225; *Convivio*, 33, 44, 48, 231; *De vulgari eloquentia*, 36, 41, 196, 209; *Letter to*

Can Grande, 151, 218; *Vita nuova*, 3, 147, 151
—*Commedia*, 1, 33, 48, 68, 117f, 162; overall structure of, 18, 119f, 146–52, 162, 228–29; compared with *Confessio Amantis*, 163, 166, 189–96 *passim*; *Inferno*, 147–51 *passim*, 161, 219–20; *Purgatorio*, 18, 33, 38, 48, 146–51 *passim*, 152–62, 189, 190–91, 219–20; *Paradiso*, 37, 73, 147–52 *passim*, 160f, 207
Delany, Sheila, 12f
De' Medici, Lorenzo, 160
De Vogel, C. J., 212
Dinzelbacher, Peter, 2, 201, 210
Discontinuous change, *see* Change
Double truth, doctrine of, 115, 136, 146. *See also* Condemnations of 1277
Dreams: liminality of, 16, 50f, 56; psychology or epistemology of, 16–17, 63–72, 87–88, 148, 155, 211; as analogous to poetry, 17, 71–76, 109, 141–42, 195–96; used to mark stages of narrator's progress, 18, 148, 153–59 *passim*, 164–65, 186–94 *passim*; as *visio spiritualis*, 51, 64, 147; Macrobian classification of, 51, 69, 74, 120, 134, 152, 165, 217; in writings of Synesius of Cyrene, 54–55; healing power of, 55, 67–70, 139, 165, 213; *daemones* in, 63, 98, 164f; as explicated by Nature in *Roman de la rose*, 133–34
Dronke, Peter, 74, 82, 103, 204, 209, 225, 230
Drycthelm, vision of, 47–49, 51, 70, 161
Duns Scotus, John, 31

Earthly Paradise, 47, 151, 159
Echecs amoureux, Les, commentary on, 40, 219

Economou, George D., 78, 81, 95, 209, 219f, 227, 233
Eden, Garden of, 91, 158, 230
Eliot, T. S., 161
Engin, 143–44, 171, 233
Epistemology: summary of high medieval theory, 16, 25–37, 59–60, 211; general poetic expectations informed by, 17, 42–45, 55–56, 75f, 193f, 204; Platonic, 17, 56–58; Aristotelian, 17, 57–58; individual poems informed by, 17–19, 119, 124–25, 145, 147–50, 167, 171, 193f. *See also* Abstraction; Common sense; Imagination; Memory; Natural order of knowing; Reason; *and under* Dreams
Eünoè, River of, 18, 160, 230–31
Evans, G. R., 82, 222

Fabliaux tradition, 143
Faculty psychology, 27–34, 67, 205. *See also* Common sense; Imagination; Memory; Reason
Fantasy, *see* Imagination
Faral, Edmond, 225f
Fisher, John H., 166f, 173, 231–34 *passim*
Fleming, John V., 10, 119, 126–27, 129f, 211–12, 227
Fletcher, Angus, 42
Fortin, E. L., 223
Foster, James Joseph, 173, 176, 183–84
Fountain of Love, 121, 136, 226
Fowler, Alastair, 5–13 *passim*, 202. *See also* Genres
Freccero, John, 162
Freud, Sigmund, 3, 64
Frye, Northrop, 5
Fulgentius, Fabius Planciades, 61f, 214

Galen of Pergamum, 28, 30, 54, 208, 215, 227
Gallacher, Patrick, 195, 232, 236

Gallo, Ernest, 208, 210, 213
Genius, 41, 93–101 passim, 112, 138, 186, 189, 220f, 233
—personification of, 7, 220, 231; in De planctu naturae, 17, 80, 82, 91, 93–106, 111, 135f, 159, 169; in Roman de la rose, 18, 129–37 passim, 169, 182, 226; in Confessio Amantis, 19, 164–98 passim
Gennep, Arnold van: quoted, 48
Genres: historical evolution and extension of, vii–viii, 7, 11–15, 120, 141–45, 163–64, 189–98 passim; influence of, on meaning of text, vii–viii, 52–76 passim, 120, 139–42; "subgenre" defined, 4–9 passim; theory of, 4–11, 78; external form or structure of, 6f, 164, 168. See also Love vision; Philosophical vision
Geoffrey of Vinsauf, 13–14, 38–45 passim, 156, 202–3, 208, 210
Gilson, Etienne, 25, 31, 148, 202, 206, 223f, 228
Godfrey of St. Victor, vii, 12
God of Love, 12; as Cupid in De planctu naturae, 43, 86, 92, 101; in Roman de la rose, 120–26 passim, 144; in Confessio Amantis, 176, 178, 186, 188
Goldin, Frederick, 226
Goliardic tradition, 139
Gower, John, 4, 7, 15; Vox Clamantis, 165, 179, 197, 231ff
—Confessio Amantis, 13, 18–19, 48–49, 77, 93, 163–98; "Apollonius of Tyre," 177, 184, 191; "Canace and Machaire," 169–70, 176–77, 188; "Capaneus," 181; "Constantine and Sylvester," 177, 191; "Eneas and Dido," 178–80, 234; "Florent," 180–81; "Iphis and Araxarathen," 174; "King, Wine, Woman and Truth," 178, 234, 236; "Nectanabus," 184; "Phebus and Daphne," 178; "Pyramus and Thisbe," 175–76, 234; "Socrates' Patience," 173; "Tereus," 184; "The Three Questions," 177–78, 191; "The Trump of Death," 180–81; "Ulysses and Telegonus," 184; "Vulcan and Venus," 183. For Gower's use of works by other authors, see individual authors by name
Grabes, Herbert, 226
Grace, medicinal or preparatory, 70, 123, 127
Grammar: discipline of, 24, 38f, 117f, 142, 224f; metaphor of, 109–10; allegorical character, 208
Grant, Edward, 224
Green, Richard Hamilton, 78, 106, 192, 222–23
Guillaume de Conches, 60f, 74, 205; commentary of, on Boethius, 35, 44, 60, 207, 213, 215, 221; commentary of, on Plato, 36–37, 207; quoted, 56
Guillaume de Deguileville, 48, 194
Guillaume de Lorris and Roman de la rose, 1, 13, 77, 156; as interpreted by Jean de Meun, 119–22, 126, 128, 139, 141, 226; influence on the Confessio Amantis, 166. See also Jean de Meun and Roman de la rose
Guillaume de Machaut, 1, 166
Gunn, Alan M. F., 225f

Hall, Louis Brewer, 179
Haly Abbas ('Alī ibn al-'Abbās al-Majūsī), 29
Hand, as symbol of creativity, 38–41, 110, 133, 156, 158, 198, 208
Hanning, Robert W., 144
Hardison, O. B., Jr., 118, 224f
Häring, Nikolaus M., 204, 218, 222
Henri d'Andeli, 24, 118, 204
Hermetic tradition, 41, 209

258   Index

Hernadi, Paul, 5
Hieatt, Constance B., 3, 5, 201, 215
Hill, Thomas D., 226f
Hillman, Larry, 226
Hirsch, E. D., Jr., 5
Hissette, Roland, 115, 224, 227f
Holub, Robert C., 10, 202
Horace, 38, 97, 208, 221
Hugh of St. Victor, 61, 85, 206, 216; *Didascalicon*, 32f, 71, 75, 142, 216–17
Humanism, high medieval, 16f, 23–27 *passim*, 98, 113–14, 203–4
Hymen, 80, 89, 91–92, 101f, 110

Illumination, knowledge as, 27, 59, 194, 204
Images depicted in visionary landscape, 120, 154, 214–15
Imagination, in medieval psychology: poetic, 16, 25, 34–39, 72, 195; function of, within medieval epistemology, 16, 26–34 *passim*, 45, 58, 148–49, 211, 233; in dreams, 16–17, 55, 64–76 *passim*, 139, 215f; Genius as figure of, 17, 96–100, 106, 130, 135f, 170–71, 182, 186–91 *passim*; as "fantasy," 28, 34, 40, 87, 147, 188; limits of, in Dante, 33, 147, 161–62. *See also* Ingenium and *under* Reason, in medieval psychology
Inexpressibility topos, 143
Ingegno, 38, 155, 161–62
Ingenium, 233; as poetic imagination, 16, 34–42, 72, 143–44, 207f; as apprehensive imagination, 36–37, 63, 84–88 *passim*, 188, 215; as *ingegno*, 38, 155, 161–62; Genius as figure of, 96–100, 106, 112, 130, 135, 170–71, 182; as *engin* or *angin*, 143–44, 171, 233
Initiation motif, 48–49, 161

Insomnium, 74, 134, 217
Intellect, *see* Reason, in medieval psychology
Intentiones, 32, 155, 157
Intuitive cognition, 27, 194, 236
Isidore of Seville, St., 37, 207

James I of Scotland, vii, 38
Jauss, Hans Robert, 5–10 *passim*, 56, 78, 202, 213
Jean de Hanville, vii, 23
Jean de Meun and *Roman de la rose*, 1, 4, 13–18 *passim*, 46, 48f, 77, 113–45, 226; use of *De planctu naturae*, 83, 93, 120–42 *passim*; compared with *Commedia*, 119, 146, 156, 162, 225; influence on *Confessio Amantis*, 164, 166, 169, 179, 182f, 190–95 *passim*.
John of Garland, 24
John of Salisbury: *Policraticus*, 64ff, 75f, 216f
—*Metalogicon*, 23, 61, 117, 224; psychology or epistemology of, 30, 35f, 85, 126, 204f, 206–7, 227
Jones, Julian Ward, and Elizabeth Frances Jones, 62, 203
Jourdain, Charles M. G. B., 60
Jung, Carl, 3, 64
Jupiter and Saturn myth, 124, 127, 130, 183

Kelly, Douglas, 38–39, 119, 233
Kerenyi, C., 213
Kiser, Lisa J., 12f
Knowles, David, 115, 223
Knowlton, E. C., 220, 231, 233
Köhler, Erich, 226
Kolve, V. A., 173–74
Kuhn, Thomas S., 202

Lament, *see* Complaint motif
Langland, William, vii, 1, 3f, 68, 76, 163, 193f

Langlois, Ernest, 122, 225
Latini, Brunetto, vii, 12, 83
Laurent de Premierfait, 119, 225
Leah (in *Commedia*), 158
Lecoy, Felix, 225
Leff, Gordon, 11f, 27, 114, 202, 223f. *See also* Change
Le Goff, Jacques, 161
Leonard, Frances McNeely, 232–35 *passim*
Lerer, Seth, 212
Lethe, River of, 18, 159–60, 189, 230–31
Lévi-Strauss, Claude, 100, 103f, 222
Lewis, C. S., 77, 106, 166–67, 170, 174, 189–92 *passim*, 197, 220, 222f, 233
Liminality, 211; of dreams and visions, 16, 18, 47–51, 56, 69, 106, 153, 162; of Genius, 103; of Purgatory, 161; of encounter with dream vision guide, 190
Literalism of dream vision narrators, 18, 82, 86, 89, 125–27, 135, 139, 153–58 *passim*, 182
Literary theory, medieval, *see* Poetic theory
Little, Lester K., 22, 203
Logic: discipline of, 24, 37, 113–18 *passim*, 129–30, 142, 224–25; allegorical character, 40, 208
Lombard, Peter, 146
Lonergan, Bernard, 205f, 227
Love vision, genre of, 4, 7, 13, 120, 165–66, 232
Luca, Costa ben (Qusṭā ibn Lūqā), 205
Lucy (in *Commedia*), 153
Luria, Maxwell, 226

Macaulay, G. C., 167, 169, 231f, 234
Machaut, Guillaume de, 1, 166
Macrobius, Ambrosius Theodosius, 36, 61; *Commentary on the Dream of Scipio*, 49, 51, 66, 74f, 120, 127, 141, 196, 216f
Maresca, Thomas E., 62, 203, 214
Martianus Capella, 21, 52, 94, 107, 208, 221
Matelda (in *Commedia*), 153, 159
Mazzeo, Joseph Anthony, 159, 211, 229
Means, Michael H., 55, 201
Medici, Lorenzo de', 160
Meerson, Daniel Carl, 61f, 207
Memento mori motif, 180
Memory, in medieval psychology: as represented within structure of individual texts, 18, 63, 81–88 *passim*, 159f, 164, 177, 189, 214f; function of, within medieval epistemology, 28–37 *passim*, 45; archetypal or Platonic, 57, 59, 68, 70, 74, 84, 135–36; in dreams, 65, 67; in structure of vision poems, 69, 150; limits of, in Dante, 147, 162; higher type of, 160, 231; in Chaucer, 233
Menippean satire, 52
Migne, J.-P., 101
Minnis, Alastair J., 204, 232
Mirror, image of, *see* Speculum
Moffat, Douglas, 77, 218, 222
Moralizations of classical stories, 173–84 *passim*
Muscatine, Charles, 122, 140f
Mussato, Albertino, 118
Mythographus Tertius, 98, 213

Naming episodes in visions, 48–49, 80, 159, 187, 189
Natural order of knowing: poetic structure informed by, 16, 44–45, 68, 210, 213; in *Commentary on the First Six Books of the Aeneid*, 44–45, 60, 63, 150, 210; in *De planctu naturae*, 82, 105; in *Roman de la rose*, 119, 139; in *Commedia*, 119, 150, 161; in *Confessio Amantis*, 177

Natural philosophy, 21–22, 37, 80–81, 113–18 *passim*; harmony of, with faith or theology, 16, 27, 99–100; on dreams, 65–67; versus poetry, 117f. *See also* Aristotle
Nature (goddess), 7, 39, 42, 49, 58, 168, 194, 217; in *De planctu naturae*, 7, 17, 80–97, 101–11 *passim*, 120–32 *passim*, 142, 170, 183, 219; in *Roman de la rose*, 18, 49, 129–35 *passim*, 142–43, 169, 226; in *Confessio Amantis*, 187, 191
Nebuchadnezzar, 164f, 177, 216, 231
Nemesius of Emesa, 28
Neoplatonism, 27, 54, 58, 215
Newman, Francis X., 2, 45, 66, 75, 201, 211, 228f
Nitzsche, Jane Chance, 63, 95, 97f, 164, 220ff
Nolan, Barbara, 3, 201
Nominalism, 14–15, 117, 125–26, 129, 142, 194. *See also* Philosophy, late medieval; Ockham, William of

Oberman, Heiko A., 202
Ockham, William of, 13–14, 24, 31, 203, 227
Old Woman (*La Vielle*), 130, 132, 140, 143, 179
Olsson, Kurt O., 232, 234
Oraculum, 69, 74, 152
Orpheus and Eurydice myth, 98, 112, 130, 221, 227
Otherworld journeys and visions, 2, 4, 46–47, 51, 151, 161
Ovid, 166, 174–79 *passim*, 228, 235
Ovide moralisé, 175
Ovidius moralizatus (Bersuire), 175
Owen, D. D. R., 2, 201, 210

Paetow, Louis J., 224f
Paré, Gérard, 129, 225ff

Paris, University of, 28, 117f, 131, 225
Park, Katharine, 205, 227
Pascalis Romanus, 74ff, 216f
Patch, Howard Rollin, 201, 210, 213
Paul, St., 50–51, 65. *See also* Vision *of St. Paul*
Payne, F. Anne, 201
Pearcy, Roy J., 227
Pearl (Middle English poem), 1, 3, 163, 193
Pearsall, Derek, 173, 232ff
Peck, Russell A., 164, 183, 202f, 232–35 *passim*
Penitential motif or framework, 153–54, 164, 172, 188ff. *See also* Absolution; Confession motif
Peter Damian, St., 43, 209–10
Peter Lombard, 146
Peter the Chanter, 161
Petrarch, Francesco, vii, 37, 43, 194
Phantasms, 31f, 64, 160. *See also* Imagination
Philosophical vision, genre of: as subgenre, 4–13 *passim*; formation and function in high medieval period, 15–19 *passim*, 47, 50, 52, 66; used in *Confessio Amantis*, 19, 163–66, 170, 185–90 *passim*, 194–95; used in *De planctu naturae*, 78–82 *passim*, 108f, 111; used in *Commedia*, 119, 147–54 *passim*, 159; used in *Roman de la rose*, 119–22 *passim*, 132, 139, 141; extension of, in late medieval period, 193–94
Philosophy, late medieval, 11–15 *passim*, 24, 31, 114, 116–17, 202f. *See also* Nominalism; William of Ockham
Philosophy, personification of, in *De consolatione philosophiae*: compared with guides in medieval vision poems, 7, 68, 79–83, 87, 104f, 123, 155, 168; function

of, in *De consolatione philosophiae*, 48, 54–59, 68, 73–74, 104f; compared with Reason in *Soliloquia*, 53–54; reception of, in broader medieval tradition, 56, 60–63, 215
Piehler, Paul, 3ff, 56, 68–69, 80f, 119, 201, 215, 218
Piers Plowman, see Langland, William
Pietro Alighieri, 147
Pilgrimage motif, 48, 56–57, 128, 152–53, 180, 195
Plato, 111, 143, 145; psychology or epistemology of, 17, 56–60 *passim*, 70; dualism of, 26, 104; and vision of Er, 53; dialogue form of, 57, 68, 70. *See also* Neoplatonism; Platonism
Platonism, 57; spirit of, in medieval period, 26, 113; of *Somnium Scipionis*, 53; of *Soliloquia*, 53–54; of *Commentary on the First Six Books of the Aeneid*, 61. *See also* Neoplatonism; Plato
Poetic theory, medieval, 13–16 *passim*, 23–26, 31, 34–45, 204–10 *passim*; authority of, threatened, 71–76 *passim*, 117–18, 141–42; in *Roman de la rose*, 127, 141–45; in *De planctu naturae*, 85–86, 108–12; in *Commedia*, 161–62; in *Confessio Amantis*, 177, 184–85, 195–98. *See also* Natural order of knowing
Pointing, poetic technique of, 173–75, 177, 182
Poirion, Daniel, 225, 227
Premierfait, Laurent de, 119, 225
Prophecy, 54, 65, 74, 159, 165, 190, 211; *ingenium* and imagination endowed with power of, 33, 37, 144
Providence: relation of, to fate, 44, 59, 103f, 197; relation of, to evil, 104, 106; relation of, to Fortune, 195

Purgatorium Sancti Patricii, 161
Purgatory, 18, 147, 152–62 *passim*, 228
Pygmalion myth, 128, 143

Quadlbauer, Franz, 210
Quintilian, 38, 207–8

Rachel (in *Commedia*), 154, 158
Rashdall, Hastings, 117, 224
Raynaud de Lage, G., 84, 94–95, 217f, 220, 223
Realism, philosophical paradigm of: discussed, 11–18 *passim*; mentioned, 25, 34f, 113, 125, 140, 142, 147, 192, 194
Reason, in medieval psychology (also "intellect"), 176–77, 215, 220–21, 230; natural or humanistic, 11, 23, 114, 158, 192; function within medieval epistemology, 16, 26–39 *passim*, 45, 126, 134–35, 148–49, 182, 194, 233; synthesis with revelation or faith, 16–17, 25, 29, 49–50, 107–8, 114–16, 131–38 *passim*, 142, 146; in dreams, 16–17, 65–68, 71–76 *passim*, 215; control of, over imagination in individual poems, 17ff, 67–70, 81–92 *passim*, 112, 126–41 *passim*, 148–60, 171, 182, 188; visionary guides as figures of, 18, 62f, 68–70, 81–92 *passim*, 96, 105, 150f, 155–58, 228–29; as faculty of artistic creation, 39, 72–76, 98; synthesis of, with imagination, 191
Reason, personification of, 7, 18f, 67ff, 168f, 186, 191; in *Roman de la rose*, 17–18, 83, 120–38 *passim*, 144, 169, 183, 226–27; in *Soliloquia*, 53, 67, 123, 212; in *Anticlaudianus*, 107f; in late medieval vision poems, 194
Richard II, king of England, 177
Richard of St. Victor, 146

Richards, Earl Jeffrey, 225
Robertson, D. W., Jr., 120, 206, 225–26
Roman de la Rose, see Jean de Meun and *Roman de la rose*

Schmidt-Kohl, Volker, 212
Schreiber, Earl G., 62, 203, 214
Schueler, Donald G., 164, 220, 232f, 235
Schupbach, William, 208
Scotus, John Duns, 31
Servius, 61
Seven sins, 173, 177, 190–91
Sheridan, James J., 77, 109, 218, 222
Siger of Brabant, 114, 116, 146, 223, 228
Silk, Edmund T., 211
Silverstein, H. Theodore, 15, 38, 207, 215, 229
Singleton, Charles S., 148, 228–31 *passim*
Singulars, as objects of knowledge, 14, 31, 227
Siren, in *Purgatorio* XIX, 156ff
Somnium, 69, 74, 120, 165
Southern, R. W., 23, 25, 27, 113, 204
Spearing, A. C., 2f, 109, 142, 144, 201, 215, 231
Speculum, 226; image of vision as a, 84, 111, 121, 136, 154, 159, 219; in Fountain of Love, 121; Nature's discussion of, 133; of Venus, 181, 188; of Middle Earth, 194
Steenberghen, Fernand van, 202, 223
Stock, Brian, 209–10, 219
Strabo, Walahfrid, 210
Sybil, in *Aeneid* VI, 60, 62f, 150, 215
Synesius of Cyrene, 38, 54–58 *passim*, 65, 212–13

Tempier, Bishop Stephen, 114–17, 131–38 *passim*. *See also* Condemnations of 1277
Tentler, Thomas N., 182, 234
Third Vatican Mythographer, 98, 213, 235
Thomas Aquinas, St., see Aquinas, St. Thomas
Thompson, David, 61, 150, 213, 229
Tillman, Mary Katherine, 129
Tithonus and Ganymede myth, 153
Translatio, rhetorical figure of, 101, 109, 111
Turner, Victor, and Edith Turner, 47–48, 49
Tuve, Rosemond, 42, 139, 198

Universals, as objects of knowledge, 14, 27, 30ff, 126, 194, 205
Universities, medieval, 23, 117–18, 142, 224f. *See also names of individual schools and disciplines by name*

Van Gennep, Arnold, 48
Van Steenberghen, Fernand, 202, 223
Varro, Marcus Terentius, 99
Venus: in *De planctu naturae*, 86, 92, 101, 109f; in *Roman de la rose*, 127, 133; and Vulcan myth, 127, 133, 183; in *Confessio Amantis*, 164–71 *passim*, 175, 181–91 *passim*, 197
Victorinus, Gaius Maurius, 61
Vielle, see Old Woman
Villani, Filippo, 147–48
Virgil, 24, 36, 45, 111, 159, 178–79; as a character in *Commedia*, 18, 148–62 *passim*, 230. *See also Commentary on the First Six Books of Virgil's Aeneid*
Vision of Bernoldus, 46
Vision of St. Paul (apocryphal), 46, 92, 151, 161

Vision poetry, late medieval, 1–4 passim, 12–13, 18–19, 76f, 144–45, 163–64, 192–94, 198
Visio spiritualis, 50–51, 64f, 147, 154, 159, 161, 211, 228
Vogel, C. J. de, 212
Voie de Paradis tradition, 139
Voyage of St. Brendan, 46, 159

Walahfrid Strabo, 210
Wetherbee, Winthrop, 78, 90, 236; introduction of, to the Cosmographia, 15, 41, 209; "Function of Poetry," 78, 80–81, 86, 94, 106–7, 218f, 223; "Literal and the Allegorical," 126, 132, 138; Platonism and Poetry, 42, 63, 98, 104, 204, 207, 227; "Theme of Imagination," 25, 36, 43, 95–97, 207, 216, 220

Will, in medieval psychology, 32, 45, 148–49, 155–59 passim, 178, 181; literary characters as figures of, 68, 230; freedom of, versus predestination, 73–74, 132
William of Ockham, 13–14, 24, 31, 203, 227
Wit, 37, 63, 170–71, 176, 188f, 233. See also Ingenium
Woolsey, Robert, 220
World or nature as book, 11, 14, 16, 34, 42, 44
World soul, 22, 60, 99

Yeager, R. F., 232, 234

Zumthor, Paul, 226

Library of Congress Cataloging-in-Publication Data

Lynch, Kathryn L., 1951–
   The high medieval dream vision.

   Bibliography: p.
   Includes index.
   1. Poetry, Medieval—History and criticism.
   2. Dreams in literature.   3. Visions in literature.
   4. Literary form.   I. Title.
   PN690.D73L96 1988   809.1′02   87-18042
   ISBN 0-8047-1275-1 (alk. paper)